TEN SECONDS FROM NOW

In action. Leaving Fremantle during the 1953–4 Royal Tour

GODFREY TALBOT

Ten Seconds From Now

A Broadcaster's
Story

HUTCHINSON OF LONDON

HUTCHINSON & CO (*Publishers*) LTD
3 Fitzroy Square, London W1

London Melbourne Sydney Auckland
Wellington Johannesburg Cape Town
and agencies througout the world

First published February 1973
Second impression April 1973

PN5123
T27
A3

92
139

© Godfrey Talbot 1973

*This book has been set in Garamond type, printed in Great Britain
on antique wove paper by The Stellar Press of Hatfield Herts, and
bound by Wm. Brendon, of Tiptree, Essex*

ISBN 0 09 114120 6

For Bess

'Ten Seconds from Now' is the news broadcaster's classic opening formula used when starting his reports from overseas. He says the words into his microphone as a preface to each of his messages, to warn receiving stations and recording engineers that he is about to go ahead and speak his dispatch.

Contents

Illustrations

The Crown copyright photographs are reproduced by permission of the Controller of H.M. Stationery Office

Among my Souvenirs

'One day you'll write a book. You must.'

People had been saying that to me for years, publicly. I sometimes said it to myself, privately. But there never was time, and I was glad really. Later, maybe. We'll see. Meanwhile, I would go on keeping a diary and newspaper clippings and the odd text of a radio piece I'd done. So it was on with the travel and the next day's reporting; on with the umpteenth royal tour; on with the ephemeral but absorbing business of broadcasting. That was the simple way out of writing a book. Sufficient unto the day . . .

But now there had arrived the moment when procrastination was no longer necessary, at any rate no longer easy. I had retired from the B.B.C. Still busy, still talking; but not on the staff. I was now able to organise my work just as I wished. And we were moving house, which meant sorting a lot of my accumulated belongings. That hoard, in fact, started me off. The things which reminded me of where I'd been and what I'd done—*they* set me writing it all down, to see what it looked like and to get it out of my system.

At the start, I sat in the attic contemplating a mountain of this book-writing ammunition: tape recordings, notebooks, old passports, souvenir programmes, ragged files of press cuttings, carbon copies of cabled messages crammed in dusty folders and twenty-five box-files spilling out old scripts. Here was material all right, though too much. Sifting was going to be a business, selecting and checking facts from the quick reportage of the time and then distilling them on to a clear mixture of reminiscences many thousands of painstaking words long. Most of my professional life had

been devoted to creative processes in a different gear: the
hurried executions of daily radio journalism. A book was a
different cup of tea. But by now I was sitting on the floor
scribbling down chapter headings and remembered stories
on the back of a large envelope, and I knew I was going to
press on, sweat and toil though it would be. I started turning
out drawers, taking odds and ends down from walls and
shelves, undoing bundles of letters and photographs,
emptying old trunks into which through the years I had
thrown the brought-home knick-knacks. And there they all
were, the mementos, hundreds and hundreds of them.

Some of the souvenirs went straight into the waste-bin:
the mouldering straw mat from then-colonial Fiji; the ugly,
useless ashtray cut from one of *the* Cedars of Lebanon; the
cheap Turkish dagger all rusted; ill-made, smelly pocket
wallets foisted on me in Kano; a nasty model camel-saddle
bought one noisy day in the Muski in Cairo when I was too
full of Stella beer to have more sense; tawdry 'national
dress' dolls and trinket trays stamped with tasteless emblems;
mugs from Munich beer houses, and a poor little dish
inscribed 'Hotel Sacher, Wien', unworthy of one of the
world's great restaurants—all those were thrown away, and
the paperweights from a Benares bazaar chucked after them.
I wondered how I could have been mad enough to bring
such rubbish home. The gaudy trifles must have looked
attractive in tropical sunshine, but they were nightmares in
the grey light of England.

Other relics were kept, nostalgically. Not beautiful
keepsakes. But they tripped all sorts of triggers of recollection: an old sepia photograph: the fierce-eyed, bearded
face of my reverend maternal grandfather. A family relic,
this. It glared at me now as it used to do from our mantel-
piece at home when I was a little boy: a focus of the Victorian
Methodism which ruled the house.

There was a large school photograph; and a report saying:
'He must concentrate on his English. He bothers too much
about what is going on around him.' My form master had a
narrow mind.

Then a yellow, brittle bit of newspaper cut from the
Yorkshire Weekly Post dated 1928, with 'my first words in

print' written at the top: two paragraphs on a Rugby League game between Leeds and Wigan. Pinned to this clipping was a letter, the date two years earlier, from the chairman of the Yorkshire Conservative Newspaper Company, thanking me for helping to keep the *Yorkshire Post* going during the General Strike. I remembered being astonished to be told that I, still a teenager then, had rendered 'signal service' to the nation by being a blackleg—and being delighted at the princely bonus of seven guineas which came with the note.

Another letter—it was an echo of my Lancashire days now —was from 1932, handing into my keeping a proud but moribund newspaper, the *Manchester City News,* of which I became editor at the age of twenty-three. The appointment was a milestone—and a millstone: the paper died under me.

And the letter inviting me to join the B.B.C., sentimentally retained, and attached to it the document ordering me in 1939 to proceed from the North to London 'in the event of war'. 'Take clothes sufficient for a stay of at least a month', it said. My stay in London lasted thirty years.

From an ammunition box used as a trunk when I left the wartime Middle East there were preserved my British war correspondent's shoulder-flashes and a batch of General Montgomery's eve-of-battle pep-messages to his men. Also a pair of still-wearable suède boots bought cheap in the officers' shop in that verminous old Kasr-el-Nil barracks in the crisis days when Rommel had almost reached Cairo and the Embassy was burning its papers. And—laughably, the most emotive of my treasures in this lot—a jam-jar full of sand scooped from the plain of Alamein where I watched the war reach its turning point and from the spot broadcast the news of Monty's famous Desert Victory.

Out of the leavings of the post-war years, stacks of stuff from the Queen's Coronation. That was one of the peak days of my broadcasting life, and the start of nearly twenty years of front seats at State Occasions. I would keep my Coronation invitation, a magnificent piece of pasteboard almost a foot wide and nine inches high, proclaiming that Bernard Duke of Norfolk, Earl Marshal of England, had been commanded by Her Majesty to bid me to the Abbey

Church of Westminster on June 2nd, 1953. It was the biggest
home date of my 'Buckingham Palace beat', and a quarter of
a million miles of royal tours came after it.

My harvest of the tours filled several suitcases. Not many
of these mementos would find room in our new bungalow.
Still, I would hang on to the unusual oddities, such as the
grass skirt from Tonga which I wore in Queen Salote's
garden beside its picture-book Pacific lagoon. And the oh so
genuine native boomerang which the Aborigine stockman
in South Australia gave me after demonstrating with it in
front of the Queen. Marvellous the way it always flew back
to his hand—miserable the way it would never return to
mine. It's a handsome stick but I just cannot throw it
properly.

I am much better at handling such a thing as my Nepalese
prayer-wheel. I sat in the attic and twirled the wheel now
as its previous owner, a wizened Sherpa, had twirled it
when we met to the north of Katmandu on the day when we
watched a British Foreign Minister take his first elephant
ride and shoot a charging rhino. The trouble was that the
prayer-wheel didn't twirl well now. It had been lying with all
manner of other stored odds and ends and its fringed chain
had become tangled with other tassels belonging to a stack of
gala programmes and decorated menu cards which were once
the garnishings of State Banquets from Guildhall to
Guadalajara.

Tired of squatting on the floor, I sat down on the only seat.
This was the biggest souvenir of all: the chair I had as an
official guest-cum-commentator at the Investiture of the
Prince of Wales. It was one of four thousand such seats
provided in Caernarvon Castle on July 1st, 1969. Guests
could buy their seats for twelve pounds after the ceremony.
Encouraged by a wife who claims descent from Gruffydd ap
Cynan, I bought mine. But the chair has hardly ever been
seen since it came into our possession: it is so hard and
uncomfortable and is painted in so shrieking a Government-
issue scarlet that it cannot be admitted to our living-rooms.
I got up and looked again at it now, and, fingering the bas-
relief *Ich Dien* motto on the back, decided not to part with it
even if it moved house with us only from loft to loft.

A perverse decision, made not so much because the chair is my own remnant of a day of historic pageantry of which I was a privileged witness as for the very unlikely yet true reason that the thing is unique. It must be the only genuine Castle Investiture Seat of 1969 in mint condition. For when the great day in Wales came I never, in fact, sat in the blessed chair at all: I spent most of the day in a broom cupboard.

Thereby hangs a tale.

It was time to get down to this and all the other tales now, to quit my attic and court my typewriter; but not, this time, to bang the keys with my usual purpose, as an instant minstrel with only the immediate broadcasting scripts of the day as the task. Now the job was different. I had to sort out as prudently as I could, and write out large and clear, three decades of experience as a specially licensed spectator all over the world—and also the story of how I got into the business at all. My own life, a personal story, of course, and full of highly personal opinions too. But, because my profession has been that of chronicler, perhaps it would be a glimpse of my generation's history too.

I have always enjoyed telling the tale—in voice. But now the aim was the permanence of print, the strait-jacket of page and chapter. I could only hope, as I began the book, that my fallibilities in writing would be forgiven as they have been in speech.

2

It Started in Chapel

It was odd that even as a small boy I hankered after being a reporter. Journalism was foreign to my family. There was nothing so bizarre in the occupations of my forbears in Yorkshire, though some could express themselves. Not that you would have called them articulate. You would just have called them local preachers or Sunday School teachers and, as their blunt friends would have put it, 'not backward at coming forward' and 'right chuffed at the sound of their own voices'.

They were for the most part 'in trade'. And in small, dull ways. But at any rate great-grandfather John Talbot did jump out of the rut for a while when he was twenty-two. He served, as a private soldier, in the disastrous Walcheren campaign of 1809 in Captain Swain's Company, 36th Regiment of Foot, part of the British force which seized the Dutch island during the Napoleonic wars. He was discharged the next year, no doubt thankful to get back to Batley alive, since seven thousand of his fellows in a garrison of fifteen thousand had died of swamp fever. But *he* had his health all right, and eventually eight Biblically-named children, of whom my grandfather James was the third. James had six children, my father Frank Talbot being the second in line.

Father was a big, nice-looking man, in character both severe and sanguine; kind, easily imposed upon, and as full of jokes as he was of sermons.

Mother was the gentlest and meekest person I ever knew. Her family, too, came from the Wakefield–Huddersfield regions of the industrial West Riding. Mother's father was the Reverend Samuel Walker. I wish now that I had known this grandparent, Walker the talker. He started his working life at the age of eight and was apprenticed to a forger of steel blades in Sheffield; he finished as a leading Minister and evangelist of the Methodist New Connexion, noted for his impulsive eloquence and striking choice of phrase. I never saw him because he died seventeen years before I was born, the Benjamin of a family of five. I only know that I was brought up to think of him as a terrifyingly righteous man. As a small boy, I disliked even looking at his photograph, which glared out of a brass frame perched high over the black-leaded fireplace grate and the burnished fire-irons.

That was in a big terrace house on a hill in Leeds, to which we had moved in the gaslit years before the First War, when I was four, from my birthplace, which was the village of Walton, near Wakefield.

Number 29, Inglewood Terrace, Leeds, stood above Woodhouse Ridge, and had four storeys if you counted the basement. Father used part of the house as an office: he was an agent for building materials, a commercial traveller, and an able though unqualified architect. He was also a seven-days-a-week Christian, one of those staunch laymen who for decades wove their patterns of hard integrity and plain speech into the fabric of the West Riding, solidly Liberal and solidly Nonconformist-Church.

We didn't ever call it church: 'Chapel' was the word—not only a word but a way of life. The Chapel habits and religious instincts of both my father's and my mother's ancestors had descended to give to our family what now seems almost a Puritan legacy and an archaic prayer-meeting ritual.

John Wesley would not have been ill-at-ease in the Talbot home. Before every meal, Father, from the head of the large table, 'asked a blessing' (I never even heard the Southern expression, 'say grace', until years later), and it was eyes-shut again and thanks to our Maker before we all got up from our eating. One of my sisters' and brothers' favourite games was 'having a service', complete with a sermon said by one of them whilst standing in an armchair turned round so that the back made a pulpit. Every night we knelt at our beds for minutes on end, whilst Mother sat and listened, and said

B

long prayers which began with 'Gentle Jesus' and finished with God-bless lists of people which enumerated not only our immediate family and scores of aunts and uncles and cousins but current friends and acquaintances. I was mouthing fixed supplications long before I knew what the words really were; and I used to wonder, I remember, why each night I had to 'pity mice', and why the mice were languishing in 'plicity', until one day, seeing the prayer in print, I was surprised to find that I was supposed to be saying 'Pity my simplicity'.

We were brought up on Bible stories, which were my first excitements in literature. And what a dramatic gallery! The wicked kings and the whiplash prophets; Moses dropping the Tablets of the Law; Jael assassinating Sisera with a tent-peg; terrified Peter saying he didn't know Christ; David stoning Goliath; and the Red Sea drowning Pharaoh's chariots—I was unselfconsciously familiar with them all. And hymns: I have known every line of hundreds of them since I was ten. Hymns perhaps started my weakness for playing with words and the sound of them. To tunes of thumping beat and splendid swing we sang revivalist classics like 'Dare to be a Daniel' and 'Only an Armour Bearer'; and *recherché* narrative numbers such as 'The Master has come over Jordan, Said Hannah the Mother one Day'. They all seemed natural and unexceptionable at the time, even the deathless ditty beginning:

> 'I should like to die,' said Willie,
> 'If my Papa could die too.
> 'But he says he isn't ready,
> 'For he's lots of work to do.'

Some of our hymn singing was done at home, especially on Sunday mornings before we all set off to walk to Chapel. After breakfast we would gather in the front room for what an irreverent onlooker might have called 'appetiser devotions'. Father not only said the prayers and read some Scripture, but with heavy fingers played a couple of hymns on the harmonium which was one of our most used pieces of furniture. After this we would leave for our Sunday services proper, down to Chapel all dressed up; Father in front, sometimes wearing a frock-coat and tall black silk-hat but more often in an ordinary black suit and a billycock; and myself, by many years the baby of the family, at the back of the procession, and clad in Sunday-best sailor suit or, as I grew older, a knickerbocker outfit complete with belted Norfolk jacket and topped by a deep Eton collar starched stiff and very uncomfortable. For me it was Chapel in the morning and Sunday School in the afternoon. For the rest— three sisters and a brother who were becoming grown-ups whilst I was still a child—it was compulsory to go to evening service as well.

Such routines were not unusual in the early years of the century. All over the North, families were making their unquestioning pilgrimages to Chapel twice every Sabbath, walking up and down streets of dingy brick back-to-backs and in steep mill-town lanes between the backs of stone houses, to worship in gaunt Bethels and Sunday School rooms whose interiors, great or small, were also the scenes of weekday choir practices and Bible classes—and all as familiar to the chapelgoers as the insides of their own homes.

In my own home every Sunday was special and solemn and busy. Father was at times himself the preacher of the Chapel sermon, and took the Sunday School as Super-intendent. Mother was the only person excused morning service, because of cooking the dinner; and always at table at the end of the meal I had to tell her, at Father's command, what the sermon had been about. Thus I had had to attend to the sermon; thus I was good at précis-making at an early age. A little later, when I was aiming to work on a news-paper, I was allowed to practise shorthand by taking down the sermon.

It was surprising that Father let me scribble whilst we all sat in the family pew, but it rather appealed to him, I think, that maybe one day a son of his might write for print. He was a great newspaper and magazine reader—but for that, I should have never been permitted to bring a news-paper into the house on a Sunday: but he, too, wanted to read J. L. Garvin in the *Observer*. He would not have a

Sunday paper delivered, though: when I brought the paper home, I had to carry it under my coat, lest somebody saw it coming to the house. Many things were forbidden on Sundays. No dusting or sweeping; no knitting or sewing. No smoking (not that anybody did) and, of course, no drinking (no alcohol ever came into the house anyway). Reading was allowed, so long as the book wasn't a novel. Music also was circumscribed: I had a small portable gramophone but could not put on any jazz-band records: only Handel's 'Largo' and 'The Lost Chord', Mother's favourites.

But, as the years went by, Sunday nights became more relaxed and cheerful, if not exactly rip-roaring. My sisters and their friends were able to gather round the piano, which proclaimed its age not only by its uncertain sounds but by its candlesticks and the front of fretwork and pleated silk. They played and sang items from the *Messiah* and 'The Holy City', and more worldly pieces like 'God Send you Back to Me', 'Nirvana', and 'Little Grey Home in the West'. Occasionally I was permitted to stay up and listen, and even to eat a sweet as I did so: a Pomfret-cake or an inscribed lozenge called 'Cupid's Whisper'. Not that the songs, or the sweets, were my favourites: I preferred my faintly scandalising Uncle Chuck doing Gilbert and Sullivan with winks and innuendos—he was the family comic—and I'd rather have been chewing liquorice bootlaces or sucking lemon-kali powder out of a paper bag. But such delightful, disgusting joys were not for Sunday.

The underlying philosophy was that pleasures were either suspect or plain bad for you, and that too much happiness was probably really rather wicked. That was why one of our house rules was 'not much cake but plenty of bread'. I had to eat bread with most things, certainly with jelly and blancmange, for indulgence in them without adulteration was almost sinful.

All the same, it was not a bad upbringing. We were taught that life was for work first, and maybe a little rewarding enjoyment second. We did not believe that the world owed us a living. We had such things as standards of conduct, no less good because they were based on the Abstinence

Pledge and the Band of Hope. Life was good—but not goody-goody.

Presently, and gradually—and this was mainly during my pretty anonymous but savoured progress through Leeds Grammar School—I began to discover a world outside the family circle, and that the wider life was not so hidebound; that, although going to Chapel all that much was not eccentric in Yorkshire then, the family prayer meetings and prohibitions were a Victorian hangover and a little over the odds. I went on enjoying Sunday School for a while, largely because the classes were more of a lark with girl friends than a religious exercise; but I remember that I used to get embarrassed over such times, for instance, as Whit Mondays. This was when the annual summer Sunday School 'treat' came, and we had to ride out to the country in horse-drawn coal carts. I was ashamed enough to crouch down on the floor among the girls in white frocks when we passed any of my schoolfellows. I was beginning to slide off the Methodist wagon.

My real treats were a week's holiday exploring the moors at Ilkley or the sea at Bridlington, a seat at Catlin's Pierrots, a visit to Bostock and Wombwell's travelling menagerie— and going to Headingley. Cricket was an integral part of life in Yorkshire, and I spent hundreds of days at that Leeds county ground worshipping Holmes and Sutcliffe, Emmott Robinson and Wilfred Rhodes. I also managed another pleasure: going to the pictures once a week, at the cost of a whole threepence, to be riveted by Pearl White, Nazimova, Houdini and Fatty Arbuckle.

Both cricket and the cinema provided comedians at whom we were pleased to laugh. But not immoderately. Yorkshire humour, and the behaviour which goes with it, is grudging, wry and dry; the best jokes are reserved for diseases, dead bodies and dropped catches. Rough, laconic raconteurs are liked rather than glib charmers.

I must have inherited infelicitous bluntness in my boy-hood writings, for the early scribblings which have been preserved in memory or on paper are flat and crude. One of the masters at school read out for the derision of the form the opening sentence of an economics essay of mine:

'Money is the bottom of a nation'. The idea was right but it might have been better expressed. Another passage which got me into trouble was in a piece on houses: 'My Auntie Nell has a two-seater W.C., but they go one at a time.' Inelegant, but a clear piece of social reporting.

I used to write precocious letters to my sisters' young men at the front during the Kaiser's War—to show off what I knew about the times, I believe. A wartime childhood in a home full of people who were all so much older than I was gave me a vocabulary of only half-understood but fascinating and emotive words like 'Mons', 'Mespot', 'san fairy-ann', 'Wipers' and 'Blighty wound'. Before I was seven I had seen khaki relatives come in on leave and unroll from their legs puttees stiff with Flanders mud; I knew the sight of a printed fieldcard telling that a soldier had been wounded. I followed the ebb and flow of the fighting like an anxious adult: when Kitchener went down in the *Hampshire* on his way to Russia I cried in our cellar for an hour and told Mother the Germans would win now. I was devouring newspapers 'before my time', and trying to write like them. I lusted after a being journalist before I knew what it meant. Why, I do not know: I was a shy and timid boy, nervous of enterprise except adventure into words, and I had no friends possessing fathers or brothers in the news professions. However, I was inquisitive and talkative, and my General Knowledge marks were always good. The Press attracted me unnaturally. At Speech Days I paid more attention to the reporters at the table below the platform than to the Governors above them.

Such indeed was my interest that when a friend of the family said he could get me a job at the *Yorkshire Post,* Father let me leave school before I reached the Sixth, and I started work at the *Y.P.* in Albion Street, Leeds. Not as a journalist, yet. At first the job was stamp-licking office boy on the commercial side; but I had a foot in a newspaper office and could actually watch those fortunate beings, the writers and the sub-editors, going in and out of the editorial door which I hoped one day to enter. And at length I did: after two years of dreary clerking in the accounts department by day and polishing my shorthand and trying to write articles by night, I managed to get a transfer to the editorial department. It was the result of getting to know some of the people on that side, persistent nagging of the news editor to give me a chance, and a good word being put in for me by Hugh Ross Williamson and Collin Brooks, who were of the Board Room, a book-lined sanctum for the august, the place where the leader writers worked. Hugh Williamson, drama critic then, gave me my first worthwhile introductions to books, music and the theatre—and to accents of speech that were not Yorkshire. From then, journalism gobbled me up, and there were not enough hours in the day for chasing the interests it brought. Home was only a place to sleep, and Chapel days were fading. I was in a new world.

To be precise, I was the junior in the *Yorkshire Post* reporters' room, an awed child amongst men. The reporters were mature and stately; they would have been unrecognisable as practitioners in news by the tearaway lads of today. They wore hats and waistcoats and watch-chains; they wrote out their reports by hand with fountain pen or 3B pencil. I was sharply rebuked and told to hush when I brought my new portable typewriter into the room and started clattering on it. No such sound had been heard in the room before, and it disturbed the snoring after-lunch nap which one of the old gentlemen ritually took, chin on chest and moustache blowing, in the armchair at the head of the the table.

But it was all changing. More young men and more typewriters were on their way; and, after I had been an inhabitant of it for six months, the room was a quiet period-piece no more. Meanwhile, though still a junior and re-stricted to writing little bits on flower shows, weddings and minor County Court cases, I was learning the trade, turning out quick, crisp English instead of the prolix, highfalutin stuff which is the mark of the beginner. In time I was reckoned fully-fledged, and was promoted to the general strength. I covered almost everything on the assignments diary: City Council, Assize Courts and big political rallies; I did some book reviewing and theatre notices, and started cinema criticism. I also spent eight months—my first taste of living in digs and my first chance to walk the Dales—in the Bradford office during the *Y.P.*'s attempt to establish its evening paper there. We printed a Bradford 'slip edition' on a new press in Nelson Street—until the enterprise was abandoned and the Wool City's own *Telegraph and Argus* reigned unrivalled again.

Ordinarily, editorial workers saw little of the thundering great presses of the printing rooms, but I had been a worker in one of them, back at head office in Leeds, in the General Strike of May 1926. The *Yorkshire Post* was one of the few papers which kept going then. Linotypes and the printing machines themselves were operated by amateurs from editorial and clerical staffs—at heaven knows what cost in apparatus damaged by our handling—and for young me it was a great adventure to be assigned to the machine room, alongside such celestial beings as editors acting as mechanics, to cycle to work in well-inked blue overalls between jeering picket lines, and to load volunteer cars with bundles of papers before sending them dashing out at speed through the mob of strikers and the hails of stones at the gates. I felt very important when I was entrusted with a copy of the management's 'secret' leaflet telling which doors we were to try to hold if the insurgents rushed the building.

That General Strike brought a new form of journalistic communication to the national consciousness: news on 'the wireless'. People turned to the infant broadcasting service for information during the National Emergency. There were not many regular listeners, but in 1926 anybody who possessed a radio receiver found his house suddenly very popular with the neighbours. In the early days, our house—surprisingly in an old-fashioned home—did have a wireless set, a funny little coil of wire with an indoor aerial trailing to it down the banisters all the way from the attic. When we got the cat's-whisker tickling the right spot on the crystal it was quite a triumph: we would press the earphones to our heads and miraculously catch the boom of Big Ben and the voice of the British Broadcasting Company's announcer, Rex Palmer.

In the late Twenties, however, I had not much time to pay attention to the novelty of broadcasting: I was working all hours; and presently I had a different job. The *Yorkshire Post*'s 'weekly' was being modernised in style and content, and I was made its Junior Assistant Editor—which sounded grand, but there were only three on the editorial staff: two senior men and me as dogsbody. But it was more experience, another string to my bow. We had fun, all the three of us, doing everything from the make-up of the picture pages to writing an 'Aunt Maud' column of advice to the love-lorn. Best fun of all was doing the children's serial story. We wrote each week's episode in turn, but with no consultation or collaboration whatever; in fact, the whole thing was a domestic game of ours, the aim being to end one's instalment with such an impossible situation that next week's writer would have the devil's own difficulty in continuing the tale at all. What the readers, young or old, made of this frolic I never dared to inquire.

I was enjoying myself. I was twenty, in love with life and love. Existence was full of talking, flirting, and playing tennis and cricket and rugby; of reading and singing; of learning to drink beer and smoke a pipe; of going to plays—and indeed making them. I joined the Leeds Civic Playhouse and was given a few parts; and at the same time became one of a group of young men in the Y.P. office who wrote one-acters and put them on in a tiny theatre made out of a barn on the edge of the moors above Burley-in-Wharfedale. The plays were awful, and so no doubt were our performances; but to us, the stage-struck, it was all pure joy.

Life at the office had its moments of unscheduled drama. We had a reporter who, though beyond retiring age, was rich in contacts and had been kept on as a part-timer to do the night calls—at which job he was a master. He knew all the police superintendents, all the detectives, all the fire chiefs and all the senior porters at the city's hospital casualty departments. He didn't actually visit these places, unless there was a big story. He would make a leisurely and dignified round of the pubs near police headquarters, very occasionally even calling at a police station like an ordinary reporter, but usually he would stand, florid and hard-drinking, for hours at an hotel bar, and his friends would pop in and give him tit-bits of news. Then he would look in at the office, write a few lines and pick up the racing intelligence, hiccuping benignly over the papers.

It was said that he could drink any man in Leeds under the
table. But there was a limit, and he slopped over it one
night when he was on duty and I happened to coincide
with him as he lurched into the reporters' room in a very
high state indeed. Once he gained a chair, he gave one loud
belch and fell into a deep and drunken sleep. It happened
that the chief sub-editor had watched the arrival, and he put
his head round the door and counselled me: 'It's nearly
midnight; we'll get no more out of him. Get a cab, Talbot,
and take him home.' The sub told me the street and the
number, and said I would find the front-door key in the
man's trousers pocket. I did, and, rather frightened over it
all, managed to get the inebriate awake, upright and
agitating his feet. I supported him downstairs and into a
taxi. I was relieved to find the front door of his house
slightly open, so I propelled him into the hall; he was now
singing unprintable songs, and recognised me sufficiently to
bellow 'Goo' night, boy!' So I left him and went off up the
street. But not far. The door I had left flew open, a night-
gowned arm pushed a bellowing figure out on to the steps,
and a voice shouted: 'Hey, you! Who's this 'orrible chap
tha's put in my passage, filthy beggar. Tek 'im off. Ought to
be locked up. Thee an' all!'

I had put my friend in the wrong house.

Episodes of this nature helped to knock my remaining
callow corners off. I was getting all sorts of experience. I
was also getting an itch to be moving. There were well-
beaten journalistic paths from Yorkshire leading to centres
of greater opportunity; and two paths especially. One went
south to Fleet Street, the other west across the Pennines.
That I took one of these roads—not to London, but
Manchester—was, however, only partly because of an urge
to 'get on'. I was on a pursuit which was more personal that
professional.

3

Made in Manchester

As the Thirties began, I went to work at 3 Cross Street, Manchester, the *Guardian* building. It was a bad time for the world: Europe was going dark, and Britain bankrupt. In Germany a strong man was getting into the headlines; in our own country a weak one was doing the same. But I was not at that time paying much attention to either Hitler or Ramsay MacDonald. Manchester, dirty wet Manchester of forty years ago, had quite enough problems and characters on the spot to absorb a young man newly come across the hills from the east. Leeds had been stimulating, but Manchester was stunning. Every one of the popular daily newspapers printed and published a full Northern edition there—that alone was enough to impress me. And, of course, *the* paper was Manchester's own *Guardian*. Suddenly, Leeds seemed just a provincial town, whereas here I was now in the midst of a metropolis. Manchester was a whole world.

The job I had landed was not on the *M.G.* itself, but on a weekly paper which it had acquired, the *City News*. I had been appointed Assistant Editor of this struggling, old-fashioned paper at a wage of eight pounds a week. Not a princely reward, and there was no promise of a rosy future. But it had not been career ambition which translated me into Lancashire: I was chasing a young woman. I had met her in Leeds where she had been studying at a training college, and when she left, to start teaching in her family's home town of Wigan, nothing would do but to be near her still. Manchester was near enough. I had looked for work there and snatched at the first post that came up, this pretty wobbly perch in Cross Street.

The *City News* was an anachronism. Earlier in the century it had been prosperous and powerful, an independent weekly outspokenly dedicated to civic and literary affairs; but now its solid columns and dated style had little general appeal; the circulation was low and the readers a few thousand old faithfuls, held together by a literary and social club called the City News Fellowship (to which, I soon discovered, I had to make my first public speeches). The editor was a remarkable man of letters of the old school, John Cuming Walters, a prolific writer and speaker, eminent Dickensian and devotee of psychic research. Cuming Walters had made a big reputation years before in Birmingham, whilst working for the *Daily Gazette,* as a much feared campaigner for slum clearance. For the last thirty years he had been in journalism in Manchester, twenty-seven of them as editor of the *City News*. It was an education for me to be, even for a short time, an associate of this veteran of unique talent and wide repute. To this day I marvel at the way in which he would sit down squarely at his roll-top desk, a self-possessed Edwardian in wing-collar and pince-nez, dip his pen in an ancient inkwell, and in twenty minutes without pause write a long and forthright leading article, felicitous in flow, indecipherable in its scrawl and inimitable in its quotations—a despair to the compositors and a delight to the readers.

It was absurd that, after a year with him, I should be put at that desk as his successor, but that is what happened when he retired in 1932. Cuming Walters, like his paper, was dying: he was gone less than eighteen months after his retirement, and I was trying to carry on his old paper. The management had hired me in an attempt to put new life into the *City News*. I was fresh and enthusiastic; I knew what newspapers were about; and I was used to pressure. I was certainly cheap labour.

There I sat, an editor at twenty-three. And I slogged. Every week, with the confidence of inexperience, I wrote the leaders, the gossip column, book reviews and theatre criticism, read the proofs and made up the pages. I introduced short stories, competitions, pictures, women's and children's features; and brightened the paper's appearance

so that at least it seemed to be moving with the times.
Indeed we began to see an increase in the advertising space
and the circulation figures. Hopes that we were winning the
fight for revival began to mount. But they were false hopes.

I had been 'in the chair' a little more than two years when,
one Friday morning, I was called to the *Guardian* manager's
office several floors below mine. There I found two solemn-
looking men: John Scott ('C.P.'s' son—the one who ran
the business side) and W. J. Haley (the man who was later
Sir William of the B.B.C. and *The Times,* but who at that
time was presiding over the *M.G.*'s evening paper, a
managing editor who was tough and dispassionately
ruthless, it was said—though that didn't square with the
glimpses I used to have of him laughingly taking on the
office boys at table tennis at lunchtimes). As soon as I got
into the room, Scott, without preamble, said: 'Bad news for
you, Talbot. It's been decided that the *City News* really isn't
viable and isn't likely to show a profit. So it's going to finish
—now. When you put the paper to bed this evening it will
be the last issue. You've done your good best, but the
situation can't go on. I'm sorry.'

Just like that. No warning. I left Cross Street that night
feeling pole-axed. The news I had to take home—that I had
no job—was all the worse because I was a newly married
man. Nine months before, I had brought courtship in Wigan
to a successful conclusion, and Bess and I were living in a
pleasant little house in Manchester's Chorltonville. Now I
had to go in and tell her that I had failed, and was un-
employed. It was one of the most miserable evenings of my
life.

Happily, as it turned out, the blow became a blessing for
me personally (and in fact all the staff soon found new billets).
The very next day John Scott, who had not been heartless,
after all, told me he had been making inquiries and he knew
there was a job for me, if I wanted it, at Withy Grove,
another centre of newspaper production in Manchester.
Moreover, he said that the directors at Cross Street were
making me an immediate cash payment (which proved to be
a handsome one) as compensation for the abrupt killing of
my paper. I started work on the editorial staff of the

Daily Dispatch forty-eight hours after closing the *City News*.
I was back to being a reporter again, though at a salary
bigger than I had been getting as an editor under the
Guardian; and I was at once happier and healthier without the
load of work and worry I had been prematurely carrying.
And, all unexpectedly, I had for the first time in my life
quite a sum of money in the bank.

I reported for Allied Newspapers at Withy Grove for
three useful years, getting a first-rate knowledge of Manchester and roaming the North of England on every kind of
story: from the Dr. Buck Ruxton murder trial (which was
the first time I heard the silver tongue of that great pleader
Norman Birkett) and Oswald Mosley's Blackshirt riots to
George the Fifth opening the Mersey Tunnel and Princess
Marina's honeymoon at Himley Hall in darkest Worcestershire. It was a carefree three years, an agreeable interlude
between the old worrying times at Cross Street and the
years of looming world war that lay ahead.

Domestically, too, they were halcyon days. I had a home
of my own in Manchester, and virtually another in Wigan
with my 'in-laws'. That pleasant, historic town—slum-
ridden only in part, and a comic dump only in the music-
hall legends invented by George Formby senior—was the
place where my wife's father, an astringent and respected
Welshman named Robert Owen, was Borough Electrical
Engineer. The post carried with it a good-sized home,
Bradford House, next to the power station in location but
next to a palace in comfort. The house was situated beside a
dirty old canal in a district of mean and squalid streets but
was blessed with gardens and high walls, so that it was in
fact an incongruous oasis of welcoming ease and plenty.
There at Bradford House I had spent almost every off-duty
day when I was a bachelor living in digs in Manchester;
there, now, was a cushioned long-stop for a young married
couple. I came almost to belong to Wigan, and to love it.
There is no more warm-hearted spot; and it commands
some of the best views in Lancashire. In short, a pleasant place
to live in.

Manchester was more grim and grimy, more ailing from
the Depression, from Japanese cotton competition, bad

housing and the loveless Dole. But Manchester, in the pre-war decade I spent there, was a rare and inspiring city to know, a box of delights. The Hallé Concerts in the Free Trade Hall; vintage elevens playing at Old Trafford; the eminent Laskis leading a talented Jewish community; the seventeenth earl of Derby, 'King of Lancashire', embellishing public occasions with his massive presence and looking like a buffalo in a three-inch white stiff collar; the richly comic characters who presided over the food shops and singing pubs in the medieval Shambles; the wild nights at the Press Club; the talent at that very different sort of club, the Salon, where you might meet a man who was then known to only a few people for his drawings of funny little figures in working-class streets, L. S. Lowry; Sherratt and Hughes' bookshop; the three big theatres where you saw most shows before London did; the tiny Unnamed Society Theatre is a Salford warehouse where Frank Sladen-Smith was putting on European classics long before the professional producers; and the dynamic Repertory Theatre in an old tram-shed at Rusholme where the young actors were mostly top-notchers of the future such as Robert Donat, Peter Glenville, Curigwen Lewis and Wendy Hiller—those were just part of the glory of Manchester.

All those and C. P. Scott too. The famous, downright man who edited the *Guardian* for over half a century and made it a great paper had just left the chair when I arrived in Cross Street, but he used to come into the building, a small grey-bearded figure bustling along the corridor. He seemed to me a fearsome period-piece. I was too late to see him perilously pedalling his bicycle through the city, but I did meet drivers who said they were still shocked at only narrowly missing him—and met members of his writing staff who were still smarting from the stylistic collisions they'd had with the old man.

Manchester was a newspaper city. Even the hundreds of little pony-carts darting through the cars in the streets as they swiftly delivered the *Evening News* and the *Chronicle* proclaimed the business in a way you couldn't miss. Journalism was a main industry, and the *Guardian*'s men led

the star-studded staffs of the dailies. The C. E. Montague–
Alan Monkhouse era was ending, but Neville Cardus was at
his best, spinning new shining webs of prose to the glory of
music and cricket; and the paper was riding high on a new
wave of finely perceptive writers including a reporter named
Howard Spring, who had already squeezed some of the juice
of Manchester into his first novels, *Shabby Tiger* and *Rachel
Rosing,* before Lord Beaverbrook bought him and whisked
him down to the *Express* in London.

This was also the Manchester which Louis Golding was
brilliantly presenting in his *Magnolia Street* and *Five Silver
Daughters.* It was the place where Walter Greenwood
was writing himself out of poverty and into *Love on the
Dole.*

To be there at such a fluent time was richness for anyone in
the writing trade: I was heady with words—and pictures
and music. Any man from those days may be forgiven his
emotion and his misty eye as he looks back, for to him
'Manchester in the Thirties' is a battle honour to wear.
He may well 'stand a tiptoe' when the epoch is named.

But, down to earth, the Thirties in reality was also an
epoch of horror and threat such as none would wish to
recall. By the time the decade was halfway through we knew
—at any rate anybody whose business was serious journalism
knew—that decencies and pleasures were under colossal
threat. The international situation was becoming so hideous
that enjoyments became spoiled by a background of apprehension—not of what was going on in Manchester but in
the wider world. Columns and columns of the newspapers
we served were heavy with reports of frenzied munitions
factories and gas-mask exercises, of Fascist dictatorships
and the persecution of the Jews. The quiet of Sundays was
shattered by newsboys crying special editions which carried
doleful and explosive tidings. It was not scare-mongering.
For this was the time of invasions and panic rearming.
The Hitler hysteria was surging to a peak, and on almost
every day a twist of the tuning-knob of our radio sets brought
from the loud-speakers the sickening screams of *'Sieg heil!'*
as the storm-troopers staged their monstrous rallies and
lusted for blood in front of the Führer of the Third Reich.

Manchester just before the war. A view up Market Street to Piccadilly, home of the B.B.C.

War comes to Broadcasting House, London, hit by bombs in the Blitz of 1940

Interviewing a soldier so new to the Middle East that he still wore an issue sun-helmet—Eighth Army never used them

My desert news-desk, 1942

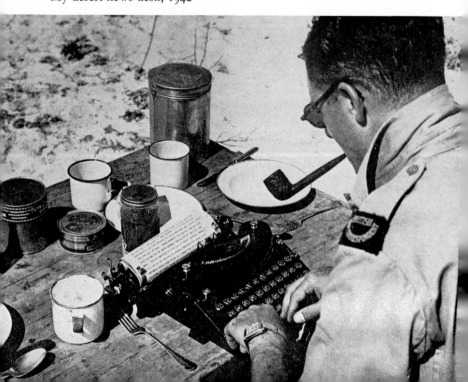

It was the time of Mussolini's slaughter of the Abyssinians and the tragedy of the Spanish Civil War.

It was also the time of the shock of the century in our own country: the Abdication.

This was a constitutional crisis without precedent, a fantastic news story both in itself and in the fact that during most of its course our Press wouldn't touch it. Although the crisis was building up throughout almost the whole of 1936, the general public in Britain knew next to nothing about it until it was almost over. Sage old King George the Fifth had died in January, and the Prince of Wales, golden boy of the Twenties, had succeeded him as King Edward the Eighth, beginning his reign as the cynosure of the nation's hopes and goodwill. But soon there began to emerge a situation which was disquieting to most of the few people in his own country who knew of it. He had become strongly attached to an American lady, Mrs. Wallis Simpson, and in that summer he was travelling in Europe with her. The 'Royal Romance' was featured for month after month in the daily newspapers and magazines of half the world—but hardly even a slight hint of it in our own newspapers or in the bulletins of the B.B.C. The King's friendship with Mrs. Simpson, and its implications—for she had already been once divorced, and it was felt that she would be unacceptable as Queen—simply was not reported. This was not because of any Government advice or Palace request to the Press: it was unprecedented self-censorship. By modern standards, it was timidity and sheep-like behaviour on the part of editors; by the code of that day, it was mass respect for the private life of the Royal Family. At any rate, although we journalists knew all the reports, our journals printed none of them. The public was ignorant of the storm that was to break.

Suddenly, at the beginning of December, the whole business burst into the open. The Fleet Street floodgates, so long shut firm by their keepers, were flung wide, and words and pictures devoted to 'The King's Fateful Choice' covered countless pages.

A news flash from the North first had split the silence. The Bishop of Bradford, Dr. Blunt, made a speech which

C

appeared to be a daring censure of the Sovereign. He hoped, he said, that the King would give 'more positive signs of his awareness' of 'his need for God's grace' if he was to do his duty faithfully. The Bradford *Telegraph and Argus* boldly splashed the story, and the news-agency wires hummed with the Bishop's words. Next morning the entire Press of the country, as though it had been waiting all year only for some excuse like this, carried at last the sensational news that the King wished to marry the American lady and would give up the Throne if that was the only way to do so.

But by that time the Abdication was virtually settled. The fact is that nine days after British readers were given the months-old story it was all over and the uncrowned King had left the country, unable, as he put it in a farewell broadcast from Windsor Castle, to continue 'without the help of the woman I love'.

It was widely gossiped that the Bishop of Bradford, in making his statement, had been used as a mouthpiece and instrument by the Establishment; that the Prime Minister, Stanley Baldwin, and the Archbishop of Canterbury, Cosmo Gordon Lang, had blessed and encouraged the Bradford words to bring matters to a head and get an unruly King out. The truth, however, was that Dr. Blunt, making an ordinary address to his diocesan conference, was doing no more than hint that, with an Abbey Coronation due, it was regrettable that the King never seemed to go to church. The Bishop afterwards told a colleague of mine that when he wrote the speech he hadn't even heard of Mrs. Simpson and that he never dreamed that his words would be reported outside Bradford, let alone cause a sensation.

Today the 1936 story of that King, the Duke of Windsor, is more than well known. So, thanks to books and television publicity, is the calmer story of the years that followed, bringing many years of happiness in each other to him and his wife—in other countries. In the perspective of the decades which have passed, his dilemma had at its heart a difficulty which his niece, Princess Margaret, faced a generation later when she had contemplated the possibilities of marrying Peter Townsend—a similar obstacle, though a different outcome. The trouble stemmed from the previous divorce of the other party—*because* of the doctrine of the Church of England that Christian marriage is binding until death.

Millions of words have been written about Edward the Eighth, but little has been told of the *effect* of the behaviour of the Press and the B.B.C. in that extraordinary Abdication Year. There really was no chance for people to say, little chance even to think, what they would have liked to happen to their Head of State. There was no time. Had it come in the Sixties or Seventies, the Abdication could not have happened in the way it did—because the ways of news have changed so greatly. In 1936 a constitutional atom bomb was exploded without a yea or nay from the King's subjects.

In any case, the climate of opinion in those days on royalty, conformity, divorce and duty was one in which existing order was largely unchallenged; and, had there been any such thing as public debate on the King Question, argument would have been so restricted and restrained that passions and prejudices would not have had full rein. Even the members of that cynical, freethinking race, the newspaper staffs, had comparatively little to say.

Had such a crisis developed today, when there are no taboos and little is private or sacred, imagine the publicity! There would probably have been no holds barred from the very start; pictures and stories would have filled the news, gossip and opinion columns; the radio stations would have buzzed with accounts of the Sovereign's parties and his family's pain; television journalism would have explored the question night after night at length—and as the programme boys love to say—'in depth'; we'd have had irreverent cameras at Fort Belvedere's gates, impulsive commentators on the Victoria Memorial, and, in the streets and in the studios, 'vox pop' interviews on what the King ought to do. With the pros and cons flogged out *ad nauseam,* with political debate prolonged, a King's Party would almost certainly have burgeoned and blossomed. The result of it all might well have been the same, but the road to renunciation immensely longer—and intrusively limelit.

As it was, that event of 1936, which should have been

cataclysmal, shaking the Throne and the country to its foundations, was over and done with very quickly and with few ripples even on the surface of our lives. It seems incredible now. A few hours after the monarch had gone into chosen exile, the Abdication was not a 'lead story' any more and the nation settled calmly down to its shy new King and its Christmas shopping, to the nuisance of the Nazis and the corruptness of France, to Franco and the Communists, the strutting Duce and stricken Haile Selassie, and to the Football Season and the English Winter. Swiftly and totally, a King was eclipsed.

I was glad enough to forget the episode myself; and to try, not very successfully, to carry on with life as though Hitler didn't exist. And what helped to keep the menace of war in the background was another change in my career— the one which took me to the B.B.C. It was good-bye to the rough and tumble of newspaper offices, and a plunge into the respectability of Reith radio. June 7th, 1937, was the date I joined the staff, six months after the Abdication.

I did not begin as a broadcaster. I had applied for, and was now appointed to, the post of Press Officer, North Region, in the Corporation's Public Relations Division. P.R. was then a relatively new and dignified calling, and the B.B.C.'s activities in this field were presided over by one of its pioneers in Britain, Sir Stephen Tallents. My part in Tallents' 'projecting' of broadcasting was projecting to the newspapers what the B.B.C. in the North of England was up to, which was quite a lot. From a small office in Manchester's Broadcasting House overlooking Piccadilly Gardens I fed to my former colleagues in the Press news about programmes—and notes about gaffes. The papers were beginning to take serious notice of broadcasting, and I was able to get a lot of publicity for our Northern transmissions. I knew the market and I had marvellous material to sell. Manchester was blazing a broadcasting trail, and the Northern output was providing the most virile programmes you could get for your ten-shillings-a-year wireless licence. London was holding the microphone up to whatever was going on—and the world's first public-service television had started at Alexandra Palace—but Manchester was originating new features and fully exploiting the arts of Sound.

The North certainly had talent. An eager young ex-schoolteacher from Tyneside, Cecil McGivern, was putting on strong regional plays; a girl with a lovely speaking voice, Olive Shapley, was beginning a long broacasting career with delightful Children's Hour entertainment; Hubert Foster Clark was the stylish Director of Music; Victor Smythe—who looked like all the cigar-smoking impresarios and showbiz kings rolled into one—had sport and the music-halls all sewn up, and his Outside Broadcasts were almost always taken by the National as well as the Regional net-works; poet John Pudney was one of our producers; the uncompromising Donald Boyd, from the *Guardian,* was making the Talks Department distinguished; and D. G. Bridson, the most original and revolutionary mind of the lot, was pioneering the craft of writing for radio, a poet making words sing and fight in such features as 'The March of the "Forty-Five"'—and creating huge programmes in which natives explored their own countryside, putting genuine moor folk and inhabitants of the mill towns on the air with unprecedented licence. I remember being on a visit to headquarters in London and hearing someone at a programme meeting in *the* Broadcasting House say: 'This Northern stuff is making our programmes sound boiled-shirt and prissy.'

Curiously enough, the creative blaze in North Region had been sparked by the arrival of a Southerner: a man who, until he made the journey from London, thought that woad began at Watford and that the North was a land of primitive darkness—Archie Harding, the most gifted and inspiring man ever to teach what radio was all about. Harding had been a features producer in London, turning out imaginative programmes of forthright reporting. When he had trodden on several official corns he was banished by the Director-General himself. Sir John Reith dubbed him a dangerous man and sent him to Manchester, where, he said, 'you can't do much damage'. So Harding was made North Regional Programme Director—and there could not have been a greater gift to the Region. He fell in love with the North

within weeks: it was a gloriously plain-speaking antithesis of
stockbroker Sussex, and he remained partial to it as long as
he lived.

I was to know Archie again a little later, when London had
realised its mistake and had hauled him back to the South
again. He became chief instructor of the Corporation's
training school, a swift killer of phoneys, a prime encourager
of literate and original rebels (he had been one of the first
people to see the quality of an unkempt girl named Joan
Littlewood, who in his Manchester days had tramped up
from London to knock on the B.B.C.'s Northern drama
door). He died sadly soon, but the mark he made on broadcasting is still there, and it owed a great deal to the spur
which life in the provinces gave to him. Nobody who worked
with Archie Harding in the North could forget his own huge
enjoyment of it all as he sat, in office or pub or studio control
cubicle, chain-smoking, wrinkling his nose and cracking
with laughter at some rude dialect joke, listening, drawing
out comment, talking slowly and shrewdly, long pauses
breaking the analytical flow whilst he waved a hand in the
air and sought for the one right word that he wanted. . . .
Those were vintage days.

But as the late Thirties became more and more clouded by
preparations for war, loathsome precautions of our own
prevented the full enjoyment of work on programmes.
B.B.C. employees had to attend lectures on air-raid drill and
such things as the treatment of mustard-gas casualties; and in
1938 staff dispersal plans were completed and made ready
for what seemed the certain coming of a national emergency.

Then, with the Munich Agreement, there came, at first, a
feeling of tremendous relief and thankfulness—before the
pact was realised to be a disgrace and a brief postponement;
and in that evil lull we carried on with our normal lives,
though knowing that peace could be shattered at any
moment. It was during the uneasy months in the middle of
1939 that I made another move, changing my job but not
this time my employer. Midland Region wanted a senior
Public Relations Officer. I was advised that it was a good
thing to move about within the B.B.C. (just as nowadays it
seems advantageous to move in and out of it), so I put in for

this post and got it. The change meant transferring to Birmingham from our comfortable Northern life; and, in the event, we removed at the most desperate time, September 1, just when the balloon was going up. For that was the day of another move: the German Army's march into Poland, the irrevocable step which started the Second World War. However, it was the day we had fixed, and on the morning of Blackest Friday, Bess and I—having parked our first-born, David, in remote safety—were flinging our furniture at random into a new house in King's Heath and listening to Government instructions on evacuation plans which were now pouring out of the wireless. That day the B.B.C. went into a single programme, common fare for the whole country. It was the signal for me to act on the instructions form, headed 'State of Emergency', which had lived in my pocket for months. The important command was: 'Report to Broadcasting House, *London*, as soon as possible.'

Most people that day, hearing of the bombing of Warsaw, expected that war would be inflicted on *us* too, within hours, by the bombing of British cities. Clearly, Birmingham was no place for my family, especially with me called away to London, so we had made a quick decision to shut up this house we had never lived in, to slam the door on the belongings we had just piled in, to go our ways and await whatever was coming. My wife would go and stay with her people in Lancashire whilst I was ordered south. I did, in fact, after Bess had been driven away north through the first nightmare black-out, spend a few fitful hours of sleep on a camp-bed in the new house before creeping out, just before dawn on September 2nd, 1939, to take my car to London and the duties in News Division to which I had now been directed.

No experience in the years of war that were to follow was as sickening and frightening as that Saturday-morning drive down the A5. It seemed obvious that I was driving to my doom. My own side of that main road was depressingly, significantly wide open and clear: I was the one solitary person being crazy enough to drive towards London. The other side of the road, the way north, was solid with traffic, nose-to-tail, every vehicle packed with families fleeing from the city to which I was heading. The roofs of the cars, the luggage-racks at the rear, even many of the bonnets, were piled high with mattresses, cots, prams, chairs, cupboards, bird-cages and all sorts of small household oddments hurriedly roped together. The people were getting out before the Germans raided London; and the effect of this exodus on my spirits was profound. I arrived at Portland Place in a state of gloom and jitters, unmitigated by the discovery that there *were* people remaining in the metropolis. I felt as though the bottom had dropped out of my stomach.

The feeling left me once I had walked through the doors of Broadcasting House. I reported to the News Room and was immediately given a desk as one of the new sub-editors needed to tackle the greatly expanded bulletins. Godfrey Talbot, Public Relations Officer, was dead; and in a flash seemed never to have existed. I was back in my proper trade, News, and down to the hard stuff of life-and-death facts as never before. From that moment I was too occupied and involved in the business of getting out the news to be scared of the terrible nature of it.

4

Words Go to War

When we became officially at war with Germany at eleven o'clock the next morning, Sunday, September 3, it was the Prime Minister who told us so in a broadcast at that hour straight from the Cabinet Room at Number 10 Downing Street. It was the gravest announcement the radio had ever carried, and it sounded so: when Neville Chamberlain said: 'Hitler can only be stopped by force,' the drained tones of that seventy-year-old voice conveyed not only the gravity of the nation's hour but the tragedy of a man who had striven for peace without force and had been palpably tricked. It was a moving message, but no clarion call.

Most of the staff on duty at the B.B.C. that day gathered in the concert hall of Broadcasting House to hear Chamberlain's words coming out of the big loud-speakers. Controllers, clerks, commissionaires, typists, engineers and announcers, they all gravitated to that lofty, windowless chamber which is the core of the building, and sat, sad-faced and quiet, on the tiers which rise above the stage. The concert hall had suddenly become a focus of our emergency life inside headquarters; and it seemed the most natural thing in the world that this place should now become each night a great dormitory and shelter full of 'sleeping-in' staff lying on mattresses laid on the steps all the way up the audience slopes, with a tatty curtain of army blankets slung right across the middle to separate the males from the females. By day, seats superseded mattresses.

On this first morning of war, nobody in that hall moved or spoke whilst the Prime Minister was speaking, though one of the canteen waitresses, who had been hovering at the door,

screamed 'Oh God!' when he had finished. Immediately the
National Anthem was played, and we all stood up.

Eight minutes later there came a noise which was to
make the heart jump and the spine shiver whenever it
sounded in the years to follow: the wailing siren of an air
raid warning. The effect was unnerving to a degree. A call
was made for six volunteers to go on watch on the roof.
The six men nearest the door departed at once, and the rest
of us felt as though they were going to their death. Someone next to me said: 'Just like the bloody Boche, to start
straight off with his first raid. And the railway stations are
still full of thousands of kids being evacuated, poor beggars.'
A colleague muttered: 'My wife's out in it.' We all assumed
that London was being bombed. But in fact the warning
had been sounded in error. No raid had taken place, and the
continuous note of the sirens, the 'All Clear', went very soon.
But out in the streets people had rushed to get indoors and
down into basements.

The incident was not made into a featured item in our
next bulletin. The News had gone to war and we had to be
careful of our words lest they should give away information
useful to the enemy and unnecessarily lower our own morale.
What we broadcast would be the truth, but nothing must
be done now which would help the Germans (that was also
why Television was abruptly closed down at the outbreak of
the war: its transmissions were on a wavelength which would
have given navigational aid to invading aircraft). There was
even a 'stop' on the climate: from the first moment of the
war we were not allowed to mention what the weather
was like on any day—until ten days after that day. Meteoro-
logical comment would have told the Luftwaffe what our
flying conditions were like.

So we had our own censorship—not to twist facts or
turn bad news into good, but simply to serve military
security. Names of regiments, numbers of troops or planes,
movements of Cabinet ministers and the Royal Family, these
were the sort of things we did not broadcast. Only when it
was clear that details of our losses and reverses, or the towns
which had been hit by bombs, were known to the enemy,
only then were the facts given. But news bulletins were

objective and unvarnished; defeats were not glossed over, grim situations not suppressed, chilling communiqués never doctored. All through the first years, when we were suffering defeat after defeat, the world and the enemy were presented with the stark badness of our state. So, when at last the tide turned and victories were coming our way, and we broadcast the stark truth of *them,* it was British broadcasting that had come to be firmly believed by the listening world, not the propaganda transmissions of the Axis powers. Such was the foundation of the B.B.C.'s reputation for honesty and accuracy and reliability.

In September 1939 all this lay ahead. But we had the censors with us from the start; not only military advisers to consult by telephone at the War Office, the Air Ministry and the Admiralty, but also experts who were attached to us in Broadcasting House. There were also teams of B.B.C. men who had been seconded to the new Ministry of Information—occupying University of London buildings in Bloomsbury—to act as liaison officers and consultants. It was all very complicated at first; and the special scrutiny of our output made life permanently difficult for those of us who were writing and editing the frequent bulletins. However, we were never 'taken over', never turned into a Government Department or even a State mouthpiece. Nor was the B.B.C. *directed* what to put out and what not to use. The editorial responsibility for the millions of words flowing out into the air in the calm and unruffled—and steadying and reassuring—voices of the staff announcers was that of the Corporation only. The B.B.C. remained independent, and trusted. Never before in an international conflict had there been such a thing as public broadcasting; and now radio was becoming the predominant source of information and a powerful instrument of war.

In the practice of my own job as a sub-editor in the News Department these considerations conditioned every day. The business of all of us in the News Room was to exercise our normal journalistic judgments and skills, and also to apply the yardstick of Security to everything we wrote for the news announcers (freed now from the peacetime injunction to wear dinner-jackets in the evening!) to read in the

bulletins which were on the domestic air from early morning
until late at night.

The large News Room was as comfortably untidy a place
as any subs-room in a newspaper office. It was scattered with
desks—and crumpled newspapers, teacups, trays of half-
eaten food, and tobacco smoke—and at each table sat a
'sub', with a typist at a small table beside him. Each of us,
well before each bulletin, was given a 'story' to write, or two
or three, according to the length and complication of the
news item. The material which was the basis of each item
came piling up on the desk: sheets of teleprinted news
'tape' from the clattering machines, messages from the few
staff reporters we then had, dispatches from the news-agency
representatives of the Press Association, Exchange Telegraph, Central News, British United Press, Reuters and the
Associated Press, plus the texts of official announcements and
war communiqués. Thousands of words on each story, all
to be read and assessed and boiled down to maybe four
hundred words, less than three minutes of bulletin time,
and only that much if the story was very important. It was
essential to get every item down to bare bones and clear
English, easy for the announcer to read and for the listener
to assimilate. In broadcasting, the listener must understand
what you are saying at first hearing—he must 'get it in one':
there can be no repeating—and yet the material must be
concise. So our constant preoccupation was squeezing all
the world's and the country's important news into a bulletin's
total number of words equivalent to only the words of
about one-sixth of one page of a newspaper. Such was the
task of preparing the material for that influential but ephemeral commodity, broadcast news.

The fact that all-out war did not come to us for months
did not mean that the News Room was without material.
There was the dying struggle of Poland, the shipping losses,
the existence (so far, a peaceful existence) of the British
Expeditionary Force in France, and the legends the French
were creating about their 'impregnable' Maginot Line.
At the same time, Government Departments were deluging
us with announcements about National Service in all its
aspects and a variety of morale-boosting instructions to the

public. I seemed to spend a lot of my sub-editing life in
writing about Finland, because, as 1939 wore on and the
Poles were silenced and overrun by Germany, almost the
only daily fighting we had to report was from that country,
where Marshal Mannerheim and his troops were putting
up a magnificent resistance to the onslaught which Russia
had launched in the snow and ice of the Karelian Isthmus.
But it was all rather unreal and remote to us in Britain.

What was real enough was the disruption of normal life.
The B.B.C. had scattered most of its programme departments, such as Drama and Music and Features, to what were
then reckoned to be safe areas up and down the country;
and Bristol, Manchester and Evesham suddenly found
themselves flooded with Head Office staff and bedevilled
by the problems of billet existence. Dispersals of broadcasting people continued through much of the war years;
and, to this day, people in the back streets of Bangor tell
each other stories of the hilarious times when the wild
comedians of the Variety Department descended upon the
city and stirred it up with goings-on such as North Wales
had never known before and has never known since.

In London, life was less jolly and more jumpy. We waited
for air raids hourly, and every bus in low gear sounded like
a siren alarm. In the early morning hours of one night during
that lovely Indian summer of September 1939, an Alert did
sound and got us out of our beds. Like many B.B.C. people
just then, I was living at the Langham Hotel just across the
road from Broadcasting House, billeted there in what in
fact was pretty luxurious accommodation. Later, the
Langham became what it still is, a B.B.C. building full of
rooms converted into working quarters (some people have a
bathroom in the office), but at the beginning of the war it was
still a hotel and all grades of B.B.C. staff, from the top brass
to the tape boys, were sleeping there. When the Alert went,
hotel staff at once began rushing up and down the wide
corridors blowing whistles and banging on doors. They
would not allow anybody to stay in bed: we were all herded
into the cellars where, in night clothes and dressing gowns,
we sat uncomfortably on the floor with a multitude of gas
pipes, electricity cables and water mains a few feet from

our heads. It was a most dangerous place to shelter in: we
would have been safer in bed. But the hotel manager—
clothed in a tin hat, khaki jacket, striped pants and brief
authority—was determined that we should stay in his
catacombs. No nonsense about it, either: he fussed up and
down, segregating the sexes, breaking up innocent conver-
sations between programme producers and secretaries,
and lining up the women in one wing of the cellars and the
men in another. Most people read books or talked sleepily;
some did crosswords; and a number of pocket chess-boards
were brought out. As time passed, and there were no
sounds of explosions or aeroplanes, the vigilance of the
manager and his henchmen relaxed, and several of his guests
wandered out into Langham Place and sat on their haunches
on the kerb in the warm, clear dawn of a beautiful morning.
The Director-General himself, Sir Frederick Ogilvie, was
there. He too had been shunted to and fro by the officious
hotel man; and now he sat with others on the pavement,
wearing an old mackintosh over his pyjamas, waiting for the
'All Clear'—a courteous and gentle man, smiling his handsome smile at the chatter of the messenger boys and office
cleaners perched unabashed beside him. (Sir Frederick was
the 'unknown' Director-General of the B.B.C. He had
scarcely begun to grapple with the awesome task of
succeeding the great Reith when he was saddled with the
shattering transitions which the war brought to broadcasting;
and he resigned in 1942.)

That Alert in the first September was a false alarm. There
were several such in the early days, but no raids; the
Luftwaffe was leaving London alone. As 1939 slipped
quietly away with nothing happening—and even the British
Army in France not engaged—we began to slip into frustration and then complacency and a false sense of security. The
situation was being called 'the phoney war'. A semblance of
normal life crept back: theatres, closed in the first days of
September, reopened; sporting events were held; the pubs
did hearty business; people took holidays; and evacuees
started to trickle back.

There endured, however, the Black-out. In London it took
some getting used to, as we groped and stumbled through

the unaccustomed gloom, relieved only by faint glimmers from the few cars that were about, by the pinpoints of brightness from the masked traffic lights, and by the flashing of torches from doorways as the prostitutes, still plying their trade in the West End streets, illuminated their silk-stockinged legs whilst they softly called their invitations.

The capital had plenty of food and plenty of entertainment. In my hours off duty I went to many films and shows. I ate well in restaurants without using coupons from any ration book. There was enjoyment in my bedside wireless set—for I was a listener to the radio as well as a writer for it. The variety broadcasts were good; and listening to Big-Hearted Arthur Askey and Stinker Richard Murdoch in 'Band Waggon' was a universal act of devotion and joy. Making fun of serious things became almost a patriotic exercise: there was a danger of the air raid wardens, with their tin hats and rattles, becoming a joke; we were no longer quick at adjusting the curtains when they shouted 'Put that light out!' and we tended to let the protective strips of brown paper on our windows peel off. We did not bother to sling those gas-masks in their cardboard boxes over our shoulders every time we went out. We sang, with giddiness and optimism, 'There'll Always be an England' and 'We're Going to Hang out our Washing on the Siegfried Line'. My wife emerged from her parental retreat and opened our Birmingham house; I went up from London and lived there during the regular strings of days-off which my spells of intensive shift-work gave me.

So we drifted along, in that 'bore war' of waiting, into 1940, whose only major discomforts at first were those of the long and intense cold weather which February brought. 'When spring comes,' said the pundits, 'get ready, for then Hitler really will start.'

They were right. The tension snapped in April when— five days after poor Chamberlain had declared: 'Hitler has missed the bus'—the Germans attacked Denmark and Norway. Then, on the 10th of May, the storm burst: the long-feared invasion of Holland and Belgium began; and, from the first moment of that blitzkrieg before dawn, Europe was plunged into all-out war. The news burst on us like a thunderclap, and brought a frenzy of events. Parliament, incredibly enough, had gone on Whitsuntide holiday the day before, and was hurriedly recalled; Chamberlain resigned and his place was taken by Winston Churchill, beginning his epic years as Prime Minister in an atmosphere of unprecedented alarm and consternation as the German forces swept across the Low Countries. Our British Expeditionary Force, moved from France into Belgium, was almost at once steam-rollered into fast withdrawal; and within a few days the enemy were at the Channel ports.

I remember my taxi driver in Regent Street one night saying: 'You're my last fare, guv. I'm getting out. The Boche are in Boulogne, so it's God help London now.'

It was hard not to be as gloomy as he was. As I sorted the 'copy' in the News Room that evening there was no item that was not either ominous or a message of sheer disaster. Britain was now under immediate threat of German assault by sea and land as well as air. We had our backs to the wall: defeat seemed more than a possibility.

Defeat—but not defeatism. Real war had brought out rare spirit, and refusal to be daunted by a desperate situation. It was a measure of the inspiration which the Prime Minister had given to Parliament and people, by the tocsin and tonic of his defiant speeches, that when the Dunkirk evacuation came that monumental retreat of a beaten army was popularly hailed as a victory. It was, of course, an extraordinary feat of bravery and improvisation for three hundred warships and four hundred other very assorted craft, including even tiny river launches, to bring back, under constant attack, 337,000 officers and men. It was, as Churchill, with superbly calculated grandiloquence, told a cheering House of Commons, 'a miracle of deliverance'. But in military terms it was a near-mortal reverse; and the delivered soldiers, whose task now was to try to defend their homeland, had few weapons and precious little equipment with which to do so.

And soon we were alone. France—of the vast and vaunted armies—France now seen with dismay to have a command rotten at the core—gave up fighting and asked Germany for an armistice. This final act of humiliation came on June 17.

Alamein front. The warning notice with graveyard crosses tells me that I am nearing the German lines

'Belinda' at breakfast-time, with the B.B.C. truck outspanned in the Western Desert. *Left to right:* conducting officer, the author, and engineer 'Skipper' Arnell

Mediterranean war reporting south and north of Tobruk — minesweeping at sea and map-reading in Cyrenaica

I was on duty that morning, and had to handle the dire news. I had been writing 'the French story' for some days; and a grisly business it had been to tell of the débâcle of a great nation and our ally. The surrenders of towns and cities, the fall of Paris, the scamper of the French Cabinet to Tours, to Bordeaux; the chill lack of response to Churchill's rallying calls; the resignation of the Renaud Government; Pétain tottering to capitulation—all this we broadcast. The daily communiqués from French Army H.Q. had been appalling; when they came in we pounced on them with apprehension and read with sinking hearts their pathetic attempts to gloss over the situation. The first sentences would extol the valour of the troops and claim large numbers of German tanks knocked out; then, at the end, would come a passage saying that a line had been established at such-and-such a place. We would turn to the map and, sure enough, the location of that place showed all too clearly that what the French had been really doing was retreating headlong. We wondered how long it would go on, and feared the worst. The worst came on the 17th. 'Pétain Seeks Armistice', was the flash.

I quickly dictated to my typist, for the announcer to read in the One o'Clock News, the story of the old Marshal's broadcast of surrender which had begun at 12.30 p.m. The story took up almost the whole of the bulletin. I wrote it with an audience breathing down my neck. Inside Broadcasting House that morning the seriousness of the situation had become apparent some hours before, as a stream of unofficial messages came through bearing reports that the French had stopped fighting and that everywhere the troops were laying down their arms. So, as I sat at my desk with a pile of tape in front of me, reading, scribbling, checking, and talking the story to the girl at her typewriter beside me, most of the other 'subs' in the room gathered round silently and helped to whip each foolscap page away smartly to the Duty Editor and the waiting announcer who was to read the news. The 'audience' behind my chair was also swollen by a succession of visitors to the News Room: controllers and heads of departments from all over the building came in, looked over my shoulder, saw what was

D

coming, whitened a little, and went out. 'So France *has* ratted,' was the comment.

There was a hurried high-level conference about the enormity of the news, the most grave and shocking since the war began. Should it be prefaced by some stand-by warning? Ought we to play solemn music first? It was decided that the 'headlines', the index to the News, should on this occasion be abandoned and that we should plunge straight into the bad tidings. Frank Phillips was the announcer on duty to read them (he spoke anonymously: we did not start naming the readers until a little later, when it was really thought that the Germans might land and set up a radio station in Britain, and put out instructions pretending they were from the B.B.C.—so the idea was that names as well as the tones of our news announcers should be recognised). Phillips read the story solemnly and sonorously, 'pulling out all the stops'. The beginning was: 'Here is the News . . . The announcement that the French Army had ceased hostilities during the night was made within the last half-hour by Marshal Pétain . . . in a broadcast to the French people.'

When the news was over, men sought each other's company. Most of the news staff went up Portland Place to the Thermionic Club to discuss what might happen next. We were now an experienced and hard-worked staff. Since the start of the German offensive, bulletins had been long and frequent; we had little time for the coffee or beer intervals, the secretaries' typewriters clacked away incessantly and the girls made poor progress with the knitting of khaki scarves and balaclava helmets on which much of their creative work had been concentrated during the quieter shifts of the 'phoney war'. A number of the girls were in the News Division crowd which gathered for a drink at the Thermionic that lunchtime after the momentous French cease-fire. There was speculation about a possible retreat now from Broadcasting House. The Germans were poised only a few miles across the water from the South Coast and, with the French no longer fighting them, they could turn their full attention to invading us. We in News had in fact prepared emergency operation rooms and communications in buildings north of London as a 'second line' for if the capital had to be evacuated; and it seemed now as though an enemy attack with men as well as bombs might come. Beer mugs in hand, we joked about what we would do when Dr. Goebbels walked into our workroom and took over the news-editorship at gunpoint; we made lots of laughs about how he would re-write the bulletins. The jokes were wild and silly, but they would not have been made at all but for a shadow of hard reality which now loomed over us, had we not felt that there might indeed be a possibility of field-grey parachute troops dropping onto Oxford Circus any day, storming north along Upper Regent Street to capture our radio station ready for Nazi propagandists to take over Broadcasting House.

Perhaps we were being fanciful; perhaps we were under-valuing our defences; and certainly we did not actually speak our fears. But on that day of the French defeat there was abroad an impression that anything might happen, and nothing pleasant. We talked to each other rather loudly, I remember. Charles Gardner (Richard Dimbleby and he, our first war correspondents, had been with the B.E.F.) called out: 'Come on, everybody, let's drink. All great empires end in an orgy.' Just words, just a jest: but the too-ready laughter with which we responded to Charles was forced by unspoken thoughts that this might indeed be the end of the world we knew.

But Winston Churchill's reaction was nothing of the sort. 'It makes no difference to British faith and purpose,' he said that day. 'We shall fight on, unconquerable, until the curse of Hitler is removed from the brows of men.' His words were colossal reassurance. Flamboyant oratory, if you like; but, at that time—and it was a time when dispassionate outside observers were writing us off as done-for—the words were worth a million men-at-arms, and they steadied and heartened the nation to a fantastic degree. It is difficult today to convey their effect to anybody who was not an adult in Britain in 1940; but to anybody who *was,* the effect was unforgettable. The nation hung on the wireless to hear such messages. Churchill made thirty-three major radio addresses during the war, sometimes reading from untidy pieces of

Number Ten writing-paper with jumbo typescript and pencilled impromptus on them. He rarely came to Broadcasting House but often spoke from his own study. One of our microphones was also ready by his desk in the War Cabinet's secret headquarters deep under Whitehall, a labyrinthine stronghold which was sophisticated in its communications but spartan in its domestic furnishing. The P.M.'s room in this burrow had bare brick walls and a very plain and small bed two strides away from the desk. Beside the bed was a cupboard, a candle, a chamber-pot with 'G.R.' stamped on it, and a 'scrambler' telephone through which Churchill used to talk to President Roosevelt—the clock above it was always kept showing Washington time.

The Prime Minister's broadcasts, whether from this battle station or elsewhere, were 'peak listening'; but his were not the only talks which had huge audiences. Listening-in was part of living; the B.B.C. was the Universal Informer.

There were the Postscripts, for instance, the long talks immediately after the Nine o'Clock News: they were a major platform and a national date. J. B. Priestley, with the deep voice and Northern accent which are such assets in broadcasting, was for a long time the regular star of those morale-boosting fireside chats, pregnant with homely philosophy and calculated pep. Duff Cooper too was good at doing them. Occasionally we gave the Postscript minutes to a hefty American journalist named Quentin Reynolds, who would fill his time with taunts against the enemy and studied insults to their leader, all in the form of an 'open letter' to the Führer. Hitler's family name having just been dug out, 'Quent' used to begin his talks with a gritty 'Dear Mr. Schickelgruber'. Other Postscripters, very varied in personal background and sound, were tried from time to time. Once the 'After the Nine o'Clock' piece was delivered with all the richness of Lancashire vowels by the ukulele-man, George Formby.

At the other end of the scale, we now and then had the First Family talking in the Postscript slot. I was once pulled out of my desk to 'produce' the Princess Royal when she arrived at Broadcasting House, in Auxiliary Territorial Service khaki, to deliver a national-campaign appeal. I liked her at once because she was so homely and said 'What a lot of fuss!' when she saw the D.-G., the bowing lift-commission-aires and the Home Guard escort in the entrance hall—and because she was humble about her script, asking if she could be shown how it might be livened-up a bit, and if she might be allowed to say 'Great' in front of 'Britain'. She was not, I fear, a heaven-sent broadcaster (which her father, the gravel-voiced and often irascible King George the Fifth, *was*: when in 1932 he gave that first Christmas Message over the air, long before the war, he *sounded* like the patriarch of his people—the Queen, when she was a little girl, hit it absolutely in calling him 'Grandfather England').

My favourite Postscripter was the ebullient Lord Mackin-tosh of Halifax (he was then Sir 'Arold), the phenomenally successful chairman of the National Savings campaigns: 'the Best Beggar in Yorkshire', himself a monument to hard work and thrift. I often looked after him when he came breezing in to say his piece (with a large tin of his firm's toffees under his arm 'to cheer up you news lads'), and he was always effective on the air with his forthright delivery and broad accents.

The funniest experience I had was in putting Lord Beaverbrook on the air one night at 9.15. The tough little Canadian had brought with him from the Ministry of Aircraft Production two bottles of Vichy water, a rubber cushion, and a respectful young speech-writing assistant who, by command, sat at the opposite side of the studio table and made extravagant thumbs-up applauding motions as his master growled and grimaced through his performance. I was terrified lest the acolyte should also cheer and clap.

Those jobs of organising V.I.P.s at the microphone were infrequent breaks in my regular sub-editor's work of writing the news. I was kept with my nose hard down at that job. Words were War Effort. Those of us whose business was words, who were producing them from the News Room, were in a 'reserved occupation', which meant that the Armed Services were not allowed to call us up for duty. But this did not preclude part-time auxiliary service; and when Anthony Eden (then Secretary for War) appealed for support for a force called Local Defence Volunteers, to deal with possible parachute landings by the enemy, most of us joined. We had no uniforms and no weapons. But when Eden broadcast he asked if anybody had any sporting arms which they might be patriotic enough to lend—and he had hardly stopped speaking before men started to arrive at police stations bearing shot-guns. It was with one of these heavy double-barrelled pieces—kept broken open by order 'for safety'!—in the crook of my arm that I as a Volunteer spent rota spells of guard duty outside the steel gas-door leading to the main B.B.C. engineering control room in the sub-basement. An armlet with the letters 'L.D.V.' on it had been strapped upon me, and I was supposed to be ready to deal with any rush of Germans down the stairs. As the two cartridges I had been lent were in my pocket, and my instructions were that I must not even insert them into the barrels without permission, the assailants would not have found me much of an obstacle.

The Prime Minister, who was never one for long phrases or fancy titles, disliked the name 'L.D.V.' and, in a broadcast talk, turned us into 'The Home Guard'. It was typical that he should find the right, robust term; and we ourselves enjoyed the new domestic label: apart from anything else, it seemed very suitable for a body of men who were drilling with broomsticks. We marched about very fiercely, the more so when after a while we were issued with a few rifles and got khaki battle-dress uniforms.

Broadcasting House itself was a camouflaged fortress in battle-dress. The handsome front doors and entrance hall were masked by sandbags, concrete barricades, wire and steel pillbox shelters. There was an inspection of passes before you were let in. For the B.B.C. was a specially guarded place, and the News Room was the nerve centre. When the bombs came—and the Battle of Britain and the Blitzes followed swiftly after the fall of France—the News Room, agency tape machines and all, was moved three floors below ground alongside the control room (and not far above the Bakerloo Tube, whose trains we could hear rumbling below when we were in the news studio). Very crowded and squalid and smelly it was too, that News Room, with bunks round the walls for sub-editors to sleep in during the few off-

duty hours they had when 'on shift'. Sordid but safe, we
said: the most tucked-away and secure journalists' workroom
in London. That is what we thought until one night when, as
we were preparing the Nine o'Clock, two brown paper
parcels came thumping down on our desks from the gallery
and a rough voice said: 'You're all dead. Them's bombs and
we're Jerry fifth-column attackers who've got yer!' We
looked up and saw four grinning men in khaki. They were
stranger Home Guards engaged in a defence exercise; their
object, the penetration and capture of Broadcasting House,
had been achieved. They had fooled our own guards. None
had a pass, none had any business to be in the place; but here
were strangers, through our defences and into the heart of
the nation's radio service. It made us think.

Now the air raids were going on by day as well as by night,
and the crump of bombs and the clanging of ambulance and
fire-engine bells were familiar sounds, so frequent that life
no longer stopped for a raid. In the daytime, people went
about their business with no clear idea whether an attack
was officially 'on' or not, so that when the sirens moaned
the continuous 'All Clear' note, you would quite often hear
the exclamation: 'Oh, was there an Alert on?' Familiar too
was the cough and stutter of ack-ack guns during that 1940
summer; and sometimes, from high in the blue sky streaked
with the white vapour trails of our fighter planes and pocked
with the grey puffs of shell bursts, there would come the
crackle of an aircraft's machine-guns. We did not realise the
fact at that moment, but up there a thousand young men of
the Royal Air Force—the fighter-pilot 'Few' of another classic
speech by Churchill—were forcing Hitler to shelve his
invasion plans.

Many people became accustomed to the war in daylight,
and bore it calmly. But the nights were hell. Sometimes,
between bulletins, I put a tin hat on and went out into the
streets not far from Broadcasting House to see what was
happening in the world outside. These excursions were not
usually prolonged, and I was often afraid as I walked, but I
always came back with first-hand impressions which were
valuable for the reports I was writing. The distant area of the
London docks was generally sending a red glow into the sky,

and, nearer, West End stores were sometimes in flames and collapsing. Fire-fighting appliances were the main traffic, but sometimes big mobile anti-aircraft guns would appear at the top of Harley Street or Great Portland Street and start banging away with a fury which rattled windows and doors and seemed as bad as the bombs.

Londoners went underground each night. I used to go down into the Tube stations to see them: hundreds of people lying on the platforms, so weary or so used to shelter life that they slept undisturbed by the trains roaring by only a foot or two from their mattresses. The Underground was their home, and an extraordinary community life sprouted there every night. People seemed positively to enjoy their cramped vacuum-flask meals, their sing-songs and their intimate bedtime chatter. It was part of the strange, incongrouus jollity of their Blitz-life. In the streets above, men, women and children were being killed and maimed and trapped in the debris of smashed buildings (during September 1940 alone nearly seven thousand civilians died and over ten thousand were injured in raids in the United Kingdom, and most of the casualties were in London); and yet the high spirits of many of the just-bombed, in the dangerous streets, matched that of the community-singing refugees down in the relative safety of the Tube shelters. Their reckless gaiety defied both Hitler and reason. Each morning, when the German bombers had gone home, you would find the inhabitants of ravaged streets wearing high spirits like a flag as they slopped about among the tangle of leaking fire-hoses in the ashes and smoke, salvaging pathetic bits of belongings from their demolished homes, sweeping up rubble and broken glass, drinking great mugs of tea from luckier neighbours who still had kitchens, and cracking jokes about not having to economise with their bath-water only up to the five-inch mark—because now they hadn't any bath.

It was a year of tragedy; yet, as I remember, cheerfulness kept breaking in. Such is the anodyne of time that recollections of small delights remain fast in the memory when dreadfulness has been forgotten. Sometimes I would be walking to Broadcasting House as dawn was coming up,

clear and fresh after a hideous night; and the sight of the
high barrage-balloons in those moments, all delicately and
rosily glowing as the rising sun touched them whilst the
earth was still dark, was marvellously beautiful. The sky
seemed to be a garden full of huge pink flowers. And
the peace of those mornings is something I shall never
forget.

For all the pain and destruction, the war days were
exhilarating days for quite a lot of people, days when it
felt good to be alive. Certainly in the 1940 Blitz dawns you
felt an upsurge of the spirit because you *were* still alive.
And, because you might die the next night, there was not
much time for bickering, not much point in moping and
moaning, not any call for beefing about hours of duty or
overtime rates. If ever twentieth-century Britain had a hard-
work and help-your-neighbour time, this was it. The worse
the situation, it seemed, the more the country joked.
Cataracts of disaster left good temper undamaged. Income-
tax was climbing from 8s. 6d. to 10s. in the pound, but there
was no revolt. German troops in invasion barges were near
our shores; we were losing airmen and aircraft grievously;
bombardment scarcely stopped; London was burning. But
the newspaper placards rejoiced and daily announced the
enemy air losses in the manner of Test-match scores under
the heading of: 'Today's Bag.' The B.B.C.'s Charles Gardner
excited everybody by standing on the cliffs of Dover and
broadcasting a commentary on a dog-fight, Spitfires and
Hurricanes versus a squadron of the Luftwaffe, as though it
was a sporting contest. (Numbers of listeners, properly and
with genuine misgivings, complained that our correspondent's description was offensive at a time of death and
sorrow, but even then, in 1940, the majority accepted the
style as part of the country's defiance and high morale; and
in the following four years, as the war came near to everyone,
even the protesters' attitudes changed, and breathless close-
up broadcasts of battles were avidly accepted.)

When Broadcasting House was hit by bombs there was an
overwhelming reaction of pride that the B.B.C. had taken its
place on the casualty lists. Announcer Bruce Belfrage,
reading the Nine o'Clock News from the bulletin studio—

now situated deep in the bowels of B.H.—paused only for a
second when the blast came down the lift shaft and burst
through the studio door; his colleague Freddy Allen, blown
out of a corridor by the explosion, picked himself off the
floor of an important room and remarked that it was the
only time he had gone through a security door without
showing his pass.

We did not announce that B.H. had been hit. The bombs
had not stopped broadcasting; and, in any case, news of
just what had been hit during a night of raids was not
normally released the next morning, for there was no useful-
ness in cheering the listening foe by announcing that his
aiming had been good or bad, or that this and that building
had 'caught it'. Often we did not name even the cities which
had been raided overnight—at least not at once.

During this period, a singularly trying morning was
experienced by me personally—and professionally: I made
my first broadcast and spoke some news myself. I was not
named, for the simple reason that I shouldn't have been
doing it: my début was an accident. The announcer due to
read the breakfast-time News overslept, and the panic
search for him during the last few minutes before the bulletin
hour failed to reveal him because of confusion over which
room in the building he had been sleeping in. It happened
that I had written a good deal of this bulletin, so my Duty
Editor said: 'You'll have to read it yourself.' Which,
shaking with nervousness, I did. The announcer, in his
pyjamas, appeared in the control cubicle next to the studio
when I was halfway through, but they signalled me through
the glass panel to continue reading, and I finished the lot
without any major fluffs. It was reckoned afterwards that I
had not done too disastrously—for an amateur in an
emergency. 'We could make out what you were saying,
just,' was the studiedly grudging reaction of my fellow subs.
Several people said kindlier things.

It so happened that, soon after this, I gave my first radio
talk in my own right. Although the Blitz was still at its
height, life was not all fire-watching; and our broadcasting
in the News periods began to include short 'news talks'.
These were topical items or occasionally sheer escapist

idylls, put in as a relief from battle communiqués and instructions about ration books. Some of the talks had to be related to items in the bulletins they followed, but often they reflected scenes and activities remote from the fighting. My wife and small son, our own house now being permanently abandoned, had gone to live in a spot as peaceful and as far removed from battle zones as could be imagined: Gatesgarth Farm in the Lake District beside Buttermere at the foot of the Honister Pass; and I had travelled up there— many long hours in a blacked-out train to Penrith, then a lift in an old car—to be with them during a few days' leave. The quietness of that Cumberland valley encompassed by high fells where only the sheep lived was in unimaginable contrast to the thundering London from which I had come; but one afternoon the peace was broken—not by the King's Enemies, but an Act of God. By a whirlwind, no less. I was out on the road at the bottom of the pass, walking with my boy and two other young children, when we saw it coming across the lake in an amazing column of spinning, sucked-up water, and making straight towards us. As it left the shore, it whipped off barn roofs and fences, and approached so quickly that there was no getting out of its path. I grabbed the children and hugged them to me. They were almost torn from my hold when the wind hit us and trees crashed down across the road before and behind us. Off it went, to lose itself up the slopes of Fleetwith. We were left shaken, but unhurt. It was a rare and fantastic experience; and when I was back on duty in London I told some of my colleagues about it. A talks producer, overhearing my tale, suggested that I might try writing a three-minute word picture of the storm—and before I knew where I was they had me on the air giving a talk about it.

That was the beginning. Listeners' letters came in, remarking on my little piece and the way it had been told. And, in the office, the Talks unit asked if I could be released from sub-editing duties from time to time in order to report 'in his own voice' on various aspects of wartime life. So I started as an occasional broadcaster, a reporter on not only city fires and sudden death but on food and farming, on salvage campaigns and Saucepans-into-Spitfires drives, on

tank factories and aircraft production, on lunchtime canteen
concerts and Land Girls digging for victory in Hyde Park.

Suddenly I was summoned to have my 'medical' before
call-up for the army. Evidently, I thought, my civilian days
of decreed exemption were about to be ended. The post-
card said my National Registration number was EXX 21181,
and ordered me to report to a drill hall in Acton at
8.15 a.m.

When I got there it seemed as though half the B.B.C.
staff had been called. We were kept for four hours. First
there were intelligence tests, presided over by an avuncular
staff sergeant who almost filled in the answers and fitted the
jig-saw puzzles for us. Then we stripped our clothes off
and, in a long line, passed before seven army doctors sitting
in a series of rough cubicles made of boxwood and sacking.
At the outset we were each required to make water into what
looked like a small lager glass; and at this stage the performances of two of my friends—both heavy drinkers and
only just out of a well lubricated night-shift—were not
appreciated by the doctors: my friends found themselves
unable to stop urinating when the glass was full, and soon
the floor was awash. Next we were stethoscoped and prodded
and measured; we were tapped on heels and soles, and had
our reflexes tested by one doctor who flourished a rubber
mallet with evident enjoyment—and who nearly had his
teeth kicked out by my own extreme reaction when he
whacked me below the kneecap. After more inspection, I
was told I had passed Grade One, and this was written on
my card. A clerk asked me to state which post office my
wife's allowance should be paid to when I became a soldier;
and finally I was paraded before a very old colonel sitting at a
trestle table piled with grey files. He asked me which branch
of the army I wished to join, and, as I had not thought about
this, I played for time by remarking that the B.B.C. had told
me that my war job was with them and that I was 'Reserved'.
I had not thought, in fact, that I *could* join the forces. At
which the colonel gave a grunt, and growled: 'Indeed!'
He then peered through some papers for a few moments,
and jerked his head up, looking at me for the first time.
'You're right. You are. We can't have you. Godfrey Talbot

is it, eh? Hum! Well, there it is. Sorry you've been troubled. Good day to you.'

But soon afterwards I did get into soldier's khaki—part-time khaki at first. The Corporation had me officially accredited as a British war correspondent, and I was issued with Licence No. 210, permitting me to carry out the duty of reporting with the Armed Forces of the Crown, or Allied Forces, in the field overseas. I was entitled, it added, to be treated as an officer—which made me feel rather grand, though rather less so when I read on and found that I was also 'entitled', in the event of capture by the enemy, to be treated as a prisoner of war (with status equivalent to that of a major). All of which was intended to tell the enemy, if I were put in the bag, that, although I would be found to be a civilian dressed as a soldier, I was in fact unarmed and still in the employ of the British Broadcasting Corporation—and that they ought not to shoot me as a *franc-tireur*.

I was furnished with uniform and equipment which included a Service respirator, a Sam Browne belt, brown boots, a camouflaged gas-cape and a long-skirted cavalry greatcoat. My shoulder-flashes said 'British War Correspondent' and my cap badge a golden 'C' on a green field. Round the 'C' was stitched a chain. I believe the chain was an emblem of communications—and *not* in memory of the original design for the badge, which had consisted (before the War Office thought what else this might represent) of *both* the initial letters of the words 'War Correspondent'.

The accreditation did not at once get me into battle in foreign fields; but it did get me out of the News Room. My broadcasting voice and the material of my reports had been liked, and I was transferred from 'subbing' altogether and set to handling news-talks speakers and doing regular talks myself. So began a career which I enjoyed then, and continued to enjoy for the next thirty years—that of a roving special correspondent and broadcasting reporter.

Not yet overseas, however. I spent months with the troops in training and on defence in Britain, and, with soldiers and with civilians (who in the cities were seeing more action than most of the troops were), covering almost every aspect of the wartime scene, becoming a frequent commentator and a known voice. I had the distinction of being quoted and jeered at by the notorious 'Lord Haw Haw', the traitor William Joyce, in one of his familiar sneering broadcasts from Radio Hamburg.

Radio broadcasting was starting to make household names of several reporters, and for the first time was also bringing into prominence staff speakers whose work was always *inside* Broadcasting House: the announcers, the men who read the News. They were being named as a matter of policy now. 'Here is the News, and this is So-and-So reading it.' The form was a novelty, but the innovation was welcomed by the public and by most of the men concerned. They were models of English-speaking: Stuart Hibberd, the Chief Announcer, kindly and sweet-tongued, the best-known voice; Freddie Grisewood, urbanity itself; Frank Phillips, resonant and reliable; Alvar Lidell of the perfect diction; John Snagge, booming and unmistakable; Lionel Marson, always the gentleman announcer; Bobby McDermot, clear and lively; Joseph Macleod, possessor of a beautifully rich voice, and a man who could read ten minutes of difficult stuff flawlessly at first sight; Freddy Allen, a very professional little all-rounder from B.B.C. Manchester; Bruce Belfrage, who read bulletins with such a virility and punch that a North Country friend of mine was once prompted to say: 'When that Belfrage reads out about how many German planes was destroyed 'e sounds as though 'e shot 'em all down 'is self'; Wilfred Pickles, who had been an announcer in North Region, and whose Pennine tones brought unaccustomed variety into the news-reading team for some months; and the imperturbable, so competent Alan Howland, to my mind the best newscaster the B.B.C. ever had.

The whole nation knew the voices of those men. They were favourites, each with millions of ardent followers. They were part of daily life; and indeed in many listeners' minds were part of the news they spoke. None, however, was more powerfully identified with his material than was Frank Phillips—at any rate in the view of one wartime listener. Frank had a break from news-reading towards the end of 1940, but returned in the spring of the next year.

On the 1st of May the Director-General received (from a lady in Stourbridge in Worcestershire) the following letter, written with dead seriousness, a *cri de cœur* if ever I heard one:

'Can't you take Mr. Phillips off the News? As long as he is on this service, the war news gets worse and worse. When he left it before Xmas, everything went well—till he came back. I have not the least objection to him personally, but felt a shiver when I heard him start on the News again this year. I said that everything would go wrong and so it has. If you look up dates, you will find they do synchronise as I have said. Do put him on to something else before we lose the war.'

. . . And some have greatness thrust upon them!

I was never a radio news-reader or announcer myself (except for that one fortuitous morning) but always a commentator and reporter of events, delivering my own material (the jobs may seem much the same to listeners and viewers, but 'in the trade' the difference is quite distinct). All through 1941 I was a busy user of the mobile microphones and recording cars, one of a handful of staff correspondents bringing in eye-witness accounts, sound impressions and on-the-spot descriptions of the fighting, the air raids, and civilian war work of a hundred kinds. Our contributions gave flesh and blood to the bulletins' bare bones of brief and often formal statement; our human reaction and the voices of the people we interviewed brought authenticity and reality to the words of the official communiqués.

As such work became my full-time business, I had to give up that sideline I had enjoyed: producing V.I.P.s' talks. For I was spending less and less time inside Broadcasting House and more and more days and nights with the armed forces—on ack-ack gun sites and wired and mined beaches, in reconnaissance aircraft and sometimes bombers, in Service training schools and camps and secret arsenals, in bombed cities and in hospitals. I had to interview pilots back from fighter sweeps and commando raids, from Atlantic patrols and the war in the Mediterranean. I went in small patrol boats on coastal sorties. Some of these were less uncomfortable than the mock battles and invasion-and-

defence exercises on land, in which I was often involved for
days at a time in various parts of the country as the army at
home gathered strength and sharpened its claws.

There were certain exercises which turned out to be more
realistic than was intended. One practice battle which I
covered—and scampered and suffered and slept with—took
place in rural Dorset and was memorable for the seriousness
with which the local militia took its part. Home Guard units
in the district had been brought into our 'battle' during the
week-end in order to give them a little experience of working
with regular troops. But it was the regulars who got the
experience. Several of the Home Guard men, bored perhaps
with being inactive defenders of their homes, so relished
their temporary role as attackers that they refused to be
'killed' and drop out when the umpires told them they had
all run into an ambush and were dead, and they proceeded to
'capture' the town which was the headquarters of the opposing side. They stormed into the place literally and dramatically, lying down on top of the carriage roofs of an arriving
passenger train—through tunnels and all—knocking down
members of the town station staff when they arrived, and
engaging in actual fisticuffs with surprised infantry soldiers
who were supposed to be defending a barracks. The eager
amateurs felled two of their opponents with rifle butts, and
broke the barracks gate. Then, thoroughly enjoying themselves, they picked up a few more fellow Home Guards and,
moving on a few miles in stolen vehicles, reached a delightful country house which was Command H.Q. of one of the
armies in the exercise. They found the field telephone wires
leading into the place and, instead of tying coloured tapes
round them to signify that they had been 'cut', they procured
clippers and actually severed the lot, and ordinary G.P.O.
lines as well, thus effectively ruining the whole communications system of that bit of the world. Whilst the general in
command was having a leisurely bath in the house (he was
not making too hard work of the exercise), the part-timer
heroes, now elated with success and the contents of somebody's flask, crept into the house and removed the general's
clothes, including his boots and revolver and favourite
swagger cane, and threw the lot into a stream.

There was hell to pay, understandably. But it was, if nothing else, a measure of civilian keenness; and when I broadcast a rather offbeat account of the happenings, I received delighted letters from Home Guards, and other hearers.

However, this was lightweight stuff. I was working hard, and sometimes in a certain amount of hazard. But I felt I was 'playing at it', a war correspondent who had not been to war—not out of the country, at any rate. I agitated to be sent abroad, but the Higher Command at Broadcasting House kept sending down the dusty answer: 'Talbot cannot be spared from the Home Front.' I protested that this was rubbish; and meanwhile it looked as though there would soon be no war to go to, for everywhere the Allies were being pushed out of their ground. True, invasion had not come to our own country, and our Home Forces were building up strength; but the general war picture was getting blacker and blacker. Our ships were being sunk. German divisions were advancing through Russia. The Japanese were swarming all over the Far East—Singapore, Java, Rangoon, Mandalay, we had lost them all—and the Mediterranean theatre of war looked no better. We had retreated out of Greece and Crete; and, although we had licked the Italians in Libya and swept far beyond Benghazi, the Germans had now taken over this North African front and were very different opponents indeed. Outmanœuvred and outgunned, our desert forces were retreating as fast as they had advanced.

Such was the situation in the spring of 1942 when Patrick Ryan, then the B.B.C.'s News Controller, told me one day to get down to the War Office at once and arrange to get inoculations and tropical kit, adding: 'You're going to the Middle East. We're recalling Dimbleby.'

This was the sort of command I had been waiting for. It was also a shock. Replacing Dimbleby? There was in fact, as Ryan explained, a melancholy story behind the change. Richard Dimbleby—the man who was to have such a distinguished career, to be the foremost, and bravest, commentator in war and in peace—had for many months been our war correspondent in Greece, Syria, Albania, and now in the Egyptian and Libyan campaign. Fortune was

E

treating him scurvily: he was reporting retreats, never an easy thing for a reporter to do. And in Cairo he had been getting a raw deal. As our soldiers in the desert fell back, and optimistic official reports were followed by disillusioning admissions of inadequacies and reverses, Richard—perforce back at base in Cairo more than he wished to be—was for some time persistently given information and 'guidance' by army public relations spokesmen which did not correspond with the position at the front; and his broadcast messages, heard by the desert fighting troops as well as Supreme Command and the listeners at home, caused complaints, and the B.B.C. was accused of peddling the official view. Dimbleby was a scapegoat. For the first and only time in his eminent life, temporarily, unfairly and uncharacteristically, he was unpopular—even, strange though it sounds now, with the B.B.C. At any rate, the Corporation decided he would be best removed from the Middle East, and I was to go and take over.

For me it was the real thing at last.

5

A Microphone at Alamein

Going overseas revolutionised my existence, established me
as a commentator, and became the turning point of my
professional career. No experience in my life has matched
the war in the Western Desert of Egypt. It was a thing apart.

El Alamein . . . Mersa Matruh . . . Sidi Barrani . . .
Buq Buq . . . Hellfire Pass . . . Sollum . . . Tobruk . . .
Tripoli . . . Wadi Zem Zem . . . the Mareth Line. It is not
fanciful to say that to this day, after thirty years, those
places on the march from the Nile are remembered with
unique nostalgia and a lift of the chin by men who were with
the Eighth Army. The recital of the names is a drum-beat
and a litany.

But in the early days of 1942, before I went for the first
time to the Mediterranean, such places were nothing but
pin-points on a map; and many frustrating weeks passed,
even after my posting to the Middle East, before they became
anything else. In London, champing at the War Office bit
over the delay in getting me shipped out, I discovered that
my movement order bore a priority degree not high enough
for swift transit. They then put me in a more urgent
category, but still I had to wait. Unless you were a general—
and went by air, high and in hazard—the business of
travelling to Egypt was long and difficult, for the simple
reason that enemy-occupied Europe was in the way.
Most soldiers went in troopships all the way round South
Africa and up the Red Sea. Eventually, I was dispatched, as a
'special case', as one of twelve passengers in a small merchant
ship—by way of West Africa, which was supposed to be a
quicker way. In fact, however, the S.S. *Thomas Holt*,

in which I had taken passage—out of Oban, of all places—
shuttled about the Atlantic in convoy, avoiding German
submarines for many days, and languished in Freetown and
Takoradi before depositing me in Nigeria, whence I hoped
to fly straight across to Egypt.

In Lagos I found myself stuck again: aircraft space was at a
premium, and all the news was bad. Encircled Tobruk had
fallen and our forces—what remained of them—had been
pushed clean back into Egypt, only seventy miles from
Alexandria, and, weary and baffled, were desperately digging
their toes in at the last natural defensive position before the
Nile valley. Only the fact that Rommel's Germans, after
their phenomenal advance, had run out of steam just as our
tired men had, seemed to have stopped them from punching
clean through to Cairo. This was the war I was going out
to cover! I was still far away from it, and it looked as
though there would not be much Middle East left if I
didn't hurry. And that was maddeningly impossible.

'My dear chap, there's a crisis on. We're filling every plane
with spare parts for aircraft and tanks. Not a hope of getting
you a flight yet.' Thus the Movements Officer in Lagos.
I pestered his office day after day in vain, until in desperation
I tried another way. B.O.A.C. were running flying-boats
across the middle of Africa and, managing to wangle myself
a place in one of them, I flew with many stops up the River
Congo and on to Lake Victoria in Uganda; from there, a
whole week after leaving the west coast, our boat flew down
the Nile.

I reached Cairo on the second day of August, six weeks and
ten thousand miles after leaving home.

Cairo was all sweat and confusion. Not panic. On the
contrary, it was a scene of such exotic normality that it was
confusing to me, the newcomer, who had expected to find
the atmosphere of a beleaguered garrison. The noise, the
smells, the flies, the shuffling crowds; the importunate
pedlars of shoe-shines and sun-glasses and dirty postcards;
the flea-bitten gharries and the clanging tramcars bursting
with caterwauling Egyptians dressed in filthy garments like
long striped nightshirts; the veiled women in voluminous
black; the glaring shops and open-air cinemas—it was all

rather overpowering. And the heat! You could have fried an egg on the pavement in Emad el Dine (one day I saw a drunken Jock reel out of a Union Jack Services Club and do just that).

Although they had dug trenches out beyond the Pyramids and stacked sandbags under the Sphinx's chin, although our Embassy and British G.H.Q. inside the wire barricades of the Semiramis Hotel had been burning secret files and treating Cairo to a rain of ash, although British wives had been sent to Palestine or South Africa for safety, Cairo did not look like a city with Rommel at the gates. The Germans were less than four hours' motoring away, and there was little but sand to stop them if they got through the hurriedly prepared positions of the 'Alamein Box' where the exhausted Eighth Army had managed to halt their retreat and turn at bay; but all this was something the capital had learned to live with and settle down to. I found soldiers, like any tourists, taking camel-back joy rides from the Mena House grounds, and there was still dancing out there every night. Officers drank leisurely coffees and ate the sweet cakes of Groppi's with calm regularity; they swam in the pool beside the cricket ground at the Gezira Sporting Club. Back-street cafés and belly-dancer cabarets flourished. Troops in their khaki-drill shorts were to be seen milling around the streets under a sun that burned like a blowlamp; they were happily buying souvenirs and singing vulgar rhymes about King Farouk, while Shepheard's watched. The old hotel, once a headquarters for Napoleon's officers, stood amongst its dusty palm trees a little aloof from the turmoil of the road in front of it and wearing an air of imperturbable permanence. Red-tabbed staff officers, the base-wallah 'Gaberdine Swine' (as fighting men out in the blue called them), sat on the hotel terrace ordering the tarbooshed suffragis to bring them gin drinks with names like 'suffering bastard and limoon'. Drinks were a long time coming, and the service always impersonally obsequious. You felt that the Nubian waiters at Shepheard's would not turn a hair if tomorrow they were taking orders on that same terrace from the *obersts* of the Afrika Corps.

I was surprised, too, by the B.B.C. situation in Cairo.

Our people, like the rest of the city, had become accustomed
to having the enemy, stalemated but menacing, 'just up the
road' at this El Alamein place. We had nobody at the front:
the war was 'uncovered'. Richard Dimbleby, an ample and
amiable figure, was about the town and, though he paused
to welcome me cordially, was socially busy making his
Middle East farewells; and our war-correspondent recording
engineer and our desert transport were also back in Cairo.

The little office which the Corporation had established in
the capital was preoccupied not with the critical state of
affairs at the front but, as far as I could make out, with timeless programmes for the Arabic Service, and was using the
recording machine which should have been at Alamein to
cut discs of an imam reading passages from the Koran. Our
office at that time—before the B.B.C. set up house in a
snob avenue of residential Garden City near the banks of
the Nile—was a poor apartment over a squalid street,
Sharia Gameh Sharkass. A robed but unwashed Arab, who
kept a sheep in his 'porter's lodge', guarded the ground-
floor gates of the ancient French elevator which served our
premises. When after a shouting match with him you
ascended aboard the lift in a series of jerks, you had to be
careful to get out at the right floor: the floor below ours
housed an abortionist and the floor above, a brothel.
Mistakes were often made: our recording sessions were at
times interrupted by inebriated soldiers searching loudly
for Madame Fifi.

My own business was not with offices in Cairo but war in
the desert. However, I had to spend a few days scurrying
round the sweltering city to pay ordained contact-calls and
'make my number' at G.H.Q. and also at the British
Embassy. This meant the first of many meetings with that
giant of an ambassador, Sir Miles Lampson, in his actions
as well as his physical stature a diplomat larger than life, a
man called by Winston Churchill 'the King of Egypt'.
It was typical of Lampson (later to be Lord Killearn) that,
shortly before this, when the security of our bases in the
Delta was threatened, he had smartly called to heel the real
king, the wayward and lascivious Farouk, by marching into
the Abdin Palace—which he had surrounded with a

battalion of troops and armoured cars—ordering the fat monarch to stop conniving at German propaganda, and demanding (and getting) a change of Egyptian Government to bring into office a Prime Minister favourable to the British.

When I did set off to the front I equipped myself with extra kit and supplies which old desert hands assured me was 'the absolute minimum for your first shufti, old boy'. I took a thousand cigarettes (to barter for eggs with wandering Bedouin), medicine against 'Gippy tummy', a crate of Stella beer, three bottles of whisky (to make the jerrican water drinkable), toilet rolls and a spade, a horse-hair fly-whisk, a bedroll and sleeping bag, and a pair of 'brothel creepers', desert boots of honey-coloured suède with thick rubber soles. Also three weeks' rations from the bulk NAAFI.

It was a new start for me and a new start for the B.B.C. in the campaign, for we rode in an army staff car of our own and a recording truck, a fat khaki thirty-hundredweight, just built by Army Workshops to take our heavy technical gear. This vehicle was to be our workroom and studio and house. It had a double skin, and from its sides we could spread tents like wings when we camped for the night. I say 'we' because I was by no means alone. There were five of us, a self-contained B.B.C. unit with the army: besides me, the party consisted of B.B.C. engineer W. R. (Skipper) Arnell, a tough and enterprising little man who had had desert experience already; two very unmilitary R.A.S.C. drivers: Sherlock, a gentle West Country boy, and Pretswell, an invincible hobbledehoy from Carlisle who didn't give a damn for anybody; and a conducting officer provided by Army Public Relations. We had, as time went on, an oft-changing series of these officers. They were always captains, and I was not always lucky with them: several could not read maps or drive or cook or comprehend radio, but they were jovial passengers whenever we had them with us, and all possessed one splendid quality—they seemed to have been at school with half the senior officers of the army, which meant that it was all Christian names in Divisional H.Q. tents from the start, and a smoothed entrée for me into the dugout

operations rooms and intelligence officers' map lorries which
from now on were my sources of information to supplement
what I saw of the fighting for myself. For desert life became
a matter of crawling around through choking dust and
crumbling rock, and din and discomfort. The hot, hard
wilderness which was called the Alamein Line was our home.

The surprising thing was that it wasn't a line at all; nor
was Alamein a place. The desert war was fought on a wide
stony plain, decorated by yellow outcrops and low, colour-
less scrub: a huge sand-tray, remote and isolated, neither
tropical nor European. There was not a tree or a stream or a
blade of grass; not a house, not a hut; and the only inhabitants, save for the occasional begging Arab who would
appear in your camp in an evening out of nowhere, were the
soldiers themselves. It was hard enough to find *them*,
especially in that August of 1942 when the lull was on and
both we and the German and Italian divisions opposing us
were building up strength for the next round, entrenched
behind deep fields of sand sown with four million mines.
You could be at an infantry command post or a forward
battery or even a divisional headquarters and hardly be
aware of it. All you saw were a few brown-and-yellow
camouflage nets over sand-blasted dun trucks widely
dispersed. The desert looked empty, for its men, its
perspiring and fly-pestered men, lived like rabbits in holes.
They were the same colour as their surroundings—all over:
not only khaki shirts and khaki shorts but khaki faces too,
with blown sand caked on the sweat of their skin.

A day or two after I joined the Eighth Army, however, a
person arrived who cut a different figure: Winston Churchill
himself. Even if he had not been the British Prime Minister
he would still have been a sensation among the troops as he
visited both the Alamein positions and the reserve areas in
the Delta. For he was dressed as nobody else. One day he
wore an Old Colonial suit of white ducks, and on the next
day that one-piece blue romper suit which we knew in
England. Whichever outfit he had on, he sported with it a
white solar topee, a white sunshade and a fat cigar. He
stumped about the camps and glared at the tents. He watched
the soldiers. When even two or three were gathered together

he gave them his V-sign. Up in the forward areas—the 'sharp end', as we used to say, nearer to the enemy—he seemed to be in his element. He had never seen the Western Desert before, and when he first arrived at Alamein, beginning a tour of some of the units at their fighting stations, he stood for a long time gazing across the sands shimmering in the heat towards Rommel's observation points, asking questions and grunting, then staring and staring in silence. Later, he spoke a message through my microphone, beginning: 'This war in the desert has to be seen to be believed. It's a wonderful thing to see the Desert Army at work. This looks unlike any other war that has ever been written about or fought.' Off the record, he had described the desert as: 'Miles and miles of arid austerity. How Stafford Cripps would like this!'

We were not allowed to 'release for broadcast' the recorded message, not until the Prime Minister had completed his Middle East tour and returned safely to the United Kingdom, for his visit was an official secret. The field censors not only banned any reference to the Churchill presence in our dispatches, but frowned on even a conversational mention of his name. They invented a fatuous code name for him—'Mr. Bullfinch'.

The P.M. had come out to see our newly appointed captains of arms, who were so recently arrived that their knees were still white; General Sir Harold Alexander, C.-in-C., Middle East, and Lieutenant-General Bernard Montgomery, commander in the field. 'Monty' came to Alamein, the scene of his greatest victory which gave him his name and his fame, by accident. One of the veteran commanders of the earlier desert campaigns, General 'Strafer' Gott—who had shown outstanding skill and endurance in the pioneer battles of manœuvre in the days of Wavell and Auchinleck—had been chosen for what on all sides was considered deserved promotion by being given command of the Eighth Army, but 'Strafer's' aircraft was shot down and he was killed the day before his appointment was due to be announced. In his place, Monty was pulled out of his job in England's 'invasion corner', South Eastern Command, in a matter of of hours, and was flown straight out to this battleground on the edge of the Mediterranean. One of Monty's new corps commanders was just as new to the desert: Lieutenant-General Brian Horrocks had been commanding the 9th Armoured Division in Newcastle forty-eight hours before he found himself reporting to be briefed in the Eighth Army Commander's map lorry at Alamein.

Monty's first desert victory was in fact before the famous Battle of Alamein. It was the throwing back of Rommel's last offensive thrust, the German general's full-scale drive with his armour in an attempt to break through in the south of our positions. This final enemy bid to get to the Nile started on the last days of August, and was known as the Battle of Alam el Halfa. Monty let his enemy advance a few miles, 'stick his neck out', and then hit him with everything. In four days the Axis forces were back where they had come from, licking their wounds—back with the loss of a good number of tanks, but back with one component intact: an Italian military band, which had been equipped with new uniforms and flags, and sheet music of the Grand March from *Aïda*, for the expected triumphal entry into Alexandria. A win for the reconstructed Eighth Army.

To get the enemy out of their defensive positions, in great depth and strength, was another matter. But Monty, with the now overwhelming strength of his Commonwealth army in Egypt, presently accomplished this task too. And it was my good fortune to be the broadcasting chronicler of his historic success.

On the morning of October 23, the day when our offensive and the Battle of Alamein began, I was one of a small party of war correspondents who stood on a patch of smoothed sand outside the Army Commander's tent—which had been pitched behind the right flank of the 'Line', near the sea—to hear a very assured and relaxed Monty tell us how he was now ready to 'hit the enemy for six' and that 'the battle, gentlemen, begins tonight'. He then handed to each of us a printed copy of his personal message to the troops, the first of his well known eve-of-battle calls which always sounded half Kipling and half school padre. 'Let every officer and man enter the battle with a stout heart,' it read, 'and with the determination to do his duty so long as he has breath in his body. Let us all pray that "the Lord Mighty in Battle" will give us the victory.'

Bronzed as well as brisk, his sharp nose peeled and red, Monty now oozed self-confidence, and looked as though he had been in North Africa all his life. He wore a sloppy khaki jersey over his shirt and shorts, and a bush-whacker's hat which men in the Australian division had given him (this broad-brimmed headpiece, for all its shade, was soon abandoned for the famous black beret). This was the man who in a short time had put new heart into what had been a baffled and dispirited army. He was ruthless, fit, austere, clear-thinking, and entirely dedicated to the profession of arms. He had spent the past weeks driving up and down his forward units like a puritanical dervish, so full of bounce that it hurt to watch him, telling the men they were the best soldiers in the world and that the sooner they stopped thinking of Rommel as a bogey-man the better.

The general told me one day: 'I had to beat the Rommel legend before beating his army.' And I remember Monty saying: 'You must never let the soldiers know there's any doubt in your mind.'

Certainly the effect of his cocky personality and the calculated crackle of his talk was remarkable to see: he simply gave the troops the idea that they couldn't possibly lose. And everybody knew him.

One day he came across a party digging a whole system of trenches. 'Who are you?' he snapped at the young officer in charge.

'Lieutenant Blank of the Durham Light Infantry,' came the reply.

'Do you know who I am?'

'Yes—sir!'

'But what are you doing?'

'Digging defence trenches.'

'Will you now please stop, and go and report to your battalion commander and tell him I have ordered you to stop.'

'Yessir.'

'From now on, remember, the emphasis is on attack. We have ceased digging defensive positions. Tell your command-

ing officer. Good day to you!' And off he went in his jeep
in a cloud of sand.

As the B.B.C. man with his army, I occasionally came
under the Montgomery lash. He would listen each night
to our Overseas Service news coming out of a small radio
set by the bed in his caravan and if there was something he
didn't agree with on my day's report on the desert situation
as quoted in the bulletin he would have an orderly find me
and haul me up in front of him for a dressing-down. He
made me feel like a small boy in front of a peppery house-
master. On the other hand, Monty sometimes wanted to
see me to ask if I could get certain soldiers' voices on the air,
because of pathetic letters he had had from their wives or
mothers at home. He had an enormous correspondence
from people in Britain as the campaign progressed; he used
to go through all the letters himself and wrote many replies
in his own hand. One day when I was in his caravan he
showed me two proposals of marriage he had received
among his mail that morning—then he brushed them on
one side and went on to talk about the importance of
broadcasting in the war. 'You, here, help the crusading
spirit.' I was surprised and pleased at this benediction. But
by then 'Monty's War', its stories told in my dispatches—
and those of my colleague, Denis Johnston—had become
the backbone of the whole wartime radio news.

The start of the Battle of Alamein gave me some of the
best recordings of that war ever to go out on the air and
into the B.B.C.'s sound archives: descriptions of scenes on
the spot and the noises and voices of the fighting itself.
On the opening night we were up with the recording truck,
ready and dug in between the guns and the infantry start-
lines. Our bombers had been going over in waves all day,
but now the desert lay uncannily silent and the sands were
still and beautiful and quite white under a full moon—until
the silence was shattered, at precisely 2140 hours, by the
crash and roar of a barrage of one thousand guns along a
six-mile front. There had never been anything like it in the
whole war, and it went on all night. The ground reverberated
and heaved (so, alas, did the truck where we were trying to
cut discs of commentary and effects), and you could have

read a newspaper by the light of the gun flashes that flickered across the desert in continuous performance. Arnell and I, and the rest of the party—on wheels sometimes, at rest where we could, sometimes on foot, sometimes on our stomachs—spent the night seeing, and ducking, talking into the microphone, and getting the voices of infantrymen.

Alamein was a combined operation but very much the foot-soldiers' job. The aircraft and the guns and tanks, and the sappers who cleared the paths in the minefields—all these were vital; but, because the Alamein position was a set one, its 'Line' a 35-mile-wide bottleneck between sea and sand-swamps where Auchinleck had in the summer stopped Rommel in his tracks, this was a battle in which there could be no outflanking. And so this was a different kind of warfare from all the previous fighting in the desert, when tanks and cars and guns had ranged about like cavalry. This time it was almost like a battle in the First World War: we had to make hard, battering attacks on a relatively narrow fortress whose 'walls' were miles and miles of thick minefields with defences which a very efficient German army had been assiduously preparing for a long time. Going up and down the confused front to report the attacks, driving and trudging through the dust and the din, dodging in and out of trouble and scampering back to get my stories through, I was tremendously impressed with the way the Germans were resisting and the weight of stuff they were throwing back at us. I was often afraid—and very afraid of showing it.

In spite of the Eighth Army's great superiority now in weapons and material, there were twelve days of terrible slogging before the break-through came. It was 'a near-run thing'. We correspondents, though reporting heavy fighting, had not been allowed by the security censorship to say that this was *the* all-out attack which simply had to succeed; and during those days there were times when it seemed to me that the Battle of El Alamein wasn't going our way at all; I wondered whether we should ever get through, whether indeed we might have to haul off, pull back, and try again later, calling the whole thing a sort of 'reconnaissance in force'. But Monty kept re-grouping and shifting the direction of his thrusts; and on November 2, with almost the last good infantry reserves available, a final gap was bored through the enemy defences to let the tanks crash through. Two days later I was able to send full accounts of the whole struggle and its triumph at last, and to announce from the spot the victory communiqué which set the church bells ringing in England: 'The Axis forces are now in full retreat.'

I was exhilarated; and I was lucky. This was the biggest story of the war. We hadn't slept properly for several nights, but there was no time to be tired, and in fact I had never felt less exhausted. Admittedly, my spirits had been uplifted by cables of congratulation from London and messages from the office which said: 'Your excellent dispatches widely used in all output.' And I should have been less than human if I had not been spurred by letters which soon began to come from people at home containing such phrases as 'Everybody's listening to you' and 'It's marvellous to hear your voice right from the spot where our lads are—so keep it up'.

For me, professionally, it was enormously fortunate to be in on this phase of the war, this turning of the tide after all the defeats which had gone before. Now we were reporting successes, not retreats any longer.

On-the-spot reporting was not a simple business, all the same. My spoken dispatch on the night of the break-through, which brought to listeners all over the world the sounds of tanks moving into battle through that gap which had been punched through the mines, was made in hazard—more from our own armour than from the enemy. I was up at the end of what was called Moon Track, describing the advance of the tank squadrons; and the microphone which I was holding in my sweaty hand was connected to Arnell's recording gear by hundreds of feet of cable stretching away to the truck. The tanks were churning up such a fog of sand that I could judge the coming of each monster only by the sound of its squeaking and grinding; and during the whole broadcast I had to keep leaping backwards and for-wards to prevent not only the cable but myself from being cut in two.

All the dispatches were recorded. It was not technically

possible, in any case, to transmit voice 'live' from the desert. The recordings were all on heavy old discs: there was no tape at that time. I made many of the recordings standing near the truck, but sometimes we would manhandle the gear out and into a smaller vehicle, or use the gear out on the sand after the truck had disgorged it and retreated to safety. For the truck—which we named 'Belinda' and which as such became well known—was too big and heavy for speedy action, too conspicuous for the really forward areas. She was occasionally most unwelcome when we were visiting an advanced position, and on arrival we would be roundly told: 'Hop it, for God's sake. Jerry can see Belinda, and he'll think a general has come up in his passion-waggon and he'll start shelling us afresh. Get Belinda to hell out of here!'

If, after scrambling about the battlefield, I came back into Belinda and typed a script of my dispatch before I spoke it, the paper had to be taken to be passed by the field censor back in his tent near Main Army H.Q.; and if it was a spontaneous and unscripted description or interview, recorded on discs, we had to take a machine and play the discs back for the censor to hear. If I had said anything reckoned dangerous to security, mentioning a regiment or location on which there was as yet a 'stop', the censor would have to deface the record and I would have to lose the dispatch or try to do the whole thing again. So 'talking on to disc' was an inhibiting business, and I had to be my own censor as much as I could. When passed, the recorded dispatches were flown or sent by dispatch riders back to Cairo, and from the studios of Egyptian State Broadcasting were beamed to London.

So a slight time-lag was inevitable; and, as the army fought the German and Italian divisions back across Cyrenaica and Tripolitania, racing to the end in Tunisia, the distances between us and a transmitter were many hundreds of miles, and sometimes the delays were more than slight.

But the reports were genuinely 'from the field'. Not all of them dealt with blood and tactics. Wars are not fought in a vacuum; and I would often describe in some detail the setting of the fighting and the way of life of the men who were in it. Into the pieces I spoke from the desert I put, deliberately, the sandstorms and the sunsets over the slit-trenches; the strange sight of the earth where it turned from yellow to snow-white at the edge of the sea; the incredible cobalt of the Mediterranean itself; the moments of personal bliss when opening a letter from home whilst lying in a secure bivouac after a gruesome day; the sheepskins and dizzy neckscarves and soft boots which made these soldiers look like no other force; the bouts of sandfly fever and jaundice and dysentery which removed almost as many men as bullets did; the new and ruder verses sung to our anthem, 'Lili Marlene'; the army's elaborate slang of bastardised Arabic words; how we cooked on fires of petrol-soaked sand—and even the suet pudding which Driver Pretswell made over one such blaze, using my one undervest as wrapping. The important trivia as well as the great military triumphs and tragedies got into my reports. I did not mind when a retired admiral in Tunbridge Wells took the trouble to send me an angry airgraph letter saying: 'Your reports are lacking in seriousness and strategic analysis. It is shocking. When you speak, it is like writing a letter home, in public.' I took more notice of the letters which urged me to 'go on telling us what it's like'.

Two of the things it was like were thirst and dirt. Shortage of water was a major privation. You had to put some of your ration aside for making tea—we pretty well lived on brew-ups of 'chai'—and some for shaving and washing: left leg Monday, right leg Tuesday, and so on; a few drops for dhobi-ing a shirt; and then you put the few mugfuls of grey laundry water into the radiator of the truck. One soldier wrote home: 'Don't forget every time you pull the lavatory chain it's equal to one week's water ration for us out here.'

In trying to make desert life real to people at home, I must have aroused pity. Anyhow, as the months went on and we travelled across North Africa I received not only letters from listeners but gift-parcels too. One package contained a large home-made cake and a tin of anti-flea powder. Unfortunately, by the time this present reached me, well past Agheila, the tin had been punctured and the powder had impregnated the cake. Once I had the gift of six pairs of thick grey socks from a ladies' knitting circle in Staffordshire; the letter said they would be glad if I would accept them 'for yourself and any Walsall man present'. The socks were lovely but loud: they had large victory-V's in purple wool all the way up the sides.

As to letters, the whole of the B.B.C. camp used to sit up and watch when my mail arrived; and when we lay sleepily talking in our bed-rolls at night, in trenches or underneath or inside Belinda (according to how cold it was or how much we were being bombed), my companions would rag me about the tender messages and intimate suggestions which A.T.S. girl sorters at the Army Post Office sometimes scribbled in pencil on envelopes addressed to me.

Anybody who broadcasts frequently will get fan-mail, even in a war, but it was not disagreeable to think that others besides family and friends were wishing me well and safe home. Happily, all the B.B.C. parties came through that desert advance unscathed, though one of my conducting officers was wounded in his hind parts by anti-personnel bomb splinters as he and I lay flattened on our faces side by side in the sand at the edge of a track one day when we had scattered from a truck convoy under air attack. I was lucky that time: he was a fat man and his bottom stuck up more than mine did. Another officer and I were nearly captured once when swanning about, and for one horrible lost hour in a no-man's-land I feared I might be joining Edward Ward, that first and first-class B.B.C. war correspondent who was taken by the Italians in earlier desert fighting; but we got back to our lines at dusk, with only our morale injured.

Those exciting months in North Africa in 1942 and 1943 have a special afterglow: they saw a long and exhilarating race forward, the 'turn of the tide' of the Second World War. But Alamein and the galloping 'Benghazi handicap', the chase which followed it, have an unrivalled place in the memory for another reason. If you had to have a war, this desert was the place in which to fight it. Here there were no civilians, no wrecked cities, no pathetic streams of refugees, but just opposing groups of soldiers spread over a vast open landscape that was a tactician's paradise (and a quarter-

F

master's nightmare). For wartime, the troops lived a decent, hard, healthy and almost monastic life. The issues before them were clear, and their *esprit de corps* tremendous. There was even an old-fashioned chivalry and respect between the opposing sides. It was the last 'clean' war, the last fling of the public-school ethos.

For me as a broadcaster it was the hardest but the most rewarding time. Our dispatches did service as the immediate link between front and home, bringing reality and combating distance and strangeness. Heaven knows, my stuff was fallible and fleeting, but there was the satisfaction of genuinely communicating. No war had had this treatment before. With the reports from the Eighth Army, radio was beginning a valuable gap-bridging operation (to be developed fully and most efficiently later by the B.B.C. during the fighting for the liberation of North-West Europe), the making of distant struggles less remote psychologically, especially to the families of the soldiers, airmen and sailors 'out there'. Sidi Barrani was known and near as the Somme had never been.

Newspaper accounts and pictures had a similar though smaller and less intimate impact; journalistic quality was bred in the desert days. Among my fellow correspondents were several who distinguished themselves then, and became widely known and popular in later years. One of them was the gifted Australian, Alan Moorehead, then writing for the London *Daily Express*, who travelled in team with his newspaper rival but personal friend, Alexander Clifford of the *Mail*. They were the best and most experienced reporters in the desert. Among the many army photographers we frequently saw 'up forward' was a cheerful, spectacled young man toting a still camera: Alan Whicker, who in peace-time was to become one of the most engaging of the professional investigators of television.

With such fellow journalists, and with my fellow workers in radio, I covered the advance westward, sending the stories of the taking of point after point from Bardia to Benghazi, the battles for Marble Arch and Sirte and Wadi Akarit, and so into Tunisia and the last 'tough one', Mareth. After a long stint in the desert, I had a spell back in Cairo and other parts of the Middle East, sometimes covering the war on the sea—and under it; and my place with Monty's thrusters was taken by the indefatigable Frank Gillard, who later won his spurs in Sicily and Salerno, led the B.B.C. correspondents in Invasion Europe, and after the war crowned his Corporation career by becoming Managing Director of Radio, our 'Head of Steam'.

My own immediate future was being decided by my bosses in London whilst I was in Cairo in the autumn of 1943; and in October a cable ordered me to fly home as soon as possible. At Broadcasting House I was told to get ready to go out to cover the war in Burma, and to have a few days' leave. But during that leave the Middle East reached out and took a last swipe at me, ironically. Having spent eighteen months out there without wounds or illness, I now, in England, went down with some sort of exotic infection which I had brought home. I was found to be full of poison, ran a temperature of 104 for six days, spent three weeks in bed, weak as a kitten, four more in convalescence, and altogether was laid off duty for over two months.

During which time another man, Richard Sharp, also a Yorkshireman, and one of the finest descriptive reporters we ever had, was sent to Burma—and I finished writing a book about the desert.

At the beginning of 1944 I was fit for action again and was sent to the Italian front.

6

All Over Italy

'I'm so cold I can hardly hold the mike. And the desolation of the scene beggars description. The villages are smashed. The mountains are barren and pitted and hostile, seared by ice as well as shells. Men here are fighting the wind and rain and mud as well as the Germans. Don't forget them . . .'

The words were some I spoke in one dispatch from the Italian front soon after I got there. They summed up the winter war. The plaintive note crept in because *my* front was now not the only one, and was being elbowed out of the picture just then. Bill Slim's Fourteenth Army in Burma was in the news; the Soviet ally's divisions were demanding attention, too, massively recovering in the east; and in the west, in Britain, the big build-up for the coming Second Front was already a leading story. Italy was bogged down—and, in the news bulletin headlines, low down.

And yet I was again lucky. Italy was not all winter and discontent. Indeed, sometimes, when we had got up as far as Umbria and lovely Tuscany, there were glimpses of the Sunny Italy of the travel posters. And to cover this Southern front, to be in this particular fight from the Mediterranean to the Alps, was a singular experience and a distinguishing mark too—as those who did *not* go through it knew, just as much as those who were there and earned the Italy Star.

'A man who has not been in Italy is always conscious of an inferiority', Samuel Johnson once lucubrated. It would not have been such a pontificating overstatement if it had been applied to British soldiers in 1944 and 1945. Not that

there was anything inferior about the D-Day-and-after men
who went into battle for the first time in the maelstroms of
the Normandy beaches and the Rhine crossings. But the
troops in Italy were trail-blazers who had been fighting
and beating Germans in Europe, in very difficult conditions,
long before D-Day; and when many of them were switched
to that later, bigger Western assault on Hitler's strongholds,
they went as picked professionals and were recognised as
such. They were the veterans who, striking north after
Africa, had found that when Churchill talked about hitting
the 'soft under-belly of the Rome–Berlin Axis' he had got
the adjective wrong. For this war in Italy was as tough, as
dramatic and destructive as anything the centuries had seen
on the historic ground over which it was fought.

When I got to it after my spell at home, Sicily had been
liberated, the foot of the mainland peninsula won by the
Eighth Army and the Salerno beaches by the Fifth, Naples
was in our hands and the front was well north of the city;
but we were halted—as we were for six months of bitter and
bloody fighting—before Cassino, where the Germans,
holding the seemingly impregnable Monastery Hill, barred
the road to Rome.

It was whilst the front was stuck there, frozen and
frustrated in the torn hills and valleys flanking Highway Six,
that there came, towards the end of the 1943–4 winter, back
over the Bay of Naples, a quite different event, one of the
strangest happenings I have ever seen in war or peace: the
eruption of Vesuvius.

The volcano began to blow its top early in March, and
soon it was doing more damage than enemy bombs and
shells. Rivers of red-hot molten lava flowed down the
mountain slopes far beyond Pompeii. Their size alone
proclaimed that this was a major eruption. One stream,
nearly two hundred yards wide, pushed its forward edge, a
moving wall forty feet high, down on to vineyards and
houses. It was a devouring horror of glowing cinders and
crackling boulders which spat and hissed as it carried trees
and walls along with it. Its slow yet inexorable advance was
the dreadful thing about it.

I went up to the village of San Sebastiano and watched

stone houses crumple quietly like tissue-paper and disappear
under the tide. Priests stood praying and holding services
at the edge of the burning flood. Sometimes people stayed
in their houses until the last moment, hoping against hope
that the devouring stream might stop; and then, when it
didn't, they suddenly dragged pieces of furniture out and
threw the contents of drawers and cupboards through
windows to friends waiting outside with carts, before getting
out themselves, sweating and singed. Half an hour after one
of these hasty evacuations, the lava was at the walls and over-
topping the roof, and you would see ceilings collapsing
gently on to a kitchen table which had plates of half-
consumed food and glasses of wine still on it. The peasants
seemed hardly able to believe what was happening: British
and American soldiers and airmen had to drag some of them
away from Canute-like stands in front of the oncoming
furnace and get them into army trucks and off to reception
camps—which had in fact been laid out to receive refugee
civilians, not from Monte Vesuvio but Monte Cassino on
the battlefront.

By night, German aircraft coming in to bomb the city of
Naples and Allied shipping in the harbour had the best
flaming beacon of all time, the top of Vesuvius, to navigate
and to turn on; but they also had to contend with the new
fog. The nightly man-made smokescreen round the docks
and on the bay, set up to protect our ships, was a mere wisp
compared to the spreading cloud of dust and sulphurous
vapour now set up by the volcano. The pall stretched
across the country and far out to sea. Bari, 120 miles away
on the other side of Italy, was darkened by the cloud; the
decks of ships forty miles from shore were covered by a
black deposit. And immediately beneath the spouting crater
and the burning slopes, hot ash rained down day after day
with stinging intensity. Men and women worked in shifts
day and night sweeping the stuff off the flat roofs of their
homes: for those roofs which were neglected collapsed after
a few days under the accumulated weight of the ash.
The stuff blocked roads round the bay: army shovellers and
mechanical bulldozers had to be put to work, digging deep
ways through banks of 'black snow' to keep communications

open. The dust settled thick on parked planes on military landing-grounds, making wings collapse; seventy aircraft were put out of action.

Day was sometimes nearly as dark as night. Lorries drove with headlights on and wipers wig-wagging to keep windscreens clear of the hail of fine coke. We walked, on the Vesuvius foothills, with tin hats on, flicking off cinders which burned our uniforms. Ears and eyes were full of ash. We held handkerchiefs to nose and mouth—and the macabre thought crossed my mind that, doing just that, people were overwhelmed and drew their final breath in the last days of Pompeii when the city was destroyed by the lava erupting from this same volcano nineteen hundred years before.

Vesuvius was an amazing story, but one we could not tell fully, at the time—our old friends the military security censors saw to that: the enemy had not to know that Allied aircraft and some of our vital supply roads were suffering from extraordinary violence of nature.

When the spring came, and the familiar war, the battle for Cassino and the key-point, Monastery Hill, was resumed, the eruption and its consequences were mentioned no more. But Vesuvius aflame remains an indelible Italian memory, vivid when many of the man-made fires of that war are forgotten.

For me, it was a war in contrast to the desert in both terrain and task. I went through the campaign in the peninsula as an organiser of other people's broadcasting as well as my own: this time I had been sent out as leader of the B.B.C.'s team of correspondents in the Mediterranean and South European theatre. The assignment gave me experience, scope and responsibility such as I could hardly have had among the cohorts of new and old reporters which the Corporation flung into the grand assault, from Normandy onwards, in the north. The B.B.C. coverage of that main front was superbly done, its huge machine of organisation long prepared; and the programmes containing the front-line reports constituted an editorial, technical and administrative triumph. But the war reporting on my front was more of an individual enterprise, organised on the spot rather than by strings pulled in London. It maintained a rogue independence.

I was fortunate in my B.B.C. companions. At one time or another my team of fellow broadcasters included Denis Johnston, the Irish playwright who was in pre-war television, a Fine Desert War veteran and a tall tower of strength to our reporting; Wynford Vaughan Thomas, the brilliant stick of Welsh dynamite, our ace raconteur, effervescent and irrepressible, the only war correspondent who stuck it out the whole time in the murderous Anzio beach-head; Douglas Willis, the devil-may-care Cockney reporter who hid his soft heart and his kindness by acting the part of a hard-case, hard-drinking newspaper man of American films; Patrick Smith, one of the B.B.C.'s most civilised foreign correspondents, urbane as a bishop; Kenneth Matthews, our Balkans war expert, toughest and liveliest of the lot under a professorial manner; Reginald Beckwith, 'Tony' to everybody, the bouncing little professional actor, who saw the funny side of even the direst ploy; and our student of military history, Michael Reynolds, tall, erudite, and so absent-minded that he permanently mislaid two jeeps during the campaign. Michael was miserable with recording sets or any mechanical devices whatsoever, but marvellous at tactical detail and at generals' press conferences: he would often voice well-founded doubts about a commanding officer's battle-plan and declare that Hannibal would never have crossed the Apennines *that* way.

Our company was joined from time to time by the Scottish writer Eric Linklater, whom the army was employing as an official observer and compiler of campaign appreciations, but who broadcast for us too; and Anthony Quayle, the actor, then Major Quayle of Allied Military Government (Civil Affairs). By those two we were splendidly enlivened. Altogether, a mettlesome team of particularly gifted and amusing talkers. I have rarely known such hilarious evenings as when this group of men, when their paths to and from this or that sector of the front crossed, sat after a meal in some B.B.C.-camp tent or billet, with the *vino* flowing and the tent's air near-lethal with dense tobacco fumes, and told tale after backstage tale from their professional pasts or embroidered the lighter adventures of the last few days of battle. Beckwith and Quayle vied with each other in outrageous theatre reminiscences and imitations. Linklater would begin the session by being very quiet, sitting in a corner behind his pipe and twinkling glasses, the hole in his head which a First War wound gave him showing and glowing, and then gradually he would enter more and more into the conversation with shrewd and earthy comments on the Italian scene. It was in those days that he was absorbing the atmosphere which later came out so beautifully in his sardonically comic novel, *Private Angelo*.

Such were the war correspondents for whom I was supposed to have some responsibility. I was ostensibly manager and chief of this rare constellation. I failed to 'manage' any of them, but muddled through with their assistance and connivance; and on the whole our operations worked. They were agreeable and stimulating coadjutors. Stints and movements up and down Italy were arranged between us amicably enough: ructions of artistic temperament were only a routine preliminary to getting down to the job.

There remained for me, however, a lot of cabling and letter-writing, and sending Service messages over our radio links; and on some days I had to spend several hours—when in Naples or Sessa Aurunca or Cassino or Rome or Florence or wherever our base might be—in satisfying London over the disposition of the B.B.C. forces. I was even embroiled in administrative bothers over our backstop base in Algiers, where the headquarters of the Allied forces in the Mediterranen area remained. The B.B.C. engineers who were with us in Italy were part of my team too—and were men whose skill and resource made them a very present help in time of trouble. Their ministrations were by no means confined to the sound trucks and portable recording gear: when it came to drawing rations, cooking, scrounging anything from petrol to wine, or making runners out of written-off motor vehicles, they were without peer.

At first we used army Signals or civilian Cable and Wireless network out of Naples to get our broadcast reports back to London for use in the B.B.C. news programmes. Then, to my great joy, Broadcasting House shipped out to us a transmitter of our own, with good studio microphones and record-playing machines (*and* more staff technicians to look after). When the gear was assembled and put into operation our output got a much better crack of the whip. Reporters, or their dispatches on disc, still had to be sent from 'up front' by dispatch rider or small aircraft to wherever the transmitter and its tent had been set up, on Roman hillside or Tuscan vineyard, but at least we talked direct from that point to London; editors in Broadcasting House could answer us back, and our spoken reports usually reached Britain pretty clearly. It was a relief to listen to Radio Newsreel coming back and hear my voice sounding like Godfrey Talbot and not Donald Duck.

Almost as much a blessing as the transmitter, I received some organising help in the shape of a man who was both practical and a good adminstrative fixer: Arthur Phillips, a friend and colleague with whom I had worked both in London and in Egypt, and who had been in the field with our very first correspondents. Phillips 'looked after the shop' and ran our base with efficiency and versatility; and I was able to get forward to the war front myself and do long spells of on-the-spot reporting, knowing that the material, dispatched as 'released and urgentest press package' to Phil, would be put swiftly over to London, no matter what the hour of arrival at our rear headquarters and transmitter.

There was plenty of reporting to do. The war was prolonged, the battles on a wide and savage scale. The Italian army had given up almost at once, but Germany, senior partner of the Rome–Berlin 'axis', took command of the whole country and fought all-out to keep it. Field Marshal Kesselring used twenty-eight German divisions in Italy against the Allies. Our radio coverage of the fighting was not easy because the war itself was hard going. No exhilarating chases across the landscape, but a life of noisy and costly hammering at some hell-hole of a strongpoint for perhaps weeks on end; the gradual and painful dis-lodgement of stubborn, top-class German soldiers from a

succession of vast entrenchments in country ideal for
defence, whether in the heat and dust of summer or the
mire and slush of two miserably cold winters. To our
own troops, it was one bloody river after another: Volturno,
Sangro, Garigliano, Tiber, Arno and Po—they were all
dirty words, and the less they had of them the better.
(When they crossed the Rubicon—in the opposite direction
to Caesar's southward march—they didn't know it or care,
though they knew that Rome was behind and not ahead of
them and that the end of the war must be near.) One hard
siege followed another, to get through Gothic Line,
Gustav Line and Adolf Hitler Line. It was a slow advance
up the map, through a ravaged countryside in which villages
had been shelled into heaps of rubble (though why, I used
to wonder, did the tall brickworks chimneys always remain
standing?), in which trees and fields had become skeletons
and stony wastes, and pitiful streams of black-shawled
refugees clogged the routes of the supply lorries.

And yet we also saw timeless Italy, the little hill-top towns
still thrusting up their campaniles in skylines that were pure
Bellini. Despite the swaths of destruction, the old blue
hills endured up there beyond the Bailey bridges; carts
drawn by white oxen serenely lumbered beneath a line of
cypresses across the terra-cotta earth whilst shells were
bursting among pearly-grey olive groves not a mile away,
and graceful poplars and umbrella pines, undamaged,
sheltered the rude encampments of fighting men.

There had been a hope, at first, that the war's centrepiece,
Monte Cassino Abbey, the huge Benedictine monastery
which was one of the treasures of Italy, would also keep its
existence and its skyline unimpaired, even though it stood
on the enemy's most commanding position: Monastery Hill,
two thousand feet high, was the strongest German-held
bastion in the whole country. But this was not to be.
As the struggle for Cassino went on month after month in
vain, it was clear that this dominating mountain would
have to be taken before any progress could be made.
Infantry and guns had not subdued it; so the controversial
decision massively to bomb the Monastery was made.
Broadcasts warned Abbot and monks to leave; and the

great place was destroyed from the air so that the Germans could be forced out of their eagle's nest.

On the day the Monastery fell, May 18, I was one of the first to reach it. It was a shocking day. In the early hours, two of my friends, war correspondents Cyril Bewley of the *News Chronicle* and Roderick MacDonald of the *Sydney Morning Herald*, were blown to pieces by trip-wired mines as a party of us edged through the ruins of Cassino town. Two hours later, after an exhausting climb with my gear, I got to the blasted summit of Monastery Hill. I went with some of the troops who finally captured it. Poles, they were, fierce and fearless men, who ignored enemy mines and bursting mortar bombs as we sweated up the stony slopes among bomb craters full of slimy green water and the stinking bodies of dead men and dead mules, until, ducking and running, we stumbled at last into the building which for so long been a hostile brooding mass, distant on its mountain, overshadowing men's bodies and minds in the agony that was Cassino. But now the Abbey was a corpse of a place, acres of ruin with hardly a wall standing, but here and there stumps of stone like supplicating arms. The Monastery was a ghost, grey-white in the dust of its death. Through this we ploughed, ankle-deep, and down into a hole where we found a small crypt chapel, evidently the last inhabited shelter. Two wounded German soldiers lay on fouled mattresses at the far end, grenades and rifles beside them among the smashed religious ornaments which littered the floor. A camp-bed and a beer bottle and a dish of decayed food were on the altar, and on a wall above it there had been plastered a poster of a smirking pin-up girl. Everything else was rubble.

It was a historic moment to be up there: the Poles waved their arms and put up their flag and a Union Jack. But I could feel no joy or triumph at being on that dust heap which war had made of a place which had been a centre of learning and Christian endeavour for fourteen centuries, even though I was able to look down on Highway Six far below and see our own columns at long last moving on the road towards Rome which this Monastery Hill had denied them for half a year.

The fall of Rome seventeen days later was a very different affair. The Germans defended the outskirts but then withdrew to the north. We found the city virtually undamaged, sunny and beautiful. The bells of St. Peter's were ringing welcome, Pope Pius XII came out on his balcony, and the people indulged in a riot of rejoicing at the Anglo-American liberators' entry. With my little party I drove into the Piazza Venezia early on June 5; and as soon as the B.B.C. insignia on our jeep and recording truck was spotted a great shout went up, and in a matter of seconds we were engulfed in a crowd of yelling and waving people, all in their best clothes and carrying flowers and wine. For the next hour we were mobbed and could not move. These were the Romans who night after night had heard our voices as they crouched secretly in cellars over tiny radio receivers, in defiance of the orders of the hated, occupying *Tedeschi* that listening to the B.B.C. was forbidden on pain of death.

It was a scene which was to repeat itself all over Europe as the liberating armies swept forward, B.B.C. men with them, and oppressed citizens, for whom B.B.C. news and the spoken reports of war correspondents had been a focus of hope, rushed out from shelter to greet not only the soldiers but the broadcasters whose voices they had come to know in the years of clandestine and dangerous listening. In Rome, on that June morning, men and women clambered frenziedly on our truck and car crying ' 'Allo B.B.C.' and 'Viva Radio Inglese!' I stood on the truck's roof to escape, but was pulled down, my battle-dress torn, and was hugged and given smacking garlic-breath kisses. My ribs were bruised, my shirt drenched with the wine they tried to force down us; my cheeks were blotched red with lipstick and scratches from bunches of roses thrown jubilantly at us. Babbling men begged for a cigarette, and offered us the freedom of their dwellings and their daughters. It was with the greatest difficulty that I made my way across the packed square and recorded a quick commentary on this Roman holiday from the Palazzo balcony where Mussolini used to stand and strut and scream his speeches, my voice now almost inaudible in the storms of cheering that could not stop.

As a news story, Rome was grade one. Our broadcasts from this first capital city of Europe to be freed from Teuton thrall swept almost everything else out of the bulletins from London. But we were only just in time. Twenty-four hours later came the news of the D-Day landings on the Normandy beaches; Italy had to fight to get into the headlines at all for a while, and the North-West front was *the* war for the final eleven months.

But Italy had its moments. There was the fall of Florence, with every historic bridge over the Arno except the Ponte Vecchio deliberately smashed by the retreating enemy, but the Uffizi's Botticellis found safely hidden in a farmhouse; the break-through to Bologna after arctic miseries up Route 65 and the dreadful Futa Pass; Milan, where I found the body of Mussolini hanging by the heels from the girders of a petrol station in the Piazzale Loreto—and widows of partisans whom the Fascists had executed coming up to spit and fire revolver shots into the corpse; and, in the last days, the discovering, on a mountain-top in the Dolomites, of a handful of once-famous men who had disappeared and whom the world had thought murdered long before by the Gestapo: Chancellor Schuschnigg of Austria; old Léon Blum, once Prime Minister of France; Dr. Schacht, the German financier who had turned against Hitler; Paster Niemöller, the heroic anti-Nazi of the German Church; and other hostages from many countries.

That last one was a surprising story. I had been up in the forests beyond Cortina and to Dobbiaco near the Austrian border, watching crowds of Wehrmacht officers driving down the roads in search of someone to surrender to, when I met an American major of the Fifth Army who told me he was just off to investigate a report of some 'important guys' the Germans were rumoured to be holding captive in a last redoubt above the snowline. I went with him and a convoy of armed jeeps. We roared and slithered up miles of steep and twisting tracks, without meeting any opposition, and found what we were looking for, remote and well hidden. But the 'fortress' was a large hotel beside a lake perched on a peak. It was called Lago di Braies. Inside this place, unguarded but frightened, abandoned a few hours before by most of their army guards who had disobeyed orders to shoot the prisoners before the Allies arrived, were that eminent bunch of missing persons. When we burst into the hall of the hotel we found them huddled together in one corner, with no food and no heat, not knowing whom or what fate to expect. On realising that we were Allied soldiery the hostages broke down and cried like children, laughed hysterically, poured out torrents of words in four languages, and embraced us and each other in their relief, almost disbelief, that they were alive and saved. The stories told to me by Schuschnigg and the others, and the wives who were with them, of being hustled from concentration camp to concentration camp until at last they were driven from Dachau to this extraordinary Shangri-La, made one of the oddest broadcasts of the end of the war.

By the time VE-Day came and the shooting stopped, I had hauled my microphone the length and breadth of Italy, into Jugoslavia and Greece and through the landings on the French Riviera as well. I had had a lot of edges knocked off me in covering the actions fought, in all weathers and every sort of country, by an outstanding, polyglot assembly of fighting men. Never were so many nationalities brought together in a single force as there were in the divisions of the Allied Armies in Italy: men from the United Kingdom, Ireland, United States, Canada, New Zealand, South Africa, West Africa, Morocco, France, Australia, India, Nepal, Italy, Poland, Brazil, Greece, Cyprus and Palestine, Jew and Arab together.

During my own Italian service with this unique international brigade I learned a great deal, suffered a great deal, enjoyed many experiences enormously, ruined five sets of uniform, and wore out two jeeps, one fifteen-hundredweight truck and a military staff car. I was much beholden to the army for our 'wheels' (they were all army vehicles)—and indeed even more fortunate than I knew at the time. During 1944—when, in spite of chaining our jeeps to lamp-posts every time we stopped and removing vital parts of engines if vehicles were left unattended, we had two

vehicles stolen in that cesspit of thievery, Naples—I
appealed in some desperation to the Commander-in-Chief
himself, Field Marshal Alexander, for help to get the
transport the B.B.C. team urgently needed. He arranged for
the transfer of a truck to our unit within Army Public
Relations, and told me: 'You'd better have something else
too,' and scribbled a chit and gave it to me. Armed with
this, I drew next day, from a vast vehicle supply dump
which had been set up on the shore of the Bay of Naples, a
brand-new army jeep, as part of the Public Relations fleet;
and we kept this jeep right through the war. I drove it
myself for thousands of miles. When I was back in England
in 1945, four months after peace had broken out, the
telephone rang in my office in Broadcasting House one day,
and a voice said: 'War Office here. Your jeep is at the docks
in Brindisi and they are ready to ship it home to you. May we
have your private address, sir?'

My jeep! They reckoned it didn't belong to the army at
all! The fact that a scrap of paper signed by Earl Alexander
of Tunis had said: 'Issue to Mr. Talbot, one jeep,' had
apparently caused the thing to be put down in the records
as my personal property. Should I accept the gift? I was
very tempted to allow the car to be delivered to me—but only
for a moment: the problems of explaining it, getting a
civilian licence, and running it at my own expense at seven
miles to the gallon would be altogether too much. No, I
said to the War Office, it is an army vehicle which was used
by the B.B.C. There the conversation ended. But in fact that
jeep continued to be used by the Corporation: my colleague
Kenneth Matthews went off on a later reporting mission
to Greece in it, and we lost it only when Kenneth was
captured by brigands. He was released, but the jeep disappeared for ever.

I was much indebted to Field Marshal Alexander during
the war for more than jeeps. As commander of the Allied
Armies in Italy, he would invite me from time to time to a
meal and a talk at his headquarters, and on those occasions
the wealth of information he gave me about the whole
military situation and his future battle plans formed an
absolutely invaluable background to my work as a war

Broadcasting a commentary in Tripoli's main square soon after the 51st Highland Division's entry, 23 January, 1943

With the Desert Air Force in Italy the following year, describing the visit of King George VI—in the back of the car

Berlin, May 1945 (Dimbleby at the Brandenburg Gate)

B.B.C. men on the spot at the fall of the two Axis capitals

Rome, May 1944 (Talbot in the Piazza Venezia)

correspondent. Thanks to him, I was always fully 'in the picture'.

As a general, as a person, 'Alex' was the very anti-thesis of 'Monty', though every bit as much the experienced and brilliant professional soldier. There was certainly no rasping egotism in his make-up. And he had the charm of self-effacement. In battle, having made his dispositions, he would keep out of the limelight; there was no fussing, no evangelical messages on the eve of an attack, no breathing down the necks of his commanders in the field. A brave man, but a quiet one, a philosopher. He was never loud in complaint or opinion; he fought for his troops but never thrust himself forward. When the Allied Chiefs of Staff tried to make his Italian campaign a sideshow and took divisions away from him, he wasted no time over noisy criticism but pressed resolutely forward up the peninsula and fought the enemy back with the forces that he had.

What he had in common with Montgomery was a flair for delegating responsibility well, and also the ability to get his mind off the problems of the day for a spell: Monty would go to bed early at the height of a battle; Alexander would sit back and paint.

He was a man who appreciated the civilised arts and pleasures of life. When his base, the headquarters of the Allied Armies in Italy, was in that southern Versailles, the vast Bourbon palace of Caserta, I used to go and see Alexander at his villa in the palace grounds, and as often as not would find him, a debonair, patrician figure, at ease on his balcony in the sun with an easel in front of him, absorbed in his work on a small landscape in oils. At my approach, he would immediately put down brush and palette and, with a twinkling welcome which suggested that I was the one person in the world he wished to be interrupted by, would declare that he had been waiting for the opportunity to break off and take a glass of wine before lunch. Over the meal, he talked gracefully and wittily, always sparkling with fun, his generous judgments of people and events salted with shrewd labelling, comic phrases and fascinating reminiscences.

Recalling the Dunkirk evacuation (he was the last man to

G

leave the beaches) he said: 'People have the wrong idea.
The little boats did well to get the chaps away, but *we* ought
to have done better. Materials and equipment could have
been got away too. If it had been an army like the fine force
I have here in Italy now, that would have been done. But
the B.E.F. was raw and had not then a lot of fighting experience, of course, and discipline was not the same. Men rowed
out to ships off the beaches and chucked the oars away
and let the boats go wasted. Some of them were near
panic.'

He talked of Churchill's famous visit to Alamein before
the battle in 1942, and how, looking across towards
Rommel's positions, the Prime Minister had said: 'I hope
they attack whilst I'm here. That *would* be exciting!' The
P.M., he said, still gave him the impression that, although his
grasp of broad strategy was splendid, he had not much idea
of how modern war was conducted: 'I think he imagines
squads of men marching about with rifles shouldered, and
horse-carts following them.' Churchill, he thought, retained
superb clarity of thought, but boyish simplicity. He had
told Alex: 'I'd like to come to Italy and you and I could
drive along the front in your jeep.' (The Field Marshal
delightedly fulfilled Churchill's ambition for him when the
great man did manage a visit to our front when the tide
was flowing strongly in the Allies' favour.)

It was one of the few sadnesses of Lord Alexander's
Service life that his final peninsula victory did not have a
good clean finish. For north-east Italy was in a mess. When
the cease-fire came and the German generals formally
surrendered a million soldiers unconditionally to him—it
was done back at Caserta Palace—there was still toil and
trouble for his troops to tackle at the northern end of the
Adriatic where Marshal Tito's Jugoslavs were trying to
claim Trieste and the region round it by force of arms and
military occupation. I went to see 'Alex' at the end of May,
after the official peace had come and I was about to return
to England, to say good-bye and give my thanks and have a
farewell talk. I found him in a rare mood of depression,
shaking his head over Tito and his obstreperous forces.
'I like the man,' he told me. 'I expect the Russians have put

him up to this try-on in the hope of grabbing some of Italy. But it's a nasty crisis in Istria, and it has spoiled the end of my war.'

That was the last interview of *my* war, and my last day in khaki. The B.B.C. had called me home to the rigours of demobilisation.

7

The Talking Journalists

The stock of the British Broadcasting Corporation stood at a peak in 1945 when victory in Europe had been won, and its reporters were as famous as film stars. B.B.C. war correspondents' fan-mail was at times excessive, the terms of some letters immoderate. Among the gems from my own collection were: 'All work stops in our factory when you come on,' and: 'Your picture from *Radio Times* is under my pillow. Here is my number for when you are on leave.'

Most of the letters were less personal and more temperate, of course, and were concerned with serious things. Heaven knows, our broadcasts had been dealing with matters of life and death; and the radio audience had become an intense and enormous one. The electronic journalism in which we served had made the spoken word transcend the written, in impact and immediacy, and in range and reality. Our public had a sense of involvement: listeners came to know the regular reporters almost as members of the family, even though the acquaintance was through voices only.

Of the fifty reporters who, by the end of the war, were wearing the war correspondent's badge as broadcasters, half a dozen were household names, men whose microphone personalities were projected into millions of homes night after night.

Pre-eminent in this company was Chester Wilmot. The B.B.C. had 'found' this sturdy and competent Australian newspaper man in the early days of the war. We snapped up and with admiration re-broadcast many of his spoken messages from New Guinea and East Africa. Soon we managed to secure him as one of our own men; and his work during the invasion of Europe was not only in the finest tradition of war reporting but came over the air with an incisiveness and virility of speech that made for first-class news-broadcasting. What was more, nobody got the soldiers telling their stories more naturally than Chester did. He was a ferret for essentials, and he scorned trimmings. His passion for accuracy would make him travel ten miles in an arctic German winter to check one fact—and the checking would just as likely be for a colleague's story as for his own 'piece'. Chester was addicted to the truth. A kindly man, but brusque sometimes on the outside. When you found him sitting brooding, bull-necked, argumentative, stubborn, it was because something had been put across that wasn't to his satisfaction, not fundamentally correct, not copper-bottomed as to source. His unerring pursuit of the full, balanced picture contributed to his development as a historian in the first years of peace. His brilliant book, *The Struggle for Europe,* a vast analysis of the campaign in North-West Europe, would undoubtedly have been followed by other writings of painstaking research and breadth of vision had he not been in a Comet airliner which was lost over the Mediterranean in 1954. He was forty-two when he died.

Frank Gillard was the backbone of the broadcasting teams on the Continent as the armies tore the Nazis off Europe's back in the last year of the war. Single-minded Frank, with a natural capacity for responsibility, a clinical organiser, workmanlike to the last syllable, his output was prodigious.

Stanley Maxted was a name everybody knew—Maxted, the B.B.C.'s Canadian, who went through the hell of Arnhem with the Airborne Division and, when those who had survived were perilously withdrawn, came out with them and got to London with a story, told with hard understatement, which few who heard it could forget.

There was Robert Reid, my old comrade from Bradford long ago, who (not of his own volition) was a little late in the war-reporting field but, when Paris was being liberated, found himself in Notre-Dame doing one of the most hair-raising commentaries ever heard, crouching on the floor, cuddling the microphone, talking and dodging bullets at

the same time, whilst a machine-gun battle raged inside the
Cathedral itself around General de Gaulle and a hysterical
congregation.

We had another correspondent whose name was Flight-
Lieutenant Caverhill of the Royal Air Force. He was well
known too—but not by that name. He was, and is, Alan
Melville, author and wit. We knew him then as an ex-
feature-programme producer, a tall Scot with a highly
developed sense of humour and an appealing flair for the
apt word and the light image. Even in the first turmoil of
the invasion beaches, he was describing the lorries and jeeps
roaring up the road from the shore 'shaking off water like
collie dogs after a swim'.

And then a man who, although he was working for an
American network, used Broadcasting House in London as
his base and was looked upon by many of us as part of the
wartime B.B.C.—Ed Murrow, the Anglophile C.B.S.
commentator with the cool, dry voice and economy of
phrase which gave added force to his far-from-dispassionate
reports which were followed with more attention than most
of the pronouncements of world statesmen. Neat, lean, dark,
quizzical, fatally chain-smoking Ed: an ace professional, and
the most entertaining and generous companion in the
journalistic business.

There was also, of course, Richard Dimbleby. After his
Middle East days, Richard was in England training the
B.B.C. teams before D-Day; then he led the Corporation's
correspondents covering the air war, and did a dozen other
jobs too. He would have made himself famous for his
broadcasts from bombers over Cologne, from the appalling
charnel-house of Belsen and from occupied Berlin, if for
nothing else. The war was only one chapter in the story of
this First Broadcaster's life to which B.B.C. history (and this
book) comes back again and again.

Such were the Talking Journalists who made their names
between 1939 and 1945. I was fortunate in knowing them, in
working with them, and in being one of the 'names' myself,
wrapped in the fame of the air, pointed out, asked out,
recognised on speaking, besought to talk to schools and to
open bazaars. It was pleasing and heart-warming to be so

known—of course it was. It would have been easy to get a
swollen head, were it not that we knew perfectly well that
we could not have achieved anything without a whole lot of
back-room boys behind us, and that our importance was the
importance of *agents,* conveyors of the fact and flavour of
great events—and 'not just a pretty voice'. Ours was not the
success of orators: platform tricks have no place in radio
commentary and news broadcasting on the spot. Indeed, if
the talking reporter is to be even moderately successful he
must be informal and natural as well as fluent, colloquial as
well as correct, easy in manner so that the listener may be at
ease. He must speak, not to a million persons, but as though
addressing one. And it is the work of preparation which
makes for a good, assured performance—the background
work he does *before* the broadcast, that is what matters.

Come to that, what also matters in quite another way is the
work an overseas correspondent has to do *after* the talking
has stopped. That includes the domestic chores of the chase,
such as caught up with me when I returned from Italy to
civilian existence: in particular, the private chore known as
'making out your ex's'. Being poor at figures and 'admin', I
have never liked this sort of clearing-up, but in the first few
days after I had flown home to London it had to be done.
A methodical person jots down what has been spent, or at
least how vanished money might be accounted for, at the
end of each day or anyhow once a week. I am not such a
person; and I was now pestered by the Corporation's
money-men to undertake another kind of reporting—on my
financial stewardship over several months: my expenses.

The backlog took me days. The B.B.C., unlike most
newspapers, required precise details of all expenditure, and
expected 'documentary evidence of outgoings' even during
a war. So there I sat, filling in pages and pages of claim
forms as best I could, sadly realising that I possessed few
receipt-slips to show, and that outgoings of money seemed
to be the one thing my diary notes did not cover. The only
joy I got from this drear compilation of spendings was
being able now and then to put on paper such unusual—and
perfectly genuine—items as: 'Hire of ox to help pull vehicle
from mud'; 'Purchase of knuckle-duster as anti-thug

precaution in night-time Rome'; 'Drinks to King of Italy';
and 'Gratuity to Nun for special services'.

Once the mass of detail was there, the B.B.C. was very
understanding: none of these claims of mine was queried.
Perhaps, after all, the eccentric touches were enjoyed during
the accountants' dull days at the ledgers. But I must confess
that my returns were boringly prosaic by comparison with
those shown to me by a colleague. His statement of costs,
far from being dull, glinted on every sheet with hints of
adventure and romance. Typical of these was an explanation
added to a hefty room-charge item, incurred apparently in a
Balkan town where accommodation was difficult. 'This is a
lot of money for a bedroom,' he wrote, 'but they said the
room cost included a girl, and when I said I'd just have the
room, they said the charge would be double because she
would have to occupy another room.'

When expenses were submitted and passed by the
guardians of the Corporation's purse, I emerged thankfully
from those by-ways of the special correspondent's road, and
went from London to the North of England for a short
leave. It was necessary to catch up on sleep, absorb the shocks
of civilian rationing—which made army food seem gorgeous
—and contemplate my future in the strange peacetime world.

8

News in Vision

At home in Britain the end of hostilities was as great a jolt
as the beginning of the war had been. We were thankful, of
course; but life seemed suddenly odd and not as comfortable
as it ought to have been. We were not used to peace. We
missed all the tension, if truth be known; we missed being on
the winning side in a fight. We even missed the hazards.
Long-familiar things had gone from people's lives. No dives
for cover. Never the wailing of an air raid siren. The
aircraft we heard were all ours. There were no gas-masks
now, and no tin hats. It was bliss to have no bombs—but a
bit unnatural. At night we slept in our beds undisturbed and
without fear, but sometimes the peacefulness woke us: the
sheer quiet—and the lights. Streets were becoming illuminated again; that was funny. My elder son, grown to a tall
nine-year-old, was dumbfounded to see a shining glow come
at night from the tops of the tall pillars in the streets: he
knew these kerbside ornaments were called lamp-posts,
but to him they were just pieces of lifeless ironmongery, for
he couldn't remember the time when they had lights. Even
to adults, the lighting-up of the streets after the years of
black-out was at first unreal, and it seemed almost as
though you were on a theatre stage. You felt somehow
naked as you walked in the glare.

In London, the B.B.C. glowed too. Shutters and bricks
were taken down from the windows of Broadcasting House,
so that the sun shone in and the neons shone out. The big
front doors lost their anti-blast walls; the wire and sandbags
were cleared from the entrance hall. None of the staff had to
show a pass.

I became a permanent inhabitant of 'B.H.' myself. On settling into England once more in the middle of 1945, and facing the chances and disenchantments of normal life, it was necessary for me to make personal decisions about my career. There had been offers which would have meant a big change of job, to go into the film or advertising world. But it seemed sensible to stay with the B.B.C. The Corporation, and the war, had treated me well and made me a name. What now, though? Back to the regions? They said there was a place for me in programme producing or in Public Relations again. But now News, the telling of events as they happened and the daily challenge of microphone work, had a harder hold on me than ever; it was too much to give up. I elected to remain on the staff of News Division, based on London.

So family life started again. We got our household goods, not much the worse for five years' storing in one of the few furniture depositories in Birmingham which had not been burned in air raids; and we moved—wife, prep-school boy and Number Two Son still a baby—to a house in suburban Surrey. I was a resident in the South of England for the first time. After the years of living in a camp-bed and the hard delights of travel it was strange to be resident anywhere.

At work, my new peacetime residence was the old News Talks office in Broadcasting House, alongside Portland Place and the large hole in the ground where the B.H. Extension was to be built. I was made Chief Reporter—and at the same time had my wings clipped. Instead of tearing round the world, I was stuck at a desk, organising our United Kingdom news coverage and 'marking the diary'. I was Chief Reporter in the old newspaper sense, chained to the office, a news-editor 'fixer' of jobs for our staff men to go out and do. The trouble was that at that time we hadn't really any reporters, and only the sketchiest idea of the daily events to which men might be assigned if we had any. Most of the people who had been news reporters during the war had gone back to other jobs: the fine big news-organising machine which the B.B.C. had created stopped dead and disintegrated the moment after victory arrived. Far-flung, our correspondents melted away, even before the captains and kings departed. We were back to 1939, or earlier, with the broadcast bulletins largely compiled from news-agency messages without the boon of stories from our own reporters. So most of my first peacetime year was spent in starting to spin our own news web, creating a news diary for the Current Affairs departments, and recruiting some staff correspondents. By the end of 1946 we had created a Home Reporting Unit to begin a new stage in the progress of radio journalism—of *Sound* radio. The revolution of broad-cast-*picture* journalism was still on a distant horizon.

In the B.B.C. this was a reluctant revolution. War reporting had created new news skills, forged new techniques, made new names; and these now had to be applied in post-war broadcasting. But whereas for over five years, with the new wonder of television killed for the duration of hostilities, our business had been with Sound only, the transmitting of topical pictures as well as words was possible again now. The Television Service had re-started—an hour or two a day at the beginning of 1946—and we in the news business ought to have been urgently addressing ourselves to the possibilities of getting the News on to the screen. But in fact hardly anybody was bothering about any such thing, and there seemed scant awareness that news would have to come to television, that Current Affairs would be the backbone of the service. My own News Division had to be *dragged* into the vision business. Many senior people in comfortable Broadcasting House, absorbed in Sound, eyeing television as a dangerous upstart and a rival, could not or did not wish to realise the power of the new medium. Radio ruled the roost; and Television, Son of Sound, receiving just a pat on the head from Father in Portland Place, was shoved into a corner and kept in place. The occasional fragments of events-coverage which were done with cameras by people up at Alexandra Palace and later at the old film studios at Lime Grove, Shepherd's Bush, had to be given a little play, of course, for they were B.B.C. too. But it was all an expensive bother, this news-picture business—the corridors of power down in Broadcasting House seemed to think so, at any rate. Many people in the Television Service itself 'didn't want to know' either, and

viewers got no reflection of the daily happenings of life at
all. Even when the first tiny stirrings of News Division
action came, they were not concerned with putting pictures
on the screen but with imposing the old medium on the new.
Why, said Portland Place, couldn't a sound recording of
the excellent Nine o'Clock News of radio's Home Service
be played to television viewers at the end of their programmes
each night? They were surely capable of listening, and could
have a caption, an emblem, or the Corporation's coat of
arms and the motto, 'Nation Shall Speak Peace Unto
Nation', to stare at for ten minutes whilst they listened.

Which is precisely all they got night after night for a long
time, when presently the feeble idea was put into practice.

Meanwhile, the News Division was working hard to
make sure that, if and when picture-news came, it wouldn't
be the TV programme boys who put the bulletins on, but
the professional journalists of the radio service. Down in
B.H. they stamped the brakes hard on the 'bunch of wild
amateurs' at Alexandra Palace who were now trying to get
bits of topical stuff into their television programmes—even
though those pioneers presently included a hostage from
News, Michael Balkwill, a brilliant duty editor from News
Division and a TV News enthusiast from the start, who had
been allowed to go and work, as an experiment, with the
B.B.C.'s topical-film makers. Balkwill was delighted with
the chance, though knowing perfectly well that he had been
sent to keep a News finger in the new pie. His feeling for
pictures soon matched his nous for news: he was the first of
the television journalists.

The film department, led by Philip Dorté, an engaging and
energetic man demobilised from the R.A.F., were for
several years the only people trying to cover current events
in pictures regularly. They had a thin time. It was difficult to
lay hands on useable film: the only newsreels the B.B.C. was
allowed to put on at first were the productions of the
commercial companies, the ones supplied to cinemas. And
even an 'illustrated news talk' was unknown. The public still
had to rely on radio, not television, for information on what
was happening in the world: the News authorities merely
pussyfooted round *proposals* for regular screened news as if

they were as dangerous as the unexploded Luftwaffe bombs which were still being dug up in British earth.

True, the slowness to start a news programme was not all reluctance: it was born of the many difficulties in the way of making news visual, of the responsibilities involved, and of anxiety that Vision should have Sound's high standards of news-giving. And there were *some* people in the Television Service who pressed hard for News and for picture-coverage of big events—predictable events, anyhow. Among them were Maurice Gorham, Norman Collins, Grace Wyndham Goldie, Cecil McGivern, and the realists of the expanding Outside Broadcasts unit. But the ginger groups were up against Corporation heel-dragging—and opposition outside as well. Fogs of nervous suspicion blew up in high places when the new medium and its cameras were mentioned: in those days television stirred apprehension.

It was only with difficulty that the B.B.C. received permission to screen any moving pictures at all of the wedding of Princess Elizabeth and Prince Philip in November 1947, even though the event was a cheerful and very welcome gleam in that austere post-war year, and though 'live' television was covering the processions *outside* the Abbey. Indeed, we seemed to have moved but a few inches along the road to Outside Events in a dozen years. Back in 1934—when there was no television at all—Westminster Abbey had frowned even on radio coverage of that year's royal wedding, of Princess Marina and the Duke of Kent, for there was a fear that if such a thing as a direct commentary and relay of the service were to take place the sounds from the Abbey 'might be heard by irreverent people sitting in public houses with their hats on'.

Now, in 1947, radio was accepted and permission given for microphones to be in the Abbey for the marriage ceremony; but our cameras got little more than a look in. King George VI did not wish the wedding of his daughter to be filmed inside the church; and when broadcasting plans for the occasion were being considered he said yes to sound but no to vision. However, backed by what had become great public interest in the romance of the young Princess and the good-looking Mountbatten, further representations were made to Buckingham Palace; and, less than three weeks before the marriage, the King reconsidered his refusal and declared his willingness to allow filming—restricted filming —by the cinema newsreels and the B.B.C. Only the procession out through the nave could be shown, 'only from the westernmost end of the choir stalls to the Great West Door, and not at any period during the marriage service itself—and no close-ups'.

A strange-sounding edict today, in an age when not only weddings but Coronations and Investitures mean not so much services of dedication as Television Spectaculars. But such was the climate of opinion in the 1940s.

Dorté and company in our film department went on fighting against odds, determined to get things out of the magic-lantern era. The News continued to be sound only, accompanied by the sight only of that maddeningly steadfast B.B.C. 'badge' on the screen, with no music and never even a flash of a 'still' photograph; but Dorté did at length succeed in putting something else on the screen: a weekly magazine programme simply called 'Newsreel'. The early Reels were fairly dateless cinema stuff, with little up-to-the-minute material or original shooting in them, but they were liked for their entertainment and polish in presentation, they showed contemporary events—and the pictures moved. It was a break-through to get *some* filming of our own into the programmes. And the programmes improved. As time went on, the planners were able to put three Reels a week into the transmissions, and then five. A new Newsreel every night, Monday to Friday, thirteen minutes long! And the News itself hadn't even started.

Those Reels were not 'the latest' in information, but they were certainly the smoothest. The voice we employed to read the scripted commentaries in the first programmes was that of Edward Halliday, the portrait painter, who had done some freelance radio reporting for us. Sweetly flowing clichés rolled out soporifically as the pictures slid neatly along. The style was vintage travelogue—until Michael Balkwill contrived to inject some adult wit and crisp sophistication into the scripts prepared for the unseen narrator. Balkwill, incidentally, was fortunate enough to find two fellow spirits in the war-for-news and the rebellion against a stick-in-the-mud News Division hierarchy, two young men named Paul Fox and Richard Cawston, both of whom were to gain rank and fame a quarter of a century later, the one as a controller of programmes and the other as a maker of distinguished documentary films, including *Royal Family*.

My own part in the first fumblings towards television news was marginal. I was still at my reporting desk in Portland Place when Television Newsreel started in 1948. Soon after that, I managed to get my feet from under the table and began to travel again as a special correspondent, though I still spent part of my time in London and in planning meetings. I was called on to contribute my mite of memoranda to the bulky files labelled 'Proposals for News in Vision', and I was able to watch, and later to take part in, some of the experiments-in-public which were achieved.

Two of these experiments constituted a landmark; they should have their place in television history: the coverage on the screen of the 1950 and the 1951 General Elections. Considering the obstructions from news agencies, from news sources inside the B.B.C. too, and a certain amount of technical defeatism, the service given on those Election Nights was remarkably fast and comprehensive. Against all likelihood, B.B.C. Television for the first time provided a quick service of results (so good that it beat the news service on radio—and was rapped over the knuckles for so doing!) and very reasonable running analyses by experts, the sort of programme which is taken for granted nowadays.

Yet those demonstrations of what News and Current Affairs could do on the screen, far from galvanising our old news directorate into action and a TV News début, only seemed to increase hesitancy. After each of those successful essays it was 'back to Square One'; back to radio news only; back to domestic squabbling and more endless discussions of plans.

When there came the most picturesque news-event of the century, the superb pageant of the Queen's Coronation in the early summer of 1953, fully and magnificently televised, outside restrictions had gone and our O.B. cameras were allowed everywhere. The tremendously successful Television occasion which this proved to be demolished any lingering public doubts about 'the Box'. Dealers were flooded with demands from people who had held out against having television in their homes. Now the cry was: 'We *must* have a set!' But even the Coronation did not set the fires burning inside B.B.C. News. We had now gone on discussing what *might* be done, not merely month by month but year after year. I had kept going off on various long spells of overseas reporting—at the new United Nations in New York in 1949, and a big tour through Canada with Princess Elizabeth in 1951—and each time I got back I expected to find that we were about to go into vision. But not a bit of it.

Not until 1954—almost a decade after the war and the rebirth of public television—did the B.B.C. start a news service on the screen. I was surprised that it was not actually called 'News in Vision', for the Corporation—rather agreeably, I thought—had a fondness for archaic labels, such as 'Director of the Spoken Word', which sounded as though newly filched from the Wallet of Kai Lung.

No, 'News and Newsreel' was the title—a regular 'illustrated news', its beginning heralded at a mammoth press conference by the Director-General, Sir Ian Jacob. The opening might not have come even in 1954 had it not been that the Corporation, and in particular its hesitant News chiefs, had a rocket placed behind them by the ending of the B.B.C.'s monopoly—by the setting up of the Independent Television Authority. The coming of commercial television was going to bring competition for the first time. Action became imperative. I.T.N., it was clear, would screen a good, up-to-the-minute news programme every evening at a peak hour. At Broadcasting House, planning-meetings were no longer enough; and the Board of Governors delivered the kick: 'There shall be news on television.'

So it was started, on July the 5th—started before the I.T.A. began *their* news. This was fortunate: had there been a rival with which to compare our output at first, our effort would probably have been judged abysmal. B.B.C. Television News is established today as eminently efficient and highly professional—and is recognised as such all over the

War correspondents, back in London at the end of the fighting, in the Broadcasting House office of Donald Boyd, 'War Report' editor. I was the first to change into civvies. Others, left to right: Chester Wilmot, Richard Sharp and Frank Gillard

Peacetime years became busy for B.B.C. Royal Tour commentators. Off to Nigeria in 1956 with Audrey Russell and Wynford Vaughan Thomas

A recent visit to the old desert battlefield with producer Arthur Phillips brought a good programme from the Alamein Memorial

Success and failure on broadcasting assignments

But an earlier vigil at London Airport brought disappointment as Winston Churchill passed the microphone without a word

world—but its beginning in 1954 was fantastically restricted, and frankly was pathetic. The nightly programme was in two parts: a straight, factual bulletin followed by a Newsreel, twenty-five minutes altogether, at 7.30 p.m. The first part consisted of a disembodied voice—no news-reader in vision; no sound effects and no moving pictures: you looked only at the words: 'The News' on the screen, or printed captions, or occasionally a 'still' picture. The Newsreel part was made up of whatever film could be obtained. This hotchpotch was the great Corporation's new production of 'The Latest Moving Pictures of Current Events'. The mountain had laboured and brought forth an absurd mouse.

But at least it was a start, a foundation, a breaking of barriers. The programmes were strung together each day by a small editorial staff assigned from the old News Room to work up at Alexandra Palace, and they were responsible to a lofty, dogmatic New Zealander, Tahu Hole, who was the B.B.C.'s News Editor. For the old News Division had won the battle for control of TV News, and it was the 'steam radio' editors down in B.H. who had absolute authority as to what should and should not be mentioned or pictured, in what order and at what length, in the new news service put out from 'Ally Pally' six miles away. So TV News was nobbled by its owners at the beginning—though that did not prevent the first news-subs who went to work in television from becoming enthusiastic converts from the start. Teaming with the technicians and producers of television, they became a News *corps d'élite,* fascinated by and devoted to the new medium. They worked all hours—and forgot Broadcasting House, and what they now called its 'blind radio'. My friend Pat Smithers organised them all.

The new programmes from Alexandra Palace were not greeted by cheers of welcome from the public. More than half the viewers thought Television News a very poor swap for the old Newsreel, which in its five years had become widely popular. Not having to worry about getting the very latest stories in, the Reel had been carefully prepared and made professionally glossy. By contrast, this infant News and Newsreel was a hurried broth of indifferent bits of film, library 'stills', and patchy studio reports, and without what

H

today seems the elementary and essential anchor of seen news
—the presenter in vision, the Newscaster. For what The
Powers at that time had, in effect said, was: 'My God, if the
announcer were to be seen, he might cock an eyebrow or
smile whilst reading a political item, and that would be
comment!'

But it had to come, of course, the Talking Head. Our first
experiments in putting announcers 'in vision', getting them
to 'speak to camera', were as painful to the viewer as they
were to those battling in the studio. We were, perforce,
making our mistakes in public. I became involved in the early
struggles of news-reading; and struggles they indeed were.

The first readers on television were some of the renowned
regulars of radio announcing: Frank Phillips, Alvar Lidell
and John Snagge among them. These men had been part of
the nation's life for years—as voices only. Now they were
required to be seen as they performed; and, although none
was ugly or unpleasant, the transition was not natural and
not a success. They looked completely out of their element.
Many viewers, including devotees of those famous men of
impeccable pronunciation, who had happily formed their
own mental pictures of them whilst listening to them, found it
odd and difficult to accept them as visible beings, to see them
with their eyes down to their scripts. What we were doing, in
fact, was simply showing pictures of men 'on the wireless';
and the announcers were irremediably poor at the new game.

For agreeable regular talking on television there are few
golden rules: you 'come off' or you don't; and success or
failure is unpredictable. It has nothing to do with film-star
handsomeness. The technique of getting the information
across acceptably, of being a straightforward, comfortable,
authoritative and dependable person as seen on 'the Box'; of
being well-spoken and clear, easy on the eye but without
the sort of theatrical personality which flavours or obtrudes
into the news which you are telling—none of this is a thing
you can learn at school or discover every day. Perhaps it
was very understandable that older announcers from Sound
did not acquire the new knack. Not journalists, but readers
of material written for them, it now alas seemed somehow
obvious that they were uttering at second-hand; and their

very perfection as *talkers* of news, their long years of
devotion to the Spoken Word, made television difficult for
them—and perhaps unfair to them.

So other news-readers were sought. The Corporation
turned rather desperately to two or three of the experienced
news-men on its staff, correspondents and reporters. I was
one of those who were tried and found passable. During
spells in England between reporting journeys which were
now taking me in and out of the Middle East and on royal
tour marathons round the world, I was called upon to spend
—sometimes 'live' on viewers' screens and sometimes on
closed-circuit—weeks of sessions in front of the cameras in
the big old barracks of a studio at Alexandra Palace.

A.P. was the place where television had begun, the home
of the first public TV service in the world in 1936. The
general television programme people had now outgrown
the place and had left for Lime Grove. News alone had
inherited the ancient halls. So there we were, beneath and
around that corner tower with the lattice mast on top of it,
in full possession of the eastern wing of the vast, crumbling
Victorian relic which Alexandra Palace is. Within this
ornate and melancholy monster of a 'culture palace', a
sleeping giant of a building perched on its North London
hill-top above the pygmy villas of Muswell Hill, we suffered
and pioneered the new trade of visual newscasting. I found
I had to do my announcing whilst crouching on an office
stool at a plywood desk in the heat and glare of the studio
lights, one eye on the scripts and the other on the winking
cue-lights operated by a sub-editor in a corner. As if this
were not enough, there was The Teleprompter, the early,
terrifying 'prompter which, though designed to help,
was to me the terror of the studio.

The idea of a device like this, of course, is to help the
presenter of news to give a natural, spontaneous performance. By its use he can look up and face the camera without
constant recourse to the typed sheets of news stories stacked
on the desk in front of him. Nowadays, almost all the items
on his script are up there on his prompting screen as well, in
outsized typewriting and brightly lit. The lines he looks at
are from a moving roll inside what might be a smallish

television box. The words appear in front of the camera, so that as he reads them he looks through them straight into the camera lens itself—and so straight at the viewer at home. Thus he seems to be talking without reading.

Tha was also the idea in my day. But I did not find the prompting device which we had then either simple or soothing. Mine was a first and, by present standards, a very primitive type of machine. I stared at it as though hypnotised whenever I read a news item; for this invention was my master. It led and I, its servant, followed. Though it should have been the other way round, the thing employed *me*; and I think even the viewers at home must have known that I was gazing at something that was calling the tune, and that I was not simply a chap with a marvellous memory who never needed to look down at bits of paper. That early 'prompter, which hung ponderously beneath the camera, was too wide and there were too many words on each line, so my eyeballs were seen clearly to be traversing wildly right to left and back again as I hunted the words roliing down in front of me. Another unfortunate thing was that the machine had a fixed speed: you could not vary its rate to match your own reading pace. You kept the 'prompter moving, as you talked, by pressing your foot on a button on the floor under the desk. As soon as you lifted your foot from this thing, the machine stopped altogether: the words in front of you were either full-speed or motionless.

So, quite often, I would see the lines streaming down too quickly and leaving the 'prompter screen before I had said them. Then up would come my foot, the device would halt and I would read the now-motionless print, only to find that I had caught up with the thing and spoken all the lines I could see, before I realised that I had run out of story and should have had my foot down again. A panic stamp on the floor switch would follow, rolling the script once more, but now I had to pad and ad-lib for a few seconds until sufficient word-fodder appeared.

I used to feel a nervous wreck when these early bulletins were over, though I was heartened one day when I was given a carbon copy of a producer's report sheet saying: 'Talbot gags better than most.'

Gradually the 'prompters were improved, becoming friends instead of frighteners. The floor press-button was eliminated, and a girl operator sat beneath the camera, working the 'prompter's revolutions so that the speed exactly corresponded to the natural rate of the announcer. Today the news is read off a very efficient and almost automatic cueing machine, a sophisticated development of the earlier 'prompters. The lines appear, large and clear, just when you want them; a deft young woman controls the script-roll from a remote news-room point. The operator can pop into the modern device important items of news which come in whilst the bulletin is going on.

Even today, however, viewers can occasionally tell when it is a very 'late flash' which is being told to them—an item which has not been put up on the cueing machine. When the announcer's eyes are downcast instead of looking straight at you, it usually means that a teleprinted 'flash' has been slipped on to his desk and he really is reading a piece of paper instead of a piece of screen-prompter.

But there are also moments when it is a 'trick of the trade' which makes the announcer keep looking down, seeming deliberately to read a word or two of the script on his table instead of the lines up on his 'prompter. These are moments when, say, complicated figures or a verbatim 'quote' come into the story and it is more natural to be *seen* to be reading, to be taking pains to get something scrupulously accurate to the last decimal or syllable. A matter of verisimilitude.

As I sat a-reading in that lofty, dirty old A.P. studio, a chaos of cables and darting men in the pioneer days, it was always a pretty frenzied mixture of both script-reading and 'prompter-following that I had to endure, looking down, looking up, with bits to read 'in vision' and bits to read 'out of shot' whilst a few feet of film were shown. Each bulletin was a journey into the unknown. But it was a stimulating experience; I enjoyed newscasting, for all the wear and tear of it.

It didn't last, however. I had preoccupations elsewhere in the world of news and, in any case, what I wanted was not other people's scripts to read. I itched to write it all myself.

And announcing is not really a job for journalists. The reporter is much closer to the real thing; his is the more exciting job, and is growing bigger. Only in recent years has the reporter's role in television been developed fully and properly, with our own men appearing on the screen in their own right, providing direct, on-the-spot reports, obtaining and linking important news 'packages', giving the story at first hand wherever things were happening.

I have always relished the out-and-about of it. Which is why I bowed out of the inside job of TV 'presenting' in those 1950s. I was only really happy in television when doing news features of my own, rounding-up royal tour journeys, telling my own tale to the tune of the pictures. So, after a few months of stints as a guinea-pig newscaster, I thankfully departed down to Broadcasting House again and, from there, to continue commentating assignments overseas.

As to 'News in Vision', it improved, slowly and painfully, and went on to become very good indeed. News Division became a TV division at last. All sorts of experiments in 'link men' continued; and finally three of the younger announcers from radio were found to be the personalities Television News wanted. Quick-minded, unflappable, smoothly skilled, they became and remained an established part of the TV scene: Richard Baker, Kenneth Kendall and Robert Dougall.

Those three were the first of the real professionals in the art of communicating information dispassionately and flawlessly whilst under the world's scrutiny. I saw them grow. I used to watch them in the days when they were learning, quickly, the whole business of appearing on the screen. For I was then still making a few pilgrimages up to Alexandra Palace, in intervals at home between foreign reporting missions, to dub an occasional feature-film commentary about the latest trip I had been on. But I was already deep in work other than telly-talk. Six years earlier, there had come to me an appointment which gave me the biggest change, and the biggest chance, of all my professional life. It meant that the Palace with which I was specially associated was not Alexandra, but Buckingham. I had been given the Royal news beat.

9

Accredited to Buckingham Palace

For over twenty years of my life I have been much occupied in talking publicly about the Royal Family and in travelling round the world with them. Because of this, people have had the idea that I was a rabid monarchist or part of the Queen's Household. Neither is the case. It happens that I believe that a constitutional monarchy such as the British one is a healthy system; it happens that I have a respect—and sympathy—for the occupants of Buckingham Palace, and think that the Queen's family are a proper and useful focus of ideals; but my job at the Palace has always been that of invited onlooker and objective recorder. I was in no way Palace property; and indeed the only Establishment to which I belonged was the one in Portland Place—and, even there, I refused to let the B.B.C. call me Court Correspondent because it sounded too much like a courtier.

Nevertheless, the view I had of the Royals was close, continuous and privileged. I was the professional 'Queen Watcher', and the watching gave me a prodigious time.

The job was unsought. It was almost by accident that I became—in the words written on the morocco-bound warrant card issued to me—'the British Broadcasting Corporation Observer accredited to Buckingham Palace'.

This is how it happened. When I was sitting at a desk as Chief Reporter, organising B.B.C. news coverage in the years after the war, I was anxious to build up a small corps of specialist correspondents who would provide us with well informed and reliable services of information on a number of important subjects, in order that we would not have to depend entirely on news-agency coverage of

events, which we often found sketchy and fallible. One of
the matters on which our needs were not adequately served
was the activities of the Royal Family. I started inquiries
to see if it would be possible to have a man regularly,
though not exclusively, assigned to this field, recognised
and helped by officials at the Palace.

A good deal of humming and hawing ensued. Certain of
my superiors, who loved a quiet life and were frightened to
death at mention of the Palace, took the attitude that I
was just fussing. Half the trouble was that the two domestic
news-agencies, the Press Association and the Exchange
Telegraph, were prickly over the idea: the only two existing
court correspondents were theirs and they did not want
anybody horning in on a cosy situation. The matter was
shelved; and months went by. Then I wrote a careful
memorandum, with the request that it should 'go to the
top'. I disclaimed any notion of wanting to 'show up' the
agencies, but pointed out that they were primarily looking
after the newspapers and that there were therefore many
hours during every day and night when the agencies did not
regard their messages as being urgent; in short, their
service was not good enough to serve radio bulletins which
were transmitted pretty well all round the clock. What we
ought to have was our own full, first-hand reporting of the
many interesting engagements which the Royal Family
were carrying out each week. I asked that a formal request
be made by the Corporation for the recognition of a B.B.C.
correspondent to report royal occasions.

This eventually worked. Our Senior Controller went off
to have discussions at the Palace. One day, in 1948, I was
told, with triumph: 'We've got it! We can have our own
man with accredited status to be with the official parties
accompanying the King or the others. As a matter of fact,
the Palace rather welcomed the idea in the end.'

'Fine!' I said. 'Now we can get our own stories. So let's
think of someone suitable to appoint.'

The reply came at once: 'No need to think. It's decided.
It's going to be you.'

Now until that moment the idea of doing this sort of
work myself had not crossed my mind, for I had got into

the groove of reporting organiser rather than reporter. My immediate impulse was to answer that if it had been decided, it had been decided improperly: I should at least have been asked or consulted; it wasn't my sort of assignment and, anyhow, who would look after the desk if I was tearing round on royal visits? I did not, however, get to the point of saying this. I did some quick thinking whilst the fiat was being delivered, and it dawned on me that here was a moment I had been itching for: an opportunity to get out from the office, to travel again, and to get back to some reporting at the microphone myself. So I accepted the unexpected charge, being told that I should be doing only the more important engagements, and that as Chief Reporter I was to be given a deputy for the work inside the office. I was also instructed to go to the Palace to be looked at before matters were finalised.

That 'appointment board' at Buckingham Palace was another surprise. There were only two people on the board: the King and Queen.

I had arranged to go to see the punctilious Commander Richard Colville, R.N., Press Secretary to His Majesty, whom I had met when reporting the wedding of Princess Elizabeth the year before but did not then know well. I expected an informal chat in his office, but he had scarcely greeted me at the heavy oak door of his room when he said: 'They are ready for you now,' and I was placed in the care of not a secretary or equerry or page but a plain-clothes detective, the impeccable Superintendent Hugh Cameron of the Special Branch, the King's Police Officer. He led me gently to the drawing-room door, outside which a uniformed page, a man of about fifty, stood sentinel; he knocked, received a 'Come in', opened the door, announced: 'Mr. Talbot, your Majesties,' ushered me in and shut the door behind me. I was face to face with King George the Sixth and Queen Elizabeth.

It was a private audience—as indeed all audiences are, with no official and no attendant present, and no record of what takes place. I was nervous, and any disposition I might have had to chatter unbidden was killed by the shyness and silence of the King, who at first seemed very stern, and left all the talking to the Queen. She, however, took charge of the situation with assurance and a welcoming smile, and soon had the conversation flowing. I was encountering for the first time that extraordinary flair she has for putting a visitor at ease by looking at him and speaking with him as though he is the one person in the world she has wished to meet. Soon the King was chatting too—and I discovered another thing also: that his private conversation was not marked by the stammer which made his public speeches difficult. Much of the talk seemed conventional: on the weather, gardening, children, and favourite programmes on the B.B.C. But when it was over and I was outside the door again, I realised that, in the smoothest and most enjoyable way, I had been led to talk about myself and my family, my upbringing and my tastes and opinions. It had all been very relaxed.

Back in Colville's high-ceilinged room, the talk was much more stiff. The commander kept to the subject of diary dates for the King's coming engagements, stressed that he could never give me any information about their Majesties' personal lives, and added that when I broadcast about royal events it would not be 'in competition with the news agencies', for that was 'part of the arrangement'. I did not tell him that I hoped I should be doing more than compete with them, but agreed that my business would be with descriptions of events rather than rushing to telephones every half-hour. The royal Press Secretary gave me the impression, at that time, that he regarded journalists with some suspicion, and that they were mostly pretty odd people who had to be watched carefully. In fact he had his guard up. But he had the most beautiful manners. In later years, when the commander was more experienced in the ways of the Press, he became very knowledgeable and shrewd in dealing with journalists and never shied away from them. He became relaxed, even imaginative. I soon came to see that his incisive and rather forbidding ways were a shell enclosing a kindly man, sensitive to public opinion once he had learned his job, and, like all of them at the Palace, a first-class organiser whose paper-work was always flawless. He was by no means the darling of the popular papers of Fleet

Street, but personally, knowing him more and more through the years, I liked him and valued his friendship.

A few days after that first interview I received my trim little card of accreditation, on which was printed Commander Colville's request to all, on behalf of the King, that Mr. Godfrey Talbot 'may be afforded all the necessary facilities to enable him to perform his duties'.

My B.B.C. work did not become exclusively devoted to those duties, but they took up a good deal of my time. I became known at the Palace and on the royal rounds. I don't think I showed that pass more than half a dozen times in all the years—and then it was only when I was in a great hurry and wanted to commandeer a telephone or park my car illegally. But I was made aware of what a special possession it was when, one day in London, I mislaid it— and casually mentioned the fact when I was in Colville's office. To my surprise and embarrassment, the Press Secretary at once picked up the telephone and informed Scotland Yard of the loss. An all-stations call whipped round the Metropolitan Police network; and within twenty minutes my warrant was found in an office at Olympia, where I had been for a short time during a royal visit that morning.

After that, I always kept the card buttoned-up in an inner pocket. I had had far too much publicity over its brief loss. For months afterwards, detectives would grin and make a routine joke: 'Are you holding the pass?' Even my friends the uniformed policemen at the Palace gate would wink as I went through to the Privy Purse door (the 'office entrance', on the right) and pretend to ask to see my credentials.

Sometimes I was mistaken for a special policeman myself. Accompanying the official parties on royal visits to provincial towns, being tall, dark-suited, and often standing close to the King or the Queen, I would be approached by a local superintendent or inspector and asked, in respectful *sotto voce*: 'Should we move the crowd back a bit from the Town Hall door?' or 'Can the photographers stand on the platform when the bouquet is being presented?' Such moments came when I was simply standing and watching the scene. When I was doing an on-the-spot commentary, and had the microphone plainly in my hand, there was no mistaking my function. The mike was badge and passport.

On day visits the royal party would be small: one private secretary, one lady-in-waiting, one equerry, two detectives and two chauffeurs. On tours overseas, or longer visits up and down the United Kingdom by the royal train (in which one morning I had a most acrobatic fifty-mile-an-hour bath), there would be more officials, besides maids and valets and clerks. In fact, 'on the road' the party was a microcosm of the world of Buckingham Palace itself.

That world has about four hundred inhabitants (it depends how many supernumeraries you count), and every one is in a fixed and distinct strata. The Royal Family belong to the private apartments on the first floor of the north wing, overlooking Constitution Hill; the Household (headed by the Lord Chamberlain and the Master of the Household and the Queen's Private Secretary) have many of their offices on the ground floor of the same wing; and then there are the Staff (the servants, never to be confused with the Household), who are to be found all over the Palace: the dressers and maids and footmen, cooks and clerks, the typists and table-deckers, the Yeomen of the Plate and the Glass and China Pantry, the Daily Ladies, wielders of the vacuum-cleaners and the long-stalked feather dusters, the cleaners of the windows of six hundred rooms and the winders of the two hundred and fifty clocks. The Staff has its own hierarchy —and a supreme being: the formidable, devoted Miss Margaret ('Bobo') Macdonald, the Queen's dresser, who has been personal maid and confidante to Her Majesty ever since the Queen was a four-year-old Princess Elizabeth. 'Bobo's' place is special and her influence very great: even senior members of the Household treat her with extraordinary respect.

From the start, I found Buckingham Palace a fascinating place; and the servants of the Queen, great or small, a remarkable collection of people, notably efficient and hard-working at their jobs. Proud, confident, and set apart; yet, under the suave veneer, very much the same sort of people as the outside crowds of rush-hour foot-sloggers surging past the Palace railings on their way to Victoria

Station. The passions and frailties of human nature were there in salutary measure, inter-departmental jealousies and all.

When the Queen and the Duke of Edinburgh moved in at the beginning of the reign, much of the place was physically uncomfortable and hard to work in: there were antedeluvian hangovers from even Queen Mary's time such as central heating which hardly worked, laughable old telephones, and kitchens so far away from eating-rooms that food became cold on the journeys. But, though the frame and fashion of Nash's old building remains, much has been modernised within. Electric book-keeping machines and teleprinters now click busily in office and study, the heating is oil-fired and good, the intercom systems highly sophisticated, the kitchens up to date; mechanised cost-accounting has come, and so have the trade unions. Sense and streamlining are manifest at once. The footman who takes your overcoat and folds it in the Privy Purse lobby is no vision in scarlet: he is dressed in plain navy-blue battledress with a simple 'E.R.' cipher on the breast pocket.

Only on State Visits and special occasions is full livery worn. Then, the servants are splendid in gold-braided coats of red and black with knee-breeches of stiff white wool or scarlet plush. The scene at a State Banquet in the ballroom, with these gorgeous figures, white-gloved, waiting at table, is to this day a tapestry of Georgian magnificence. Even the B.B.C.'s royal microphone—one used only by the Queen at Palace dinners when the speeches are being broadcast—is an elegant ornament which would not appear out of place among the Regalia kept in the Tower. Slender, silver-plated, double swan-necked, this unique device is always placed on the table in front of Her Majesty by her Page only a matter of moments before she rises to speak. She herself presses a button to switch it on, make a small red light glow, and put herself on the air. It is in fact an ultra-modern device, but made to look like part of the royal plate which richly adorns these glittering banquets.

With such pageantry and State ceremonial I became increasingly involved. But there were more personal royal occasions too. The birth of Prince Charles was the first of many times when I was a kind of radio midwife, standing on

the plinth of the Victoria Memorial—the Great White
Queen's statue is permanently wired as an outside-broad-
casting point—to describe the scene as the crowds outside
the forecourt surged and cheered and then queued to read
the handwritten announcement, signed by the doctors and
pinned on the railings, that Her Majesty (it was the Princess
Elizabeth then) had been 'safely delivered of a Prince'.

Matters of life—and death. A sombre background to my
first years as Palace man was set by the fragile health of the
King, the illnesses and operations, including the removal of
a lung, which he endured with a quiet braveness as little
known to the public as the family anxiety which attended
them. When I went to Canada in the autumn of 1951 on a
full-scale Sovereign's tour undertaken by the Princess because
her father was too ill to travel we knew that his life hung by
a thread. In Churchill's phrase: 'He walked with death as if
death were a companion, an acquaintance whom he recognised and did not fear.' The end came, suddenly, barely
three months after that Canadian journey made by his
daughter and Prince Philip. During the Christmas and
New Year season the King had seemed to be recovering a
little of his strength—not robust enough for overseas tours,
however, and the Princess and her husband presently set off
on another long-planned odyssey in place of the King and
Queen. They should have been away for several months,
spending much of the time in Australia and New Zealand.
In the event, they had only got as far as Kenya when the
King died. They were back at London Airport—as Sovereign
and Consort now—one week after they had left.

The story of how that girl of twenty-five became Queen
up a tree in a remote game reserve in the middle of Africa,
for many hours unaware of the fact that she had succeeded
to the Throne during a night spent watching wild animals
at a water-hole, has been told often enough. King George
the Sixth, who had been out shooting during the day, died
in his sleep at Sandringham four thousand miles away from
his daughter, the Heir; the royal tour was immediately
abandoned, joyous flags were struck in Nairobi and Mom-
basa, and the young couple hastily flew home in the black
clothes of mourning.

The story of how the news of the King's death came to most people in Britain is less known, but no less unexampled.

I had not myself gone off on this tour. Having watched and described the moving scene of family farewell at the airport when the Princess and her husband left—the frail father standing hatless in a bitter wind until the departing airliner was but a speck in the sky—I had remained in London. The King and Queen went for a few days' stay at Sandringham. On the morning of Wednesday, February 6th, 1952, I made some calls on the way in to my office in Broadcasting House, and when I reached my desk, the telephone was ringing. I answered, and heard the voice of Commander Colville, very curt: 'Godfrey, *when* are you going to announce it over the air? What *is* going on?' Cheerfully, in ignorance, I replied: 'Announce it? Announce what?'

Heavy with exasperation, the voice said: 'The King is dead. It is on the tapes, and has been for some time. We are waiting for the B.B.C. Will you please see why your people are delaying!'

I flew to the News Room. There, and in the offices of programme heads, all was huddle and flap. The news had indeed been in the place for some time but nothing of it had been broadcast. The first news-agency flash was disbelieved and somebody had telephoned both the Press Association and Buckingham Palace to ask if it was true. The Home, Light and Third programmes were continuing their merry way. In those days there was no such thing as breaking smartly into programmes with news-flashes—certainly not with news like this. The B.B.C. had no formula to cope with sudden death. So there was utter consternation and panic inside Broadcasting House. Nobody knew the drill. There wasn't any drill—not for this emergency. A confidential file labelled 'Demise of the Crown' did exist, and it was found and consulted after some delay. But it contained little more than notes of policy meetings and recommendations to announcers and planners on how they should act during grave illnesses of royalty. Meanwhile, the News Room scratched through rule-books; departmental duty officers consulted each other timorously on the telephone; hurried meetings were held; and there were searches for High Authority so that grave decisions might be taken and wording of grief agreed. The only clear thought in the emergency seemed to be that a 'suitable programme junction' common to all three domestic radio networks must be found before the news could be given. All this took time. Meanwhile, jolly sounds continued to emanate from the B.B.C.; Buckingham Palace listened with mounting surprise and distress; and the country was unaware that the reign had ended.

The Overseas Services were not so inhibited, and brief statements of the King's death began to dart from the wireless sets of the world. Indonesia was the first land to hear the news from the B.B.C.

Listeners in Britain were told it at 11.15 a.m., thirty minutes after the tidings had come in. John Snagge, deep and solemn, read: 'It is with the greatest sorrow that we make the following announcement. . . .'

The B.B.C. then proceeded to go off the air. The bare announcement was repeated a few times until the full One o'Clock News. After that, absolute silence until the Six o'Clock News. Five hours of radio black-out: no information and no explanation. Loud-speakers were dumb: listeners wondered what was amiss. There was a television service closure too. Solemn music followed; another news bulletin, and a statement that all persons were expected to wear mourning. February the 6th was a sepulchral day of hush.

That night London was as though paralysed and under a pall. Lights were dimmed; theatres and cinemas closed; dances and parties were cancelled. Parliament, the Stock Exchange, all courts of law, had put up the shutters. Business houses had closed early—so had shops, after assistants had removed brightly coloured goods from windows and put swathes of black crêpe in their place. Newspapers came out with their columns heavily black-bordered. And outside Buckingham Palace people stood, silent and staring in the chilly drizzle.

Next morning normal life began to flow again in the city— but not at the B.B.C. A period of monumental mourning had set in. For nine days, until the King's funeral on the 15th, radio and television programmes were cancelled right and left. Whether you tuned to Home, Light or Third, you got the same mixture: dirge-like music, news, and solemn talking, little else. No comedy shows, no dance bands, no light relief; never a smile. Altogether a doleful business. Was somebody atoning for unpreparedness by organising public misery? Respect and remembrance were one thing, but this long blight over the air waves was quite another, a pointless and misconceived thing—or so many people thought. There was loud and widespread—though not universal—public complaint. Dr. Heenan, Roman Catholic Bishop of Leeds and the future Cardinal Archbishop of Westminster, went out of his way publicly to castigate the Corporation for 'wrapping the nation in organised gloom'.

I was myself remote from all this programme-killing, for my business was away from Broadcasting House. I was heavily involved with what we *did* broadcast: the public events which followed the King's death, which were in fact covered very well indeed by radio and television news and outside broadcasts.

On that unhappy morning of the death, having remained in the office for the panic and the ponderous programme break, I took a cab down to the Palace, stopping in Jermyn Street on the way to buy a black tie and a new bowler, and began to piece together the story of what was happening at Sandringham and to make arrangements to report the new Queen's homecoming, the proclamations, the Councils, the processions and all the State obsequies which would mark the first days of the new Elizabethan era.

The lying-in-state of the dead monarch in Westminster Hall produced extraordinary scenes. For three days and nights the purple-draped coffin of Sandringham oak, with banner and crown, orb and sceptre upon it, stood high and lonely on its catafalque in the centre of the old stone chamber which adjoins the Houses of Parliament. It was flanked by six candles, each taller than a man, and guarded without cease. Yeomen of the Guard, Gentlemen-at-Arms and officers of the Household regiments, four at a time,

I

took turn to stand sentinel at the corners of the dimly lit platform.

Members of the public were admitted to pay their last respects to the memory of the shy and dutiful man who, brought to an unsought-throne by his brother's abdication, had reigned over them, painstakingly and with courage, through fifteen hazardous years of war and peace. Nobody knew how many people would come to the hall. In fact, three hundred thousand did. The doors had to be open from early morning until far into the night. Men and women waited silently in the bleak streets to go inside for three minutes. On all the days the queues, six persons abreast, stretched from the steps of the hall, back along the Thames embankments and river bridges for two miles, and it was a common experience to reach the steps of the hall only after an outdoor wait of three hours in very wintry weather. But I never heard a complaint. I interviewed people at all hours, when they had passed through the hall and out into the Westminster air again, and the comments were all the same: it was something they were satisfied to have done. Even those who seemed to me to be ill and unwise to be there, who looked frozen to the verge of pneumonia, whispered through chattering teeth that their wait had been infinitely worth while.

I wonder if such atmosphere as there was in Westminster Hall will ever be known again. It was stiller than an empty church, sadder than a family deathbed, more dramatic than a theatre production, as the thousands, in two streams on either side of the coffin, shuffled endlessly and soundlessly past the uplifted body and its guardians who stood, each man for an hour at a time, motionless, with bowed heads and sword-points to the ground—a vigil as physically testing as any Trooping the Colour parade on a scorching summer's day. Old Yeomen and young Guardsmen alike, they never moved a muscle as the crowds streamed past, to look, to bow, to kneel for a second, and often to cry.

For those of us concerned with outside broadcasting, it was an exhausting time. We were, I think, sustained by the superbly staged and moving pageants we had to describe.

The State Funeral had so much sombre pomp that it

almost stunned the senses. The burial, in lovely St. George's Chapel at Windsor Castle, was a rite apart, removed from the vast audience of the metropolis; but there was a congregation of nine hundred and a great gathering of Kings and Princes and Heads of State at the service. I watched it all, from a screened perch in the Catherine of Aragon Gallery above the chancel where the Family stood, veiled in black, pallid and poignant, as the coffin sank from sight through a hole in the floor to the burial vault below, and the bearded figure of old Lord Clarendon stepped out and broke the white wand of his Lord Chamberlain's office above the grave to symbolise the ending of a reign.

10

Behind the State Curtain

The reign of King George the Sixth had ended, constitutionally, on the day he died; and that was the day on which the reign of his daughter began. But the new reign was a year and four months old before this Queen Elizabeth was crowned. It took them all that time to transform Westminster Abbey into a vast theatre for the Queen's Coronation, even though the planning was begun on the day after the King was buried. The crowning was a non-stop news story from that day onwards; and inevitably—although I continued to be involved in other organising and reporting duties as well, including an exhilarating stay in Finland for the Olympic Games at Helsinki in 1952—one of my principal jobs at this time became the covering of the vast preparations for the great event at the Abbey, and then the making and arranging of broadcasts on Coronation Day itself, June 2nd, 1953.

The Earl Marshal, the Duke of Norfolk, and the Minister of Works, David Eccles, were the impresarios. At their orders, the Abbey's monuments were muffled in felt and boarded-up, stands and galleries for seven thousand guests were erected and became handsomely furnished as the months went by, and the church's west end was extended by the building of an elaborate annexe, its entrance guarded by lines of sculptured animals, the Queen's Beasts, and garnished with flowers by Constance Spry. It cost a million pounds to get the place ready and stage the ceremony. A hundred millions had been spent by Government and public by the time the crowning day was over, such were the forces of national pride, euphoria and licensed commercialism which gathered round the occasion. The Coronation became big business, the processional route five miles of expensive grandstand for pageantry. A whole souvenir industry blossomed; robe makers and sword cutlers flourished exceedingly; peers, and firms hiring lordly finery, shook the mothballs from furred mantles last worn in 1937; and couturier Norman Hartnell, with the new Queen's blessing, designed an alternative form of court dress for those peeresses who didn't possess the standard robes. He still used crimson velvet trimmed with miniver and ermine tails, but at a cost of a mere forty pounds—as against a probable two hunded for a new rig from the traditional tailors. Peers were paying twice that.

Magnificent uniforms and cloaks and very formal suits were officially the raiment of the day, though the Earl Marshal had declared that a compromise in clothes might be allowed. On the day, I saw only one person who seemed to have acted on this dispensation: Aneurin Bevan, whose black double-breasted jacket made him quite conspicuous.

I was one of the workers, not a gilded spectator, on the 2nd of June. I did eleven 'live' news reports during the day. But, as I was also an official guest in the Abbey, the possessor of a coveted seat, I too had to be dressed for the party—not in silk and fur, but morning-suited. From the start, there was never time for me to change; black-and-stripes was my broadcasting clothing for the day. Indeed, because my first descriptive 'news spot' into the Overseas programmes had to be spoken from Westminster at 6 a.m., I had to wear my finery from dawn onwards. I was staying in a hotel in the West End and had to be out and away from there by 5.30. There was no taxi to be had, so I walked to the Abbey in the early morning drizzle, a strange spectacle for the opening eyes of the crowds who had been sleeping out on the pavements all night. They stared at me from their sleeping-bags and makeshift groundsheet tents: I was comic relief for them as, in the uncertain light of a cold and miserable day, I marched down the middle of Whitehall clad in tail-coat and grey topper, sped on my way by the whistles of the wags and shouts of: 'Ascot's *next* week, Guv'nor!'

When that morning began there was plenty to report. As if

the Coronation was not itself enough, another news story of epic dimensions broke at breakfast time: the conquest of Mount Everest for the first time, a triumph for the British expedition led by John Hunt. The summit was reached—by a New Zealand bee-keeper and a Nepalese porter, Edmund Hillary and Sherpa Tenzing—on May 29th, but Colonel Hunt's terse signal reporting the success took four days to reach London. No public relations expert could have timed its arrival better: the multitudes gathered in the bedecked capital received the tidings with jubilation. Here was a sensational present for the Queen—Crowning glory from the roof of the world.

The news also buzzed up and down the rainbow ranks assembled inside the Abbey, and was an unexpected bonus of a talking point as the long time of waiting went by: we were inside the church for seven hours. Even lords had to be in their seats by 8.30 a.m. for a service which began at 11.15 and went on for nearly three hours. No wonder many a packet of biscuits and cheese came out with stealth and crumbs from beneath the folds of a peer's robes in the hours before the processions started. No wonder there was occasional surreptitious recourse to pocket flasks. No wonder scores of lavatories had been built behind the stands in the church. No wonder the four hundred ushers—called Gold Staff Officers and looking as gorgeous as the name— were kept busy assisting ladies and gentlemen of advanced years to and from those comfort-stations, which, incidentally, were graded and boldly labelled. Irreverent visitors remarked that the 'Peers Only' signs were misleading.

When the service at last started, all tiredness was dazzled away. The music was stupendous; the unprecedented pageantry transcended any preconceived ideas. And the ceremony itself, faultlessly and resoundingly carried through, was intensely moving, not least because of the bearing of the young Queen, her dignity and composure, the sense of sincerity of a human being which somehow shone through the trappings, and the air of dedication with which this Second Elizabeth invested the preordained formality of it all. Many professional watchers—even men who had been publicly snide about 'puppet performances'—told me afterwards that they had never before been so personally stirred by a spectacle. It would have been easy to sit back and sneer. Nobody did. Hard-bitten foreign correspondents were caught with tears in their eyes. B.B.C. sound engineers and cameramen confessed to being so carried away at certain moments—carried away by a feeling that they were taking part in the service rather than recording it—that they almost forgot their jobs.

The liveliest spectator in the Abbey was Prince Charles, not yet Prince of Wales and not yet five years old. There he stood, watching it all, goggle-eyed: a slicked-down little boy in a fairy-tale white satin suit. He was brought in to the Royal Gallery when the ceremony was halfway through, and he stayed until a little before the end, jumping about and asking questions of his neighbour, his grandmother, Queen Elizabeth the Queen Mother. He had expected his great-grandmother to be there too, but old Queen Mary had died ten weeks before her grand-daughter's great day.

One member of the Royal Family watched without being present: the Duke of Windsor, the king who was never crowned, sat quietly in a room in Paris and saw it all on television.

One lesser, but very likeable, royal person who *was* in London that day almost stole the show in its later stages. The second most popular woman in town was undoubtedly Salote, Queen of Tonga. As the military contingents and the Coronation procession, two miles long, flowed back from Westminster to Buckingham Palace after the service in the rain and chill of a climatically most uncivil day, the eighteen-stone Polynesian lady captured the imagination and affection of millions of spectators wherever she passed. All the horse-drawn carriages except Salote's had their hoods up against the downpour; but she, benign and beaming monarch of 150 British coral islands in the South Pacific, insisted that her landau remained open. Soaking wet, the rain streaming down that big dark smiling face, she rolled along with regal air quite unimpaired, sitting bolt upright, waving and waving for the whole two hours of wheeled processing: a commanding figure, giving delight and hugely enjoying it. Her dress, made from tree bark with an overskirt woven from dried leaves, the traditional habit of Tongan rulers on parade, outdid the silks and satins of all the rest who followed.

'I would have travelled with my carriage open even if it had snowed,' she told me next day. 'I wanted to see the people; the people wanted to see me. I had come a long way. I was proud to be in the Number One Queen's train. What did the rain matter! In my country it would have been grave discourtesy to put a hood or an umbrella up in the presence of the Queen.'

The Queen herself, with the Duke of Edinburgh beside her, riding through the echoing streets with the Imperial State Crown on her head and the Orb and Sceptre in her hands, had no need of hoods or umbrellas: she was enclosed in a flamboyant, picture-book coach, a great golden casket of a conveyance which had been built for George the Third two hundred years before—and, mercifully, had been re-slung and re-tyred for the Sovereign of 1953 so that she sat as comfortably as in her own Rolls.

Her Coronation Day was only the beginning of a summer of pomp and celebration, of State visits to every part of Britain, and of dinners, receptions and parties, some in honour of the Queen and some given by her, including big Coronation Year garden parties.

By far the biggest social gatherings in the country are these outdoor parties, given every year by the Queen and Prince Philip in the 45-acre garden of the Palace. There is nothing like them anywhere in the world. The Coronation parties were no more swollen and splendid than the gatherings which take place each summer, usually three of them, in July. I have attended the garden parties often, and have always spent a fascinating afternoon. They are neither State ceremonies nor exclusive Establishment meetings. They are opportunities for all sorts of people to see the Royal Family in close-up, and to meet and talk with them if they are lucky. Welfare workers from remote villages and chairmen of obscure rural district councils, trade unionists and Commonwealth students mingle with the bishops and the generals and the famous officers of state. Invitations go to men and women who serve the community in small, quiet ways as well as to statesmen and captains of industry.

By four o'clock on a garden party afternoon, which is the hour when the Royal Family emerge from the house and the National Anthem salutes them with a great flourish, eight thousand people are on the lawns. It is quite a scrum. Everybody wants to see Her Majesty and Prince Philip, and the throng is ten deep on either side of the two lanes along which, separately and with many stops, they begin to move. Women in silks and feathers and fancy hats—and trousers nowadays—shove and wriggle in their efforts to get a good view; and the men, standing with top hats in nand, are mercilessly elbowed aside. I have been more pushed and kicked at a Buckingham Palace party than ever I have been in a soccer crowd.

The way in which a space is kept clear around the Queen in the midst of the jostling thousands is miraculous, and very British. One or two figures in Tudor scarlet, Yeomen of the Guard, are standing sentinel here and there, but they rarely make even a restraining gesture. Nor are any ropes or barriers used. The trick is done by a handful of casual-looking men dressed exactly like most of the male guests at the party. They are the gentlemen ushers; there are fifty of them scattered all over the gardens where royalty is strolling. As ground-keeping 'policemen' they are superb. Tall neat men, beyond their middle years, retired colonel types with clipped white moustaches, carnation buttonholes, ramrod backs and regulation smiles, they walk gently up and down with an air which blends deference and nonchalance; and they seem to find no difficulty whatever in stemming the tide of humanity that surges round the monarch. With their beautiful manners and military bearing, they stand with their backs to the front row of the scrum and murmur over their shoulders: 'You will let Her Majesty have plenty of room to see you all, won't you?'—and, despite the pressure from the straining ranks at the back of the crowd, no one puts a foot out of line at the front.

The Queen slowly advances, a lady in waiting and an equerry behind and the Lord Chamberlain beside her. She talks to people on the way. Most of those spoken to are men and women who have been pre-selected, have made themselves known to the ushers, and by the ushers are brought forward to wait in the path of the Queen. The Lord Chamberlain presents each person—it is usually a man and wife—to Her Majesty (he has a little 'crib', a list of names on a bit of paper in his hand underneath the grey topper he is carrying). The Queen shakes hands, smiles, and asks questions about home towns and work. Sometimes, people who are not in fact 'seeded' guests but who have been waiting hopefully at the front of the crowd are rewarded by an impromptu talk— and almost always, when this happens, I have noticed that the people concerned, although this presentation is just what they have prayed for, are absolutely dumbstruck when it happens, and afterwards cannot remember a word the Queen said.

Prince Philip, in his lane, is meanwhile chatting away non-stop to his presentees, putting searching questions, cracking jokes and easily loosening the tongues of those he speaks to. His is a breezy passage.

Along another part of the garden Queen Elizabeth the Queen Mother, in a brightly flowing dress and pretty chocolate-box hat, will be making her own progress, sparkling away and thoroughly enjoying herself as she always does. The Prince of Wales may be there too—a real crowd-puller. And in still more lanes across the lawns, Princess Anne, Princess Margaret, Princess Alexandra or the Duchess of Kent may also be walking along. They are not so encompassed by ushers and massed onlookers: the gentlemen in attendance on these 'minor Royals' have smaller crowds to charm into order, and more work to do in finding people to introduce. Eager guests who wait with an air of assurance in front of those other than the Queen and Prince Philip have a good chance of catching the eye of a gentleman usher and getting introduced when royalty reaches the place where they have taken their stand.

And the band plays on, non-stop indeed. Two bands take turn. There is one lot of uniformed military musicians in an open-sided tent on the Constitution Hill side of the garden and another in a similar tent far away on the south side near the lake and the flamingos and the 'Ladies' and 'Gentlemen' marquees which, though only there for the parties, have perfect plumbing and Palace servants in attendance inside.

The toilet tents are, of course, tucked away under the trees. The Royal and the Diplomatic Corps refreshment tents, on the other hand, are in full and decorative view; and when the Queen reaches her own tent enclosure the crowds which have banked the lanes swing round and mass outside the enclosure's picket-fence to look at her whilst she takes her cup of tea.

Ordinary guests have a two-hundred-yard-long tea tent to go at; and the tea, provided and served by J. Lyons, is excellent. Never strawberries and cream nowadays, but a vast variety of sandwiches and cakes. Best of all, and most refreshing as you sip it and sit and rest your feet at one of the hundreds of little café tables on the grass, is the iced coffee.

An invitation to a garden party is still much prized. Newcomers look forward to seeing inside Buckingham Palace. In fact, they only see the entrance and the Bow Room as they pass through to gain the terrace and the lawn. A much more satisfying glimpse of what the Queen's house is like is gained by those who are fortunate enough to attend an Investiture, one of the regular ceremonies at which people who have been named in an Honours List are given the insignia of their awards. Then, at least, the visitors have a walk up the Grand Staircase and along the Picture Gallery into the cream and gold State Ballroom. In this huge room, the invited relatives of those who are receiving honours (you are allowed tickets for only two of your family to watch) have a two-hour sit on gold chairs flanked by walls decked with Gobelin tapestries devoted to Jason and the Golden Fleece; they listen to a Guards orchestra playing musical comedy numbers in the gallery, and they see the Queen, standing in front of them at a canopied dais beneath medallion portraits of her great-great-grandparents, Victoria and Albert, bestowing medals for one hour.

The men and women who are being honoured have been assembled in anterooms in batches according to their class of award, and have been soothed and told the drill by half a dozen suave officers of the Lord Chamberlain's department. Each person has a little gold hook pinned on jacket or dress in advance so that the Queen will simply have to hang, and not laboriously pin, the medal on the visitor's chest.

The Queen enters the ballroom at precisely 11 a.m. and takes up her position at the centre of the dais with members of the Household grouped around her. She is ready for the prizegiving. In single file, a sedate snake 150 people long and curling down the side of the room to emerge at the front, the people who are to be decorated move slowly into the ballroom and stand one by one in front of the Queen with a bow or a curtsey: knights first, M.B.E.s at the tail-end. The new 'Sirs' receive the accolade by kneeling at a footstool and being tapped on each shoulder by the Queen, who uses a very slender sword (and, by the way, does *not* say: 'Arise, Sir So-and-so').

Investitures are prim and glittering events in their procedure and setting, and yet they have always seemed to me the most enjoyable Palace occasions of the year, partly because everybody is comfortable and gets a good view of the goings-on, but largely because the Queen herself seems to enjoy these mornings and is relaxed and talkative. By no means all the smiling and speaking goes to the K.C.V.O.s at the head of the line: your grade of honour does not indicate your ration of conversation with royalty. When the Beatles went up for their M.B.E.s—in the days when they did not despise honours and were a performing group of sober-suited boys with well-trimmed hair—they were the most awestruck and frightened people I have ever seen inside the Palace: they shuffled in front of the Queen all four together, bunched up and almost clinging together with nervousness. But the Queen kept them talking for several minutes, and soon had them at ease and chattering—so much so that in the end they had to be shooed on to allow the next people in the queue to come up and the ceremony to proceed. Paul Macartney afterwards said to me: 'She was just like a mum.' Ringo Starr found the encounter far from inhibiting after all: so pleased and unwound was he at the royal interest shown that when the Queen asked the routine question: 'How long have you been together?' he laughed out there and then and 'hammed' the lines of the music-hall song: 'We've been together now for forty years, and it don't seem a day too much.'

But the least starchy of all Investiture moments in my

experience came one morning when I was myself receiving a decoration. It was in February 1960, and the ceremony was being taken by the Duke of Edinburgh. The Queen was not there for the very good reason that she had given birth to a baby, Prince Andrew, four days before. Great public interest had centred on this royal birth, for it was ten years since the last child; and crowds gathered day after day at the railings in front of the Palace when the expected time came. The B.B.C. was ready on the spot too: we had mobile studios and television control vans at the foot of Green Park and microphones and cameras on the Victoria Memorial, all trained on the Palace. Unfortunately we got there too early, for the baby did not arrive until over a week after we had assembled our men and machines. But it was decided that the facilities should not be idle. Each day the television and radio news programmes 'went over' for short periods to the waiting people and the waiting commentator, me, for descriptions of the scene and interviews with men and women in the crowds (even at that wintry season hundreds of people hung around there for hours, and they came from many parts of the world). At last, on Friday afternoon, February 19th, the news came: 'It's a boy!' and the doctors' bulletin, framed, was put up on the gates. This was what everybody had been waiting for, and queues formed outside the forecourt to read the handwritten notice. From the O.B. point, we launched into a series of final commentaries on the general jubilation. After which, I went thankfully home, having been on watch, volubly, outside the royal house for ten days.

It was on the following Tuesday that I went on parade for my investiture inside the Palace—and discovered how closely the Royal Family look at and listen to the B.B.C.'s programmes. For when in due course I stood in front of Prince Philip to get my 'gong', he solemnly took the medal from the velvet cushion held beside him and gravely hooked it on to my lapel. Then his wardroom grin spread across his face as he said: 'So this is what you were hanging round our front gate for all last week!'

H.R.H. then made a few pithy comments on our broadcasts. Unfortunately I had no time to regale him with our adventures during that vigil at the gate. For instance, the telephone call I had received in the mobile studio when we were all rather frantically occupied just after the news of the birth had come: the caller said he was in Wichita, Kansas, and could I tell him what was happening? I thought the call was probably a spoof but I explained, testily, that I was busy preparing a broadcast and it was taking us all our time to operate microphones and cameras in the hullabaloo going on outside, without answering outsiders' phone calls. But I did open the window so that he could hear the cheers and said they were all glad that the Queen had had a boy. I was about to bang the telephone receiver down when the voice, a little faint, said: 'That was Godfrey Tallbert, British broadcasting's Buckingham man.' And, after a slight pause, the same tones boomed in my ear: 'That was just fine, man. You have the thanks of Radio Wichita. You have been on our air for two minutes and we're sure grateful.'

Just an enterprising telephone call—and a free broadcast.

Without the telephone, radio would not happen. It may be 'the wireless', but all broadcasts start by passing through G.P.O. lines before they reach the transmitters and the customers. In emergencies newsmen's reports are put on the air from a phone—by arrangement, not in the pirate style of my Wichita friend. As a B.B.C. correspondent, I always had to be in telephone touch with the office wherever I was, at home or on the high seas.

Only three days after the Prince Philip investiture, I had one of the most startling phone calls of my career. It was early evening. I was in the bath at home when the bell went. The voice at the other end was a familiar one from a familiar source, the News Room in Broadcasting House; but it was talking fast and not at all calmly: 'For God's sake get in here as fast as you can. Margaret's got engaged. I wish you'd warned us. It's just announced on the tapes. To a chap called Armstrong-Jones, photographer.'

Half dry, half dressed, I dashed up to London, pipping the ambers and one or two reds as I drove through traffic lights. All the time I was framing words to use in putting in perspective this bombshell about Princess Margaret. There was no time for elaborate scripting: I was on the air to give the story and its background within ten minutes of arriving at B.H. It was a 'lead story', for this unexpected love-affair was the best-kept secret of the year. Nobody in the news business had any inkling of it. I was supposed to be the man in the know about royal affairs but I had not expected this. All Fleet Street was taken completely by surprise too, despite the fact that the Princess and her boy friends were in the news and the gossip columns almost every day. Tony Armstrong-Jones had never been even mentioned. True, his name had been noticed among lists of guests at Windsor, but he had the perfect cover. More than one news editor had asked his reporters about him, only to be told: 'No, old boy; he's in the house party because he's taking pictures of the Queen's children.'

As indeed he was. Which is how Lord Snowdon and his wife met.

Almost ten years later, in the summer of 1969, though an earl and a Royal-by-marriage, he was still spending some time working as a professional photographer, even whilst, as Constable of Caernarvon Castle, he was arranging for the Investiture of the Prince of Wales.

That Investiture was *the* State Occasion of modern times. Its monumental ceremony had little in common with the jolly little parties with the same name in Buckingham Palace. It was—again thanks to the Duke of Norfolk's masterminding of such events—an elaborately prepared set-piece. It caused me to spend many weeks in Wales in preparation for the news broadcasting of it, covering its long preliminaries, and watching the Prince emerge into the public ken during the spring which led up to the controversial event itself. Part of this process was Prince Charles's successful and surprisingly peaceful term at the University College of Wales, Aberystwyth—a break in the three years at Trinity College, Cambridge—and his appearances on small eisteddfod platforms, bringing the house down by suddenly speaking Welsh like a Welshman. These and the frank and very human interviews he gave on radio and television were to my mind more important, more rewarding, and much more fun, than the great show itself beside the Menai Straits on July the 1st.

And, for that matter, the events which came immediately *after* the Investiture stay in my mind more than the Day. Charles at once made a four-day journey—a Progress in the old sense—through his Principality; and it was then that the young man really won his spurs by the hugely enjoyed hours and hours he spent among the crowds (a hundred nationalist-extremist bomb scares notwithstanding), a prolonged and entirely unforced public relations performance which wasn't really a performance because it was done naturally and of his own volition. 'Meeting the people' would have been the label for it if the phrase had not become debased sales-talk. The Progress stretched over four hundred miles through the hills and the valleys, towns and tiny villages. The Prince walked through it all as though he had been doing this sort of thing all his life; he was both shy and articulate, diffident and assured, both serious and amusing. He charmed everybody, from arthritic old quarrymen to adulating young shopgirls.

For me, the journey was one of the broadcasting-by-telephone tours, a whirlwind rush which gave me no time to divert to studios or even send tape recordings to be transmitted from Bangor or Cardiff. Whenever the Prince got out of the car and began a walk round, I dived for the nearest telephone and reported into it. At one village—it was Llanuwchllyn near Lake Bala—I burst through the door of Mr. Jones the Butcher, told them who I was, and asked if I might use their phone (the tour was running late and in London the One o'Clock News, which had been expecting a piece from me well in advance, was almost over). Mr. Jones waved me to the ancient telephone instrument behind the counter, and I got through to B.H. in London in a few seconds—to be told by the 'World at One' anchor-man, Bill Hardcastle, that they were anxious to know how His Royal Highness had survived his morning of touring and they would connect me up and put me straight on the air. So there I was, talking 'live' from a remote village store. When the butcher's family, sitting in the back parlour listening to the radio, heard the announcer say: 'A report from Godfrey Talbot direct from Merioneth,' the miracle of modern science was too much for Mrs. Jones. 'Now I *know* they don't tell us the truth,' she gasped. 'He can't be on the wireless 'cos he's sitting next door, in our shop!'

But of course the Investiture itself was the Big Story. Caernarvon that day was a triumph for its central figure. The Prince of Wales went through his act of dedication as flawlessly as his mother had done at the comparable ceremony, her Coronation, sixteen years before. It was an ordeal for him, those three hours of parade and complicated ceremonial, uniformed and quaintly robed as he was, his hands full of regalia made of Welsh gold, for three hours the cynosure of all eyes. Thousands staring on the spot, and four hundred million television watchers. Every time he licked his lips with a momentary twitch of boyish nervousness the world saw it in close-up. The experience was enough to daunt a tough adult with a lifetime of public appearances behind him. Yet this boy went through it with confidence and without a fluff: he exuded calmness, whatever butterflies there might have been inside him. It was, in fact, a day of tension for him and his family and all those responsible for the conduct of the occasion. There had been a prelude of not only bomb threats but explosions, engineered by a handful of protesting anarchists under a camouflage of Welsh patriotism. Tremendous security precautions attended the ceremony. Thousands of policemen, uniformed and in plain clothes, were scattered about Caernarvon and the processional routes. Detectives in morning suits were among the guards at the Castle gates. Passes and tickets were scrutinised by a whole series of officials; handbags were inspected, spectators' lunch-boxes and musicians' instrument cases opened and searched. It happened even during rehearsals; and during the night and early hours of the morning before the ceremony police and troops went over every inch of the Castle's prepared interior, the roofless arena which was the theatre of the investing. Men with torches crawled diligently about under the stands and 'hoovered' the slate dais and every square inch of bright green turf with mine-detectors. Everyone was alert for suspicious wires or parcels, for sounds of ticking.

Our television compound was also a source of worry. Such was the coverage being given to the spectacle that it

K

involved not only eight hundred assorted broadcasting-
services personnel but five million pounds' worth of big
broadcasting equipment. This was massed at the Castle,
where hundreds of B.B.C., I.T.A. and Post Office technicians
had worked for months to prepare for the disseminating
of the Investiture. Immediately outside the Castle, and
stretching down to the river quay, a palisade, high and stout
and looking almost like an extension of the fortress walls,
had to be built to enclose all the gear and its huddles of
pantechnicons and huts and cables. The compound was
guarded like the Castle itself: there was no going in without
a permit. Even so, we had at least one panic per day as
July 1st drew near. Anonymous telephone calls would come
in, saying: 'There is a bomb in your TV enclosure—you've
got fifteen minutes.' All the calls proved to be hoaxes, but
the police could not without investigation assume that they
were, so the whole area had to be evacuated several times in
order that searches could be made and the area declared
safe.

Trouble spread during the hours immediately before the
ceremony. I never got to bed at all during that night. News
was breaking all over the place; news editors became as
jumpy as the police. Two terrorists carrying a home-made
bomb in a Denbighshire village thirty miles away blew up a
building and themselves. Bomb-disposal teams were busy
all night along the railway line from London to North
Wales, investigating sinister parcels and assorted 'security
alerts'—with the result that the Royal Family's overnight
train was considerably delayed. For me and my colleagues in
Caernarvon all this meant a night of scouring the district
and telephoning reports to London.

When dawn came and the day of the great ceremony began
to unfold I was not exactly the most rested and rarin'-to-go
commentator in the world. A sleepless night is not the ideal
prelude to a hard day's reporting. What is more, I had been
building up to this event for so long that, now it was here, I
felt not only a sense of anticlimax but that the peak had been
passed already (it is a feeling I have often experienced on big
predictable stories). But a shave and a wash, and the automatic stimulus of our news rooms' anxiety that every

moment of this flamboyant and dangerously overwrought day should be covered, soon had me on my toes.

My own particular job was to keep the story going from morning till night. I was responsible for our reporting team, and was expected to do the main narrative—for Sound—in voice myself. For this work, and because of my accreditation to the Palace, there had been put at my disposal not only a microphone on the Castle battlements overlooking the whole scene of the investing but also a coveted seat in the arena: I was, in short, one of the four thousand guests officially invited to occupy a chair in one of the specially erected stands within the walls. The original plan was that I should occupy this privileged seat and should slip in and out of it when it was necessary to go to the microphone for a progress report—or if an unexpected 'incident' occurred. But when July the 1st came it had become clear that London's demands would make it impossible for me to occupy either my seat or my post on the walls. I had to be in touch with London, in two-way talk, *all the time*.

There was only one thing for it. I had to abandon my handsome red Official Guest chair and go to a place where I had all Caernarvon's information at my elbow and a microphone constantly open to London and linked to the B.B.C.'s domestic and World Service outlets.

That place was just across the square from the Castle. It was in fact in the large Sunday School room of a Presbyterian chapel which had been taken over by the B.B.C. as a headquarters for the whole Investiture operation. It was a chaos of telephones, typewriters, teleprinters, cameras, sound engineers' gear, and makeshift desks occupied by loud people. But it was the nerve centre: into it came word and sight of everything that was happening, minute by minute, from our outside reporters and roving microphones in the streets as well as from inside the Castle.

In one corner of this organised madhouse was a slightly oversized broom cupboard, normally the chapel caretaker's junk hole. This was the only refuge from the general pandemonium; and it was made into a studio for me, our one peep-hole point with a line open to London permanently. And this airless box was my post of duty throughout the long day. Hour after hour I sat there, on an old stool, with a lip-microphone and a telephone and a television monitor in front of me and two technicians and two tape recorders beside me. I talked almost non-stop down the line. I watched the television screen, I listened to the Castle output—and the occasional explosion round about—I scanned the incoming news messages on the teleprinter, I had colleagues popping in and out with tidings from the crowds, and I kept stepping across to the Castle to watch—and all the time reeling off dispatches to the B.B.C. 'in voice' down the line. Before, during and after the central ceremony, editors and programme producers in Broadcasting House demanded running descriptions and summaries for news bulletins. I lost count of the number of programmes I talked into. 'Can you do us a three-minuter, live, in five minutes, at the start of the next bulletin?' became a routine request. And the broom cupboard always managed to produce the goods.

When the service teleprinter clacked out its last message to us late that night, I had packed up and was stumbling out of the chapel. 'Tell London I'm not here,' I said. 'They can't *possibly* want another piece.' But someone ran after me with a slip of paper. On it was the signal no journalist is ever too tired to like: 'Congratulations and thanks from all on first-class service. Sleep well.'

I had had a ghastly perch for the glamorous day; but the cupboard had worked. And on my Presbyterian stool I was no more uncomfortable than I should have been on that crested seat in which I should have sat in the Castle that day— as I found when, a few weeks later, I acquired my unyielding Investiture Chair as a souvenir.

I ought, of course, to have known by 1969 that, for me, Royal Occasions were not relaxed, sitting-back affairs. I had been leaping around in covering them, all over the world, for two decades.

11

On Tour

'It must be marvellous to go on all those overseas royal tours. First-class treatment. Everything laid on. Seeing the world and getting paid for it. The travel holiday you dream about.'

That sort of thing has been said to me a thousand times. And not surprisingly. I *have* indeed had the time of my life, and much of the education of my life, in covering the journeys of the Queen and her family to every continent. I *have* seen the sights of the world. I *have* relished it, and held myself fortunate to experience all the 'faraway places with strange-sounding names'. The list of countries and towns from my tour diaries is like the index of a gazetteer; the mileage total is getting on for 300,000.

But—holidays? Rest-cures? A succession of gilded parties? No. Not by any stretch of the imagination.

The tours are no picnics: not for the Queen, not for the chronicler in her train. To any journalist, they are the most difficult, slogging and dusty assignments, not only because he—or, quite often, she—is always on the move but because, unless his reports are to be repetitive Court Circulars drearily logging who cheered whom, he must watch constantly and search critically for what is new and real and significant behind the inevitable pomp and protocol. And he has to work hard for unusually long hours. No question of ever taking a wife along.

Going to banquets, travelling 'Priority', front seats at displays of historic splendour—certainly this has been my life. But so has living in a suitcase and washing my drip-dry underclothes at two in the morning in tropical hotel handbasins, knowing that I had to be up at six to catch the advance plane to the next province. So has acrobatic typing in lurching entourage cars and hugging tape recorders in canoes and rattling trains. So have been the perspiring drives to remote airfields and radio stations, with tapes and television film, long after a royal day was done. So has the professional grousing at acrimonious press briefings. So, too, the heatstrokes and debilitating bouts of 'tummy palaver' in lands far from home.

But I am an inveterate rubberneck. There wasn't one of the scores of long trips that I didn't enjoy, right from the start of it all. And the start was the biggest journey of all, the fifty-thousand-mile Commonwealth Tour which lasted for a solid six months from November 1953 to May 1954.

The palm-tree islands of Tonga and Fiji were visited on the way to New Zealand and Australia; and it was on a sweltering December Saturday morning only six months after her Coronation that the Queen stood on the little wooden landing jetty at Nuku'alofa and again met the benign Salote, this time as *her* guest. The Queen of Tonga had pride at being host written all over her—and she almost burst with delight and unrestrained laughter when—rare occurrence in that paradise of southern sun—a sudden shower of heavy rain fell as they were driving away from the shore. Queen Salote dredged an umbrella from the back of the old car, held it over Queen Elizabeth, smiled her famous smile, and whispered: 'Remember London? Now we're quits.'

In Salote's unfenced Palace garden, beside the coconut groves, the road made of powdered grey coral and the blue lagoon, the Tongans put on an unparalleled royal feast. We all sat down to dinner, garlanded, cross-legged, on the scorched grass, and with our fingers ate into mountains of tropical food stacked in long lines before us. Two thousand sucking pigs, roasted whole, were only a small part of it. We drank palm wine out of half-coconut shells. Our napkins were of tree bark. Young girls fanned us as we ate, using large leaves both for that task and for swatting the flies off the piles of fruit. It seemed perfectly natural, when I was presented with a ceremonial grass skirt, to put it on as apron over my shorts.

The young Queen from London had never had an experience like that banquet without knives or forks or plates or a chair to sit on.

Stranger things were to follow. That night Her Majesty slept in Salote's Palace, a rambling Victorian house of wood. She was guarded by relays of Tongans who built fifty little watch-fires in the grounds, ringing the building, and sat by them throughout the night. It was hot; the crickets were noisy; and even the whispering of the squatting sentinels sounded like a rushing stream. Probably the Queen slept little. Almost certainly not after dawn, for at dawn she was serenaded by a small group of musicians who gathered outside her windows playing insistently mournful nose-flutes. Hundreds more people then arrived in the garden with the early daylight, and, itching with curiosity, squatted beside the fire-watchers outside the Palace windows. When the Queen got up and walked from her guest apartment through room after room to reach the ground-floor bathroom which had been allotted to her, she found the shutters wide open and half Nuku'alofa expectantly gazing in.

The Kingdom of Tonga is well named 'The Friendly Isles'.

As we sailed away from those islands and on through the Pacific towards New Zealand—in the Shaw Savill liner *Gothic,* in use as royal yacht because the *Britannia* was not then completed—it was getting near to Christmas and the Queen was rehearsing the Christmas Day broadcast she was due to make from Auckland, the only one of these annual messages she has spoken away from home. As I was the B.B.C. man travelling in the royal ship, I was involved in the script conferences and the stand-by recordings of the message. These took place, in sticky weather, in the Queen's lounge, with my microphone on her desk, myself with stop-watch in hand in one corner of the room, Prince Philip as critic in another corner, and the Queen's Page and the Sergeant Footman hovering in the background—wearing their usual deferential air despite their unusual 'livery' of cricket shirts and white shorts and sandals. The Queen read her script without a fluff from the first run-through, com-

posedly and coolly, unworried by either the temperature or
the slow rolling of the ship.

We arrived in Auckland on December 23rd, and the Queen
was able to make her broadcast 'live' from Government
House. It was the traditional Christmas message, spoken in
an untraditional setting: a sultry room with windows flung
open to a tropical night.

We were now beginning the most tight-packed tour
through Australasia that royalty has ever made. Journeying
to it, sailing down from Panama, had been an agreeable
experience (except that, like half the men in the ship, I came
ashore limping, my ankles bruised and painful after three
weeks of deck hockey with the Queen's very rough-playing
husband), but it was good to be on land and to tour New
Zealand for six weeks and Australia for a full eight, soldier-
ing-on through itineraries which were staggering but which
gave an unforgettable tourist's cross-section of the countries.

It was good fortune to get such a trip—there has never
been anything like it in all the visits since—but, exhilarating
though it was, I got it the hard way. For the experience was
gained by way of a daily toiling through parades and receptions, children's rallies and State drives, tours of schools and
hospitals and factories, seeing the Queen open Parliaments
in Coronation gown and jewels, watching her shake a
thousand hands every twelve-hour day of clamorous public
duty, almost without any rest days, and rarely spending two
nights in the same town. In little New Zealand alone we
travelled thirteen hundred miles in cars—quite apart from
all the journeys by assorted aircraft and trains and ships;
and in Australia we had several spells of eight-hundred-
miles-a-day flying, coming down three or four times in the
day to carry out two hours of engagements and then take off
again. Broadcasting quick dispatches from O.B. points and
strange studios, I had to think hard to remember where I
was and what day it was. Places of call became telescoped in
the mind as we rushed along. I never unpacked.

Such was the pattern of the first royal tours, their
programmes rousing but relentless, their exciting but
abrupt changes of scene and climate testing both one's
capacity to marvel and stamina to endure.

But everything was meticulously planned and magnificently organised. Each night I would receive, pushed
under my hotel-room door, a card telling me what time
next morning my baggage had to be ready, what car I was to
ride in, which aircraft to take, which train, which compart-
ment, and which town, which hotel, and which room I would
reach at the end of the next day.

Smooth though the arrangements were, it was tough
going for the Queen. However, she herself is tough and
healthy: it was not her fault that the Big Tour struck a
snag over a health hazard in the final week of the long
Australian journey. This was an unprecedented to-do.
A poliomyelitis epidemic broke out in Western Australia
just when the Queen and the Duke and the whole lot of us
were due to go there and it caused all kinds of troublesome
precautions: inoculations all round, no handshakes with
Australians, no eating-out and no staying overnight
anywhere. For a week, before finally sailing away, we lived
on board the *Gothic* as she lay in the Swan River at Fremantle. From the ship, the royal party made a sally each day
to carry out a careful, clinically pruned round of engagements. The Queen's car was followed every time by an
unaccustomed line of vans containing food and footmen; for
wherever the Queen went she took her own meals with her.
Every item of meat and drink, every plate and cup and
knife and fork was from the royal stores; Palace staff prepared
and served the food, even at Government House, Perth.
All the dirty crockery and cutlery was carted back to the
Gothic to be washed up in the ship's non-Australian water
and dried on the ship's towels by the ship's hands ready for
the next day's picnics.

It was all rather austere; but in fact it probably suited the
Queen very well. One of the things she found most overpowering on her first official overseas travels had been the
elaborate lunches and lavish banquets laid on time after
time by her hosts wherever she went. She had no wish to
cramp the style of governments and municipalities eager to
to proclaim their welcomes by putting on huge spreads,
but ten-course meals—such as we had quite often at
banquets in Canada, for instance, when she first toured there

as Princess in her father's stead—were quite ridiculous. She could only peck a little of half the dishes put before her, but had to put knife and fork to all of them for the sake of the appetites of others—for most of the company would wait for her to begin a course and wouldn't eat until she did. Indeed, there was one enormous dinner in Quebec when the Princess was absorbed in conversation with her neighbour, didn't notice that another dish had been set before her and didn't touch it, though all the other diners had been watching her and waiting, with forks poised—so the royal plate was taken away with the food on it untouched, and nine hundred other dishes were also removed, uneaten.

Soon after the Queen came to the Throne and began travelling, the word quietly went forth that gastronomic extravagance was not one of the pleasures of either Her Majesty or her husband, and that long Lucullan evenings at table were hardly the best way of showing loyalty and affection. As the tours went on, the menus got shorter and shorter. Nowadays, big meals are out.

When hosts-to-be seek guidance from Buckingham Palace —and, for that matter, when a Household planning and reconnaissance party goes out to a country which is to have a State visit—advice is given to keep the meals plain but well cooked, and the courses few. The Queen is not a great eater, or drinker, nor is Prince Philip. Certainly no oysters, no shellfish at all, and no caviar. Nothing very strongly flavoured. And no need for ashtrays on the table for the visitors' sake: they don't smoke.

The Queen and her party can be self-sufficient when they travel. It did not need a polio scare to make the royal yacht's commissariat capable of being a supply base: the *Britannia* is well stocked always, being the British Sovereign's palace afloat, the place where the Queen herself entertains and returns hospitality.

And even when the tour is a very short one in a near country, and no *Britannia,* the Queen, like most of her subjects when they leave home, has her own items of comfort and independence in the baggage. The personal 'musts' packed will include family photographs in travelling frames, a bedside clock, a hot-water bottle, a book of crossword puzzles, probably a few mint chocolates, and certainly bottles of Malvern spa water, her favourite China tea and a small electric kettle.

The Queen, Prince Philip and the family always return from a tour with more possessions than they had when they left: gifts from the countries they visit. The State rooms and private apartments of the Palace and Windsor, and cellars and storerooms too, are enriched by presents after a long trip (and every item is carefully logged and indexed). The gifts range from ornate chairs and jewelled caskets to sailing dinghies and large models of the Taj Mahal. Prince Philip, I imagine, could set up a shop selling gold tie-pins exclusively. As to the swords, sticks, guns, knives, carpets, elephant tusks, landscape paintings and volumes of photographs, the very inventories of them must fill whole shelves of the Palace library.

Livestock is presented too: horses often. Some gift horses go into the Royal Mews, some are raced or ridden personally. The mountain Haflingers, given in Austria, have been put to work on the hills above Balmoral. Other animals go to zoos: boa constrictors cannot be kept in Pimlico; and the young Prince Andrew was unable himself to look after the pygmy hippo presented to him by the late, but in life the most ebullient, President Shadrach Tubman of Liberia.

The present-giving is a two-way traffic. The *Britannia* goes out laden with carefully assembled supplies of mementos for the Queen herself to hand out. From inscribed silver inkstands downwards, these are graded according to the recipient's position and the services rendered. There are brooches and watches, cigarette cases and lighters, three degrees of cuff-links, and signed photographs of Her Majesty and His Royal Highness—framed and unframed, large, medium and small. For governors-general and for junior chauffeurs there is usually a treasured something at the moment of farewell before the visitors' journey back to Britain.

In these days the journeys back are swift and the homecomings quiet: no crowds or ceremonies. Even the detective —'The Queen's Police Officer' is the proper title—has little to do. There is hardly a photographer to chase, so the sedate and authoritative Commander Albert Perkins can concentrate on being the most experienced coat and umbrella carrier in the world.

But that mammoth tour which ended in the spring of '54 was different. The return trip was protracted, and the welcome back to Britain prodigious. After the final stages in Ceylon and Aden and Africa, the royal party boarded the newly commissioned *Britannia* in Tobruk harbour and sailed to home waters by way of Malta and Gibraltar. For the last stretch of the voyage home to an expectant London, the royal yacht—with Winston Churchill too on deck for the final day—was escorted up the English Channel by the entire Home Fleet.

The Queen's new ship was itself a splendid sight, the hull a polished blue and the upperworks an almost incandescent white, as the yacht sailed east along the South Coast, wearing a large Royal Standard at the tall mainmast, the anchor of the Lord High Admiral at the fore and the Union Flag at the mizzen. The *Britannia* was, even then, the most unusual and the most smoothly efficient vessel of the Royal Navy, her company hand-picked and her drill impeccable— the silentest ship in the Silent Service: never a whistle or a shout or sound of a footfall on board, but all orders given by hand signal or walkie-talkie, and all the sailors in rubber or canvas shoes.

Not all the vessels in that magnificent convoy were quite so trim and calm. From Gibraltar, for our broadcast coverage of the journey's ending, I had taken passage in the Daring-class destroyer, H.M.S. *Duchess,* for she was leading the royal yacht and the whole Fleet through the Channel, and we had B.B.C. gear and microphones and a transmitter aboard— with three engineers and I scurrying about the decks in an unavoidably untidy style, in contrast to the ship's company which was smartly 'manning ship', lining the rails and facing outboard in immaculate formation. My colleagues and I rather spoiled the picture. From the shore, from other ships, from the *Britannia* herself, all eyes and all binoculars were on us, the leading ship; and when I was preparing to go up to the bridge, where my microphone had been set up, to give the first of many running commentaries that day, the

Admiral commanding the escort—he was doing it from the *Duchess*—looked flintly at me and said: 'I'm not having any civilians making my bridge look disorderly. Get Talbot into a uniform!' The wardroom thereupon scrambled about looking for some disguise which would fit me. The navigating officer, who was about my build, produced an old spare uniform from his locker; and, wearing this, masquerading quite unlawfully as a lieutenant of the Royal Navy, I stood on the destroyer's bridge all day and made my broadcasts.

Between transmissions I helped the *Duchess*'s men to clear the sea for the armada that was coming up behind us. We almost ran down several small vessels of various nationalities which had not only failed to obey Admiralty instructions banning ships from the sea lane that day but did not seem to comprehend, or at any rate took no notice of, our signals and orders over the loud-hailer to sheer off; and I was given the job of holding up a large board on which had been chalked in large capital letters: GET OUT OF THE WAY. THE FLEET IS COMING.

It was a very makeshift means of communication; and my own blackboard performance was a laughably unorthodox part to play in the grand finale of the grand tour.

But then royal tours, when you are with them, are seldom the staid and unruffled progresses which they no doubt seem to the distant ear and eye. Even that fiercely regimented and double-checked first Commonwealth journey had its disturbing moments. On the penultimate stage, flying north from Uganda to the Mediterranean, the Queen—though she was unaware of it—had been in hazard when the hydraulics of the airliner failed and the captain and half the crew resorted anxiously to hand-pumping to get the undercarriage down for the landing. The touchdown at El Adem was, in the event, achieved with perfect smoothness, but it was a landing almost without brakes and with no flaps at all. They laughed about it afterwards.

Sometimes the Queen has been in danger, and *has* known it. In Quebec City in 1964, for instance, when desperados amongst the French Separatist extremists had threatened to kill her and many advisers in Canada had counselled her (unavailingly) to cut Quebec from her itinerary. The Queen insisted on making her drives and public appearances as planned, and seemed extraordinarily serene and unafraid—which is more than the police were—on the journeys through eerily empty streets which gave the whole Quebec day a sinister air. The streets were empty because the citizens stayed at home rather than risk being involved in some demonstration or worse, so there were only troops and police lining the routes. A strange day, for most French Canadians are not Republicans but noticeable and vociferous royalists. It was a royal visit in a vacuum.

In 1966, when the Queen was driving through cheering crowds along Great Victoria Street in the centre of Belfast, a 12 lb block of concrete was thrown down at her from the fourth floor of a building under construction. It missed the Queen and her husband by only about four feet and crashed on to the bonnet of the Rolls. The Queen drove on and continued her programme as planned, meeting people in city streets immediately after the incident and behaving as though nothing had happened. Later, when she inspected her damaged limousine, her only remark was: 'It's a strong car.'

One tour, in England, almost came to a premature end when an old telegraph pole, insecurely in use to hold up decorations, crashed across a West Country road when the procession was passing. It just missed the royal car, and the following Household car too, and fell harmlessly on to the highway.

In India in 1961 a million people effervesced over the royal route in the great texile-mills city of Ahmedabad, capital of Gujerat state, and thousands got out of hand during a long drive which the Queen made one hot and oppressive day. Dhoti-clad hordes came yelling and pressing up against the open royal car and halted it, bowling over the police guards in their efforts to touch Her Majesty. Again, the tour officials were beside themselves with frustration, anxiety and screaming anger; but the Queen seemed unworried and was apparently enjoying it all. She simply climbed up and sat on the folded hood of the car, with her feet on the back seat, and rode out the storm for all the world as though she was its spectator and not its centre.

One of the nastiest moments ever experienced in a public street was in Valparaiso during the State visit to Chile. This also was caused by over-enthusiasm. The Queen and Prince Philip were walking along a wide, palm-lined avenue when the huge crowds watching and waving from the side-walks strained forward so much in their efforts to see the visitors better that they broke clean through the flimsy barriers and thin lines of police and came surging across the road in a tidal wave of humanity, impelled by sheer pressure from the rear ranks. In a few seconds the Queen was lost to sight in the midst of a wildly shouting and scrambling mass. People fell and were trampled underfoot in what became a dangerous mêlée. I was myself squashed breathless and lifted off my feet. Local police stood about helplessly and held up their hands in despair. Only the Herculean efforts of Prince Philip, Perkins and another detective, who linked arms and shoved backwards to keep a tiny space clear, prevented the Queen from being felled to the ground. There were five minutes of panic and alarming chaos before the Queen got clear, bundled into an open car in which she and Prince Philip stood up as the vehicle inched through the now-sob-bing Chileans and reached the safety of the next street. Three minutes later, the Queen, looking normal and relaxed, was taking the salute at a march-past of naval cadets.

Then there was the unnerving episode at the end of a visit to Canada—it was the long one the Queen made as Princess Elizabeth in 1951—when the tender taking the royal tourists to a liner, *Empress of Scotland,* waiting out at sea was caught in a winter gale at Portugal Cove, Newfound-land. The little boat heeled frighteningly, was lost to view in deep troughs between the waves, and was almost wrecked as it clawed away from a reef of jagged rock.

The Queen—who, persisting legend has it, is an excep-tionally bad sailor, but in fact isn't—displayed no alarm whatever.

The truth of the matter is, I believe, that through the years the Queen has so schooled herself to the hazards as well as the hurrahs of public appearance that she is able to remain preternaturally cool in the face of each.

12

Mentioned in Dispatches

In the first years of this Elizabethan reign the tours of the Sovereign and Consort were enthusiastically reported, at length and in detail, whether they produced newsy 'incidents' or not. But by the early Sixties the pattern of State visits had become familiar. The special correspondents from the Fleet Street daily papers no longer retailed the parades and the flags and cheers. Their jaundiced news-desks in London required an 'angle' in the story each day, if the tour was to be reported at all: some sharp departure from custom, some row, perhaps, among local councillors about invitations to meet the Queen, some whiff of criticism of the Palace people, maybe some over-forthright comment by Prince Philip on hilarious capers by native chiefs. Reporters frantically pursued novelty and contretemps.

This wind of change did not blow too disagreeably on me. The B.B.C., though soon wanting 'something different' like the other news media were seeking, still required my reports to include also the unvarnished facts of each day's travel; and the sound effects and news film we sent back did help to keep the stories fresh. In any case, I tried, even at the beginning of the years of travel, to speak neither flat catalogues of stuffy ceremonies nor mawkish paeans to the glory of a Fairy Queen. I saw the royal travellers as human beings with human reactions, not pasteboard figures; and I also liked best to look over their shoulders to see what *they* were seeing—because the settings, the backgrounds and the fringes of the scene were always different and usually rewarding to the sharp eye. Thus I gave the red carpets and the loyal addresses short shrift, and tried to pop into my

On her six-month tour after the Coronation, the Queen spent two of the months in Australia, where Sir Robert Menzies was her host; she saw the majesty of Gibraltar on the way home, and visited Tonga and the great Queen Salote, who garlanded Prince Philip

Her Majesty spoke on Christmas Day 1953 from Government House, Auckland. She was gowned for coolness in 'a sultry room with windows flung open to a tropical night'.

The Commonwealth returned the greeting when, in the Indian Ocean later in the Tour, sailors in the escorting Australian aircraft carrier *Vengeance* formed up to make the royal signature

pieces the illuminating incidentals, even the comic things that happened to me personally as I plied my trade: these were what very often brought a tour to life.

Sometimes an astringent news editor in Broadcasting House, London, would jib a little at the light style and the tales I told—though they were more often thankful than reproving. Sometimes a listener would object (one choleric colonel in Cheltenham wrote to demand that I should be more sober and also should 'stop exalting peasants and the discourteous habit of referring to our Dear Majesty merely as "she"'). But a majority of the customers appeared to relish informality and the funnies which I mentioned in my dispatches; and they were often good enough to send letters to say they were addicts of my reporting. I particularly cherished a warm note from a lady listener in France who wrote, in experimental English, beginning: 'Dear Monsieur Godfrey, I am a fervent of your emissions. . . .'

Oddities of wording—my own, indeed, but also other people's struggles with the Queen's English—frequently got into my broadcasts. Most of my inadvertent errors seem to have been made in hot countries. In India, particularly. After I had ridden precariously, clutching a tape recorder and talking excitedly, on elephant-back in a fantastic procession which took the Queen down to the Ganges in Benares, I was appalled at the tape playback to hear that I had punctuated my commentary by a 'whoops!' every minute or so. I knew that I had kept slipping from my perch on the elephant (and was grabbed each time by the Queen's doctor who was riding with me), but the exclamations were quite unconscious.

It was altogether an unfortunate commentary and, understandably, very little of it was ever broadcast. Never since that day have I wittingly used the verb 'enshrine' in a broadcast, for fear of getting it wrong as I did then. 'In a comfortable howdah high on the front elephant,' I said, 'Her Majesty, Head of the Commonwealth, sits *entwined* with the Maharaja.'

A different sight was suggested by a young African commentator with whom I shared the microphone in steamy Freetown, Sierra Leone, as the royal carriage

L

procession went by. 'Oh my goodness,' said this broadcaster fervently, 'this is a wonderful thing we are seeing. Mrs. Queen is *so* decent!'

A little later came a description of the Duke of Edinburgh —in words refreshingly more succinct than would have been achieved had *I* been detailing H.R.H.'s admiral's uniform and dazzling medals. 'Here he comes,' declared my friend, 'Prince Philip, looking beautiful and wearing his sailor suit.'

Equally memorable were the words of a lady speaker one splendid night in Georgetown, Guyana. She was captivated by a garden party attended, in the cool of the after-dark in the lovely garden of Premier Forbes Burnham, by the Queen and Prince Philip, and was swept off her verbal feet by the glamour of the occasion—and especially by the sight of the Queen's husband. She concentrated most of her report on him, confessing that she had 'gone overboard' on seeing him. She described him as 'a dish', and excelled herself in her peroration: 'When the royal pair left the garden at midnight, after a great succes, that handsome Prince Charming from England left there, on the lawns, a whole string of enchanted and ravished ladies.'

The ample African ladies of Accra were charmed too. During the tour of Ghana, market mammies danced backwards in front of the royal carriage holding up posters proclaiming: 'Lizzie Queen we love you' and 'Dear Phil come again'. Even their clothes declared their ardour: they had wrapped themselves in royal visit cotton cloth on which were printed large portrait medallions of the visitors in widely spaced patterns. The diverting result was that most of the mammies who had dressed in this material bore pictures of the Queen on their bosoms and Prince Philip on their behinds.

In Brazil, the booming city of São Paulo produced several young women who stood in the Queen's path clad in mini dresses made out of imported Union Jacks (but the flag upside down).

In Dunedin, New Zealand—a city very loyal, very Scottish and very thrifty—some street decorations had been bought second-hand, in ready-made job lots. They included naval signal flags, already strung. The pennants facing the Queen when she appeared on a hotel balcony were read with joy by her husband standing beside her: they were making the signal: 'Danger. Am loading explosives.'

The most unconventional greeting by banner, however, was seen in Nepal, whose people had been encouraged by their king to make some of their own welcoming flags and put English words on them. This they did. Between Katmandu airport and city we passed beneath strips of bunting stretched high across the road, and on these the repeated message was simply: 'God Save the Queen', well spelled and spaced—but monotonous. Halfway to the town however one enterprising sign-writer had sought to vary the words and to bring the blessing of heaven down on the Queen's husband too: his banner said: 'God Help the Consort.'

It was in Nepal that the offbeat occurrences most thickly sprinkled my dispatches. There it was that the Queen's Foreign Secretary in attendance, Sir Alec Douglas-Home (he was the Earl of Home then), was placed in an uncomfortable seat of honour at a royal tiger-shoot in the jungle, a hunt in which hosts and guests and beaters rode on three hundred elephants, and in which the chief guest was to have, by tradition, the first shot at anything emerging from the bush. The Queen—in slacks, bush-shirt and broad-brimmed slouch hat—was shooting only with her ciné and still cameras; Prince Philip was not shooting at all because of an injured trigger-finger; so the Nepalese decided that the Number One State Visit Foreigner was the Earl. So Lord Home, who had not ridden an elephant before, let alone shot from one, and who had never seen a tiger outside a zoo, found himself blazing away with a bucking gun at vague shapes in the grass whilst the rest of the party respectfully held back. In the end, in dust and confusion at the close of the outing, he was credited with bagging a rhino.

The whole party spent the night in a vast tented camp which had been set up out in the blue eighty miles from Katmandu. King Mahendra and his men had gone to great pains to equip the camp well, one-night stand though it was. The fire-brigade was removed from the capital to pump water from a swamp into the Queen's tent; the White Russian chef and his whole staff were removed from Katmandu's main hotel to see to the food; and half the army was removed to guard the encampment.

The Nepal visit was undoubtedly 'different'. The Gurkha parade in the Himalayan foothills was something to remember when all the reviews of redcoats in London have been forgotten; and the appearance of Sir Edmund Hillary and Friend at the Embassy garden party in Katmandu is unlikely to be forgotten either—for the friend was one of the Sherpas who had been on the Everest expedition, and from the mountains he had brought something unusual to show to the Queen: a grisly parcel which he undid for her on being 'presented', and announced that he was proud to show Her Majesty 'the skeleton of a yeti's leg'. Whether it was really a bit of abominable snowman or not, the Sherpa went home at the end of the party proudly bearing a pair of royal-gift cuff-links (mark III) and a signed photograph.

All the Katmandu arrangements were made by the Nepalese chief of protocol, who was their only real State Visit expert. At that time he was serving a prison sentence for a political 'crime', but was let out of gaol for the period of the British Queen's visit—so that the programme should be well organised. He was due back in his cell on the day after the Royals left.

Extraordinary efforts are made by host countries to make a good show of the places to be visited. The Germans took paint-spray guns to a hill-top in Stuttgart where the Queen was to walk: they felt that the grass and the tree-trunks were looking shabby, so they doused them in artificial greens and browns (the result was awful—*and* sticky). The Portuguese planted instant gardens down Lisbon's Avenida da Liberdade in the week before they were to be visited. They also installed a mile of electric sun-ray lamps down on the ground to make the newly-sown grass borders grow more quickly. Chicago distributed fifty thousand paper Union Jacks for the populace to wave and make the streets gay. To make the streets tidy, they had a mechanical road-sweeper follow immediately behind the last rank of horses in a cavalry procession which escorted the queen.

The Queen's well-publicised love of horses inspires odd manifestations among the anxious-to-please. Horseflesh is paraded on every possible occasion. Race meetings bestrew the tour programmes. Aged hacks and tiny Shetland ponies are brought from near and far to stand, bedecked, at the sides of roads down which the royal car is to travel. In Nigeria, the Northern capital of Kaduna staged a fabulous Durbar during which two thousand richly caparisoned horsemen passed in review in front of the royal dais. It was like episodes from the Arabian Nights and the Crusades rolled into one Hollywood spectacle (on which three of us did a non-stop radio commentary 'live' for three hours). The farmers' carts surrounding the polo ground of the parade were almost as striking as the show itself. Many wagons and lorries were painted red, white and blue. Some carried boards on which special slogans were inscribed. 'All our steeds are in Her Majesty's Service', said one. Another, wider in scope, announced: 'Praise the Lord— Britannia is the Woman I love.' Men and beasts were proclaimed alike loyal. At the entrance to the ground I noticed a big truck with the owner's name and 'Hides and Manure' not very effectively obliterated by the announce-ment, in rough but bold capitals, that: 'Over four million Northern Cattle are Delighted at Queencoming.'

In twenty years of processions, nothing has come near that Kaduna Durbar in splendour and noise, size and variety. In the midst of all the music and movement and shouting, the most impressive things were the cohorts of the emirs who had ridden for days to be there and pay homage to the Head of the Commonwealth. White-robed Moslem chiefs, they trotted by in dignified silence and gravity whilst all about them were their retinues of capering acrobats, holders of giant rainbow umbrellas of state, fan-bearers, praise-singers, and ceremonial trumpeters mounted on super-cilious camels. There were devil-men dressed all in straw, stilt-dancers, massed drummers in gorgeous uniforms, half-naked Pagans from the Plateau, official sorcerers wearing fearsome masks, and scores of feathered 'do-do' magicians.

The final greeting of the Durbar was the 'Jahi', a royal salute peculiar to this part of Africa. Wave after wave of horsemen came charging across the arena, each rider wearing either chain mail or some other kind of armour from the days of Saladin, and each brandishing a sword or lance or spear as they all thundered full tilt towards the dais, faster and faster in clouds of red dust, until we thought they would crash into the royal platform or mount the steps and overwhelm the royal party. But each line of riders, when only a few feet from the saluting base, suddenly reined in and reared their horses up on hind legs. Then, in tornadoes of shouts and cheers, they wheeled back in line and galloped off.

It was marvellous horsemanship and to be in the 'Jahi' was for every man the honour of a lifetime and the thrill of thrills. But there was a terrible moment. In one of the wild charges a tribesman fell from his horse and as he lay on the ground was unavoidably ridden over by his fellow warriors. You could hear a horrified intake of breath from the thousands of spectators round the field as soldiers ran forward to the lifeless figure, kicked and broken by the tide of hooves, and carried the body from the scene. From the dais a message of sympathy was sent, and an inquiry whether the victim had left a widow and children.

In fact, there was no widow because there was no corpse. The man had been spurring along joyously in the charge when one of his stirrup leathers broke, and off he fell. Miraculously, he was not hurt by the other horses, but he had remained prone and motionless on the earth, perfectly conscious and very ashamed at being unhorsed in front of the Queen. He did not wish, he said later, to get up and walk off the field with everybody laughing. Rather than that, he 'pretended' and allowed himself to be borne away. His own words were: 'Better be like fallen hero, so I lay for dead.'

The pride of far-off people often made the story of the day for me. The pride, for instance, of the forty-one fierce old bearded maliks, tribal chiefs, who stood shoulder-to-shoulder across the Queen's road at the foot of the Khyber Pass to make sure she would stop to receive the gifts they had brought down for her: four fat-tailed sheep with silk cloths hung over their backs. They had been told that they musn't slaughter the sheep in front of the Queen, which was their original idea; and they obeyed. There was also a Pakistan Government order that they should come unarmed, but this they did not obey. As the Pathans raised their hands in salute, the blankets round them parted to disclose habitual revolvers, knives and bandoliers of bullets. It would not have been courteous, they said, to leave off their 'normal clothing'.

During that day there was an embarrassing moment which could hardly get into the broadcasts. I went up to the top of the Pass, ahead of the royal party, in order to be at the frontier post when they came to look over into Afghanistan; and I was sitting in a ditch at the side of the track, changing a tape on my portable recorder, when numbers of English-speaking people who were also waiting up there came and chatted to me, flatteringly interested to meet the B.B.C. man they had often heard on their radios. They asked so many questions that I wasn't getting on with my tape-threading, and I said: 'Do you mind, I can't talk now as the Queen will be here any minute and I must have this machine ready.' So they left me alone—but not long enough. I soon heard feet coming near me again, and called over my shoulder: 'Please don't worry me just now. I must get this damned awkward tape threaded before they come.' This produced laughter behind me, so I turned round. I was addressing Her Majesty and Prince Philip, who had left their cars and walked up the track. I don't know how much they heard, but I got up, red-faced, and spilled the tape. They didn't go until I got my machine right, understanding no doubt the difficulties of a ham-fisted commentator.

Small-tape recorders are of course as useful as cameras on such journeys as these. I have made many a day's dispatch from a car in the royal 'motorcade', as I did on the day after the Khyber when we drove over an even more rugged pass, the Malakand, to visit the Wali of Swat in his enclosed and enchanting valley beneath the spurs of the Kindu Kush. The people of the hill villages along the route, unable to afford any flags or welcoming arches, simply brought out their most precious belongings from their homes and laid them at the side of the road as decoration and greeting to the

travelling Queen. Thus we were at times between what
seemed like walls of junk-store: heaps of tin vases, artificial
flowers, bamboo tables, antimacassared armchairs, kettles,
cooking pots, hideous local oleographs, and chamber-pots
bearing portraits of Queen Victoria.

In the towns where a halt was made for local councillors to
exchange handshakes with the travellers, both the Queen and
Prince Philip took snapshots and turned their movie-
cameras, whilst purdah women twittered from screened
balconies at the wonder of it. It is not only the professionals,
the press photographers and television cameramen, who
picture the royal Progresses. When the chief travellers
themselves return to Buckingham Palace from an overseas
trip, they have a lot of pictures of their own to develop.

On one occasion the Royals and the Press changed
places. It was in Portugal. Driving through Oporto, the
newspaper photographers complained that they were stuck
in a bus at the far rear of the royal procession as it wound
through the city, too distant from the Queen to get any pictures. Their moans reached the Queen and Prince Philip at
lunchtime. It was the last day of the tour and everyone was
feeling very relaxed. 'They ought to be able to get pictures
of this city and all the crowds,' said Prince Philip. 'Let them
be at the front.'

On the afternoon drive, two London press cameramen—
to their astonishment—travelled at the head of the column in
the Queen's limousine; and—to everybody else's even
greater astonishment, especially the vigilant and now rather
embarrassed Perkins—the Queen and her husband rode in
the very last vehicle, the one which had been the press bus.
This was an old open charabanc, normally used by the
Oporto police; and it looked like something out of an
early Mack Sennett film comedy. In this unlikely chariot, the
royal couple—perched up on the back, with feet on the rear
seat, and with no other passengers in all the rows of seats
until Perkins and the driver far away at the front—made their
final circuits through the city streets and then out to the airport.

You could hardly be more informal than that.

I think it was a happy swap and a relief for them to ride in that charabanc. They laughed all the way to the airport. The whole journey was fun and they could 'let go'. After all, there are so many occasions when they *could* laugh but mustn't. Such as the time when a self-abasing politician, walking backwards, fell over an aspidistra. Or when a woman made a curtsey so ostentatiously low that she sat on the floor and had to be helped up. Or indeed when, on a State Visit to the Netherlands, the travellers, brought into the great fourteenth-century New Church in Delft to be shown the vault where members of Holland's royal house of Orange-Nassau are buried, were solemnly told by the 'English-speaking' guide: 'Here, Majesty, is where we store our Oranges.'

With such strings of entertaining fallibilities threading their way through the stiff tapestry of the Progresses year after year, I did not want for lighter material to leaven my reports. There was no need to *make* the tours human: to me they were never lifeless. I cannot think they are dull chores to the Traveller-in-Chief herself.

13

The Queen Herself

What *does* the Queen really feel about it all?

The question must have come into thousands of minds when the royal car has swept past and the crowds, released and chattering, spill over the roadway, discussing the glimpse that has come and gone in a flash after all the waiting. For every comment of 'Isn't she lovely!' there are three of 'She wasn't smiling!'

It is true that the Queen does not go about grinning like a tooth-paste advertisement. In any case, she can't smile every second of the day—nobody can: you'd get lockjaw. She smiles and waves frequently during any given hour of driving along in public, but there will always be large numbers of people looking at her at moments when she happens not to be doing so. At every single moment she is a specimen under the microscope, the cynosure of all eyes and binoculars. Should she relax or sigh or pass a hand across her brow for a second, that second is the one and only sight of royalty that *one* lot of people get as the car passes them.

This is one of the problems of a life of public appearance; the strain of a long day in a big town—listening, questioning, watching, sitting up, and taking a lively interest in everything—has to be experienced to be appreciated. By both habit and inclination, the Queen *is* in fact interested in what is going on around her on her tours and visits; and, no doubt about it, she often does look serious as she listens and watches and talks, or as she rides by. She makes very few of the usual sightseers' gestures. Her solemn expressions in some newspaper pictures and television close-ups have been widely remarked. She is more photographed than a film star, yet there are times when the results present a formal, not to say formidable, figure, as remote in this prying and permissive age as the pasteboard kings and queens of history.

So—is she enjoying her life? What is she like, truly, this Super Ambassador, this national P.R.O.?

Any attempt at an answer, indeed any journalist's effort to present Queen Elizabeth the Second as a human being, runs the risk of seeming like keyhole-peeping sycophancy, guesswork, or gossip-column intrusion. The Queen does not give press interviews and does not relish being written about. Only her family and close friends know her well—and the protective secrecy they maintain is absolute. Royal servants do not talk, even after retirement from service: it's in their contract anyhow. The Queen, in short, lives the most public and also the most private—and restricted—life in Britain. Writers on royalty, usually, have little to bite on.

But because it has been my business for so many years to see the Queen in so many aspects and situations, because I think she eminently merits 'straight reporting', and because I hear so much rubbish talked about her, I would be less than human if I did not here put down a few points, for the record, on Her Majesty as a person. They are from my own experience.

First and foremost, the Queen concentrates quite exceptionally on the job she has inherited, and is far and away the most diligent, most experienced and now the most professional Head of State in the world. Heir to a thousand years of monarchy, Britain's constitutional linch-pin, she is not only the emblem of tradition but the instrument of change: not just The Crown but The Wearer too, inescapably the bearer of the pains as well as the prerogatives, sentenced for life to serve an institution. The Queen is always aware of this, and has accepted her life as dutifully as her father did before her, with quietness and reserve and dignity. And a treadmill of a life it is. Every day is a working day. In addition to whatever other tasks there may be, two boxes full of Government papers and official communications land on to her desk every twenty-four hours, wherever she is. She studies them with care—not because the law says she must, but because that is the way she works, carefully and assiduously.

The engagements which to other people would be unalloyed frolics—the parties and the film attendances and the race meetings—cannot be sheer relaxation to her; even the two late-summer months at Balmoral cannot be pure holiday: the boxes go there too. She not only 'lives over the shop', but the shop pursues her no matter where she goes. Unlike other people who work hard, she cannot look forward to a period of retirement from her post.

All of which makes the Queen notably deliberate and thoughtful in carrying out her public duties. She is a good listener. The shyness of the early years has gone, but not the concentration, not the patience, not the anxiety to avoid rash or hasty actions, and not the dislike of gimmicky innovations. She is modest and—though she never attended a school—still has something of a schoolgirl's directness and simplicity. Under the limelight of public occasions, her sense of responsibility overlays her innate sense of fun; and there are times when, intent on the job in hand, her face seems expressionless or downright censorious. I have seen that look when someone is being a smarmy smart-alick in front of her. She must, however, be at all times politically neutral. As the nation's and the Commonwealth's 'Universal Representative', and as our Number One Public Servant, she cannot voice personal opinions on public figures and matters of controversy—except in private. Whatever she may think, she must not as an official say it out loud. She is far from a free agent.

But this is not to say that Her Majesty frets under the burden of the job or seeks to lighten it; or that she finds it distasteful. She is unequivocally absorbed in it, and shows surprise and displeasure when others go trumpeting about that she is overworked. *She* does not complain that she is. At any rate I have never heard any criticism of any aspect of a heavy tour programme coming from her.

The Queen's seriousness and conscientiousness can be misleading, and her detailed knowledge—from the intensive 'homework' she does for weeks before a tour—a little intimidating. Local officials worry themselves into a nervous state when a hitch occurs during a royal visit, thinking how cross she will be. If only they could see her laughing, later in her own room, at the funny side of the mishaps of the day.

It boils down to this. The popular image of the Queen does not do her justice—and perhaps she does not care that it should. It is not her nature to 'perform'. She is not a TV natural (the delightfully relaxed bit of film of her with her two youngest sons, looking through a photograph album, which we saw on Christmas Day 1971 was an exceptional gem, the Queen natural at last—but was the product of long labour by the discreet Richard Cawston, the documentary film maker who had patiently gained the trust of the whole Royal Family). Many of her photographs, and at times the Public Person herself, belie the warmth and sparkle of the woman she is. Trained like a trooper to resist displays of emotion, and never 'putting on an act', she brings down an inscrutable curtain of stiffness when many people would be clapping their hands and kicking their heels up. She loves children—and her own happy family life is a sustainer of her existence—and yet I have seen her 'freeze' extraordinarily during a young people's rally or a walk round boys' and girls' hospital wards. These severe moments are not frequent—as I have said, royal tours are more light-hearted and informal than you would imagine—but the moments are noted. Remembering them, and the press pictures, most people on first meeting the Queen are surprised to find how much prettier, gayer, easier, and smaller (5 feet 4 inches) she is than the newspaper page and television screen suggest. Having seen her only through camera lens and cathode-ray tube darkly, they are, as the soap advertisements say, 'astonished at the difference'.

In private, you find another person, eyes sparkling, hands waving, voice bubbling, nicknames flying; she is lively and spontaneous, full of fun and repartee, a raconteur. Not an intellectual, but a shrewd observer of the passing show, quick on the uptake but given to pondering. Her own sense of humour is as acute and strong as the publicised wit of her husband and eldest son. They are a jokey family: laughter and mimicry ring round the house—a more relaxed house than the dwellings of the bicycling monarchs of Europe.

It is not a bad thing that Britain's ancient and ambiguous monarchy should in this day and age have at its heart this cheerful and sensible woman, this nice and unassuming Lady of the national Manor, living a life every bit as full of personal delight as it is of professional dedication. The only trouble is that the real Queen is often obscured by an image of a sort of inflexible Instant Britannia eternally in robes and tiara. The reality is the lithe, girlish figure in the headscarf whistling up the corgis for a family walk.

And her husband? The Duke of Edinburgh is part of the picture of the Queen, for they are a team and each has learned from the other. Officially, Prince Philip is nothing: he has no position in the constitution. But amorphous idleness was never for him. From what might have been a dead-end position, he has made himself a constant and valuable helper of the Sovereign, his primary concern always for her and her position. But he has also constructed a very busy world for himself. The number and variety of this vigorous man's personal interests is almost beyond calculation—and he is never a figurehead only: if he becomes president or patron of an organisation he really becomes part of the business, not merely a name on the notepaper-heading. He can and does go where the Queen cannot go—but comes back to the Palace to tell her all about it, a liaison officer *par excellence,* in addition to the indefatigable life of engaging in public affairs which is all his own.

Is he the Queen's Number One Adviser? Probably not. He is a very able man, he gives counsel readily, and his cleverness has been useful at the Palace; but the Queen, who has a sureness of judgment, may quite often decide against his line of thought.

They are opposites in character. He is impatient, incredibly energetic, restless, athletic, quick to judge and to see (physically short-sighted in fact, and uses spectacles). He dislikes walking for walking's sake, doing anything slowly, being a spectator or a passenger. He wants to *do*, not watch. He is a ceaseless seeker after adventure; he travels even more than his wife does—about 75,000 miles a year. He is a fair listener; but, particularly, a questing and compulsive talker. He writes his own speeches—and not infrequently makes himself unpopular with this or that section of public opinion by expressing frank opinions on controversial issues. He does not enjoy the times when he is censured, I think, but will shrug off the rebukes. One of his characteristic remarks about himself as a speaker was: 'If you get off the clichés you are immediately setting out across rather thin ice. Occasionally I go through—this is one of the hazards and it is just too bad.'

Prince Philip—like his uncle, Earl Mountbatten—*is* a TV natural. You hardly need rehearse him at all, and his memory and fluency are exceptional. He is at ease with people, in private or in public. It does not follow that everybody is at ease with him. He quips amusingly, sometimes a shade cruelly: his jaunty wardroom arrogance can occasionally be very cutting to people who have not his own razor-sharp mind. He dislikes bootlicking and backslapping as much as the Queen does—the difference is that he can, at any rate does, say so. He is a highly articulate one-man ginger group.

Yet the real Prince Philip is not the extrovert Gabby Duke, but a sensitive and vulnerable man who is at heart self-deprecating. Those close to him find him a prime encourager of others, who will take pains with other people's problems, a man who need not toil for a living but who works harder than most captains of commerce. And surprisingly kind.

They are complementary personalities, Prince Philip and the Queen. They match—partly because they do not always agree. But many of the Consort's views *are* identical with the Sovereign's. About the bringing up of their young, for one thing. They have always believed in letting the children live their lives in ordinary privacy (though not in seclusion) until they are grown-up, in sending them quietly away to school like other children, and not parading them about on State occasions. That is why the Prince of Wales was almost unknown until he emerged, an agreeable and natural young man, at twenty in his Investiture Year. Prince Charles, in his character, owes a great deal to the atmosphere of his family rearing—and to the freedom he enjoyed as a boy at Gordonstoun School (though he blossomed even more in his two blissful terms at Timbertop in Australia than in all his terms on the Moray Firth) and the normal life he had at Trinity College, Cambridge. Through the years of boyhood and adolescence he was kept happily out of the limelight of official engagements; but from time to time, from an unobserved sideline, he watched and learned the sort of events those engagements were.

Occasionally, when I was at the microphone in the Aragon Gallery of St. George's Chapel at Windsor Castle during a royal service, a small boy would be slipped in to sit beside our broadcasting point as we worked, to look down through the gallery screen on the scene below—and Prince Charles was always quiet and well behaved. A dozen years later, Prince Andrew, when *he* was about eight, came up to the gallery to watch similar occasions—with equal interest but less quietly than his elder brother when he had watched at the same age: the governess had her work cut out to prevent the bouncing Andrew from craning over our shoulders and talking into the microphone too, and from leaning so far out of the gallery in his excitement that he almost fell on to the Dean and canons in the chancel below.

The Queen has seen to it that the newest generation of the Royal Family are likeably uninhibited and have lively ways of their own. Anyone who has talked with the Heir to the Throne or to Princess Anne (with the conversation by no means confined to horses) does not need to be told that. And there is nothing cloistered about the Prince Andrew and Prince Edward I have seen tearing about the deck of the *Britannia* in carefree concord with their companions, two ordinary seamen of the yacht's company.

If royalty is to continue—as probably it will, for this country has had a break of only eleven years during eleven centuries of monarchs, and a republic now would certainly be even less popular than Cromwell's became—then it will continue in good hands. I cannot see much to worry about in the First Family's personal qualities in the years to come.

Invested—unlawfully—with naval officer's uniform on the bridge of H.M.S. *Duchess* when the Queen was sailing home up the Channel in the spring of 1954 (page 157)

Invested—lawfully—with the M.V.O. at Buckingham Palace in 1960. Wife and sons inspect the insignia after the ceremony

Crowning moment at Caernarvon, 1 July, 1969

A moment of reflection by the Prince of Wales under the weight of full regalia at his Investiture

14

The Life and Death of a Broadcaster

The B.B.C. has been called—among many other things!—the ace image-maker; and it has been said that the Corporation built up the image of the Queen. The truth is that over the years it unveiled rather than upheld the monarchy. And often through the words of one commentator particularly identified with State events: Richard Dimbleby, who illuminated and orally adorned national occasions for twenty years after the war. Then I knew him well.

In my day-to-day traffic with royal affairs, the big public ceremonies were the best-remembered highlights, not only because they were peaks of my own working life but because they brought this imposing colleague to the commentator's seat, often beside mine. He became part of royal occasions; and it would be eccentric of me if in an account of this kind of broadcasting I did not tell the Dimbleby story, the one that lay behind his own image.

He was already well known when the war ended. But in that summer of 1945, back from Berlin where he had immensely added to his stature as a reporter, he returned to a harsh Broadcasting House. Absurd though it sounds now, on the books of the Administration he was still, in status and almost in salary, the young man who had joined the Corporation as a prentice 'observer' almost ten years before. Richard now asked for a rise: he suggested £1,100 instead of £1,000! And was told that the staff reporters' structure made an upgrading impossible. He would have a better chance if he came inside and sat at a desk in the editorial department,

M

they said. But that was not the Dimbleby idea at all. He suggested alternative terms of service of his own, but they were turned down flat.

So he resigned. He went off to look after his family's newspapers in Richmond, with the B.B.C. news administrators bleakly confirming that he couldn't possibly be on the staff and at the same time be a director of an outside concern. He was uneasy, if not desperately worried. Having a newspaper publishing business behind him, he was not penniless, but his resignation was to him a gamble all the same. Nobody really knew what opportunities post-war radio was going to offer to an outside contributor, however able and experienced; and television had not restarted. 'I want the chance to broadcast,' I remember him saying, 'but I'm going to chance my arm as a free-lance.'

He was soon on the air again. Producers became as quick to hire him as the administrators had been to let him go. He never came back on the staff—and was anything but a sufferer because of that. The Corporation's attitude after the war had been myopic as well as miserably parsimonious: probably a free-lance was paid not £1,100 a year, but twenty times that. He remained a free-lance to the end of his life, but as far as broadcasting was concerned he was unswervingly loyal to the B.B.C., turning down many fat offers from commercial television.

Moving his expertise effectively from radio to television, he became the foremost Outside Broadcast commentator and, in the studio, our Anchorman Extraordinary. 'Panorama' programmes or Election Night marathons found in him an assured, fluent, good-humoured, well-informed and imperturbable professional. As an interviewer, unlike some of his contemporaries and would-be successors, he extracted information without ever being gratuitously offensive. He was both exuberant and urbane, master of the apt phrase and the graceful sentence. He felicitously matched word to picture; in his case, the commentator was not subordinate to the scene on the screen. Some critics found him unctuous and pompous—a charge which always made him angry and which he vigorously denied. What he had was a feeling for pageantry and English tradition. He saw the monarchy as a bulwark of order and decency. He respected our great ceremonies, and prepared mightily to get the words right when describing them. Speech came trippingly on his tongue; the commentaries were very human and essentially clear and simple, besides giving a sense of the national importance of what was going on. Many listeners felt that he was speaking for them too, and they were made proud of being British. If that is old-fashioned, then he was and so am I. He was the Churchill of the broadcasting business.

But Richard Dimbleby died in his prime. What the public did not know was that for the last five years of his life—the most powerful and prolific years—he was suffering from cancer.

If anyone had told the viewers and listeners that he was ill, they would have found it very hard to believe. For there was scarcely a week in which he did not make several major television appearances, the bulky, genial figure always radiating smiling energy and a robust enjoyment of whatever he was doing. Nor was that picture a pose: Richard was indeed living life to the full, tirelessly keeping up his staggering working hours, travelling the world, editing and managing newspapers which were now his, running a film company, a finance trust, a yacht, a farm and a family. All this and television too. His Rolls and his chauffeur were not just status symbols, not props for a poorly man, but instruments employed in the swift fulfilment of crowded schedules. Warm-hearted and friendly as ever, he pursued his career with unflagging ambition, relentlessly driving himself, anxious to keep at the top, relishing the position he had achieved and the life he was living. And all the time knowing that he was in the grip of cancer.

It was 1960 when they discovered that he had the disease. He took the knowledge with characteristic courage, at once putting himself at the disposal of the doctors for all the treatment possible and for all the help which could be given to let him go on with his work. 'Keep me going,' he said.

His illness was known to very few people besides his family. Doctors and staff at St. Thomas's Hospital in London, where he was treated, sedulously kept the

secret. Inevitably, when he was coming away from the
radiotherapy department and was walking along the busy
'main road' inside the old St. Thomas's, the broad corridor
which ran through the whole length of the hospital, people
would turn and say: 'Hello, that's Richard Dimbleby!
What's he doing here?' And the answer from nurses or
anyone else on the staff would be: 'Yes, he's a friend of one
of the doctors.' Incidentally, they were not lying: though he
was there as a patient, he was through all the years the friend
of all who looked after him; he and the consultant who had
charge of his case used to go on sailing holidays together.
He developed a special affection for the hospital, and was as
popular there as he was at Television Centre.

At times he would go straight to the hospital from
the studios, making the visits after normal hours and so
helping to keep them unknown. After treatment, he liked to
go to the canteen or to a pub nearby for a chat with the
doctors and nurses. At other times he received his treatment
over the week-end so that he would be able to cope with
Monday's 'Panorama'. When the programme was in recess,
when he was supposed to be away on holiday, he might be in
fact arriving regularly, perhaps six days a week, at the
hospital. There came periods when the illness seemed
conquered, when he was physically untroubled; then the
symptoms would appear in another part of the body, and
treatment would start again. For five years he was subjected
to massive X-ray doses. For five years nobody knew.

Then, in July 1965, unwell but refusing to stop working,
he went on an exhausting trip to New York to cover the
Pope's visit to the United Nations. He gave commentaries of
his usual high standard. But the strain told. He was looking
drawn and haggard with pain. He returned to London with a
high fever; two weeks later he was admitted to St. Thomas's,
an in-patient now and a sick man. It became known that he
had undergone an operation; and messages of sympathy
flooded into the hospital. Richard and his family received
seven thousand letters and cards.

In bed, in a private room, he kept up his cheerfulness and
infectious sense of humour. As he had done from the
beginning, he took an intense, not morbid but highly

intelligent, interest in his treatment and in the progress of any aspect of the fight of medical science against the disease of which he himself was one victim.

In November it was publicly announced that he was suffering from cancer. He wished that it should be said. In the words of his son David: 'My father is strongly opposed to the idea of cancer being an unmentionable disease. The reason that he has not mentioned it is that in the last five years he has not lost a single day's work because of it.' But it was sadly clear why the secret was now being told; and when Richard died, in the hospital, three days before Christmas, the news was melancholy but not unexpected. He was courageous, cheerful, considerate for others, to the end. He died, as he had lived, with dignity.

He was given a Westminster Abbey memorial service, the sort of service a great statesman gets, and the sort he had so often described. It was an act of remembrance which itself took on the aspect of a national occasion; it was an unprecedented salute to a broadcaster. People queued for hours to get into the church. His widow asked that anybody wishing to send flowers should instead make a contribution to cancer research; and, such was the wave of mourning, such the admiration for the forthright bravery of the man as well as for his gifts as a communicator, that money poured in: large amounts and small from almost every country in the world, in coins and stamps and gifts for selling as well as cheques and every denomination of postal order.

Two years later, at St. Thomas's—just across the Thames from the Westminster of so many of his Outside Broadcast *tours-de-force*—there was opened a permanent memorial, the Richard Dimbleby Cancer Research Laboratory. Fittingly, it was opened by the Queen.

For those of us who, in war and in peace, had grown up with him in news broadcasting, the gap in the ranks remained large and recurringly lamented. It is still there. With Richard's death, a classic style died too. Life and broadcasting went on, of course. Two of his sons followed his trade, inevitably in his shadow; and other studio chairmen, other commentators emerged. Two or three have become very competent indeed. But, by comparison, most seemed little men with large egos, clinically competent, abrasive, with respect for nothing. Some were good at this, some at that. None was the polished all-rounder commanding confidence. Several had the efficiency, none the authority. Human computers struggled for a human being's mantle.

15

Americana

For all its looser styles and lower standards, the post-
Dimbleby era did produce extensions of broadcasting—
greater *quantity* at any rate: more hours of talk and a wider
spreading of the B.B.C.'s talking and picturing resources.
Public events and news occurrences were smothered in
correspondents and cameras as never before. Coverage was
strenuous and often strident. My own odysseys increased,
taking me all over the country and again round the world.
It would be disingenuous to pretend I did not welcome this.
I toted a microphone through fifty countries; gluttony for
travel persisted; and my collection of unlikely sights and
experiences became richer.

Especially in the Americas.

I made my first appearance on commercial television when
on the other side of the Atlantic. What is more, I made it
whilst I was still on the staff of the B.B.C.—which was quite
unlawful; but it seemed very permissible when so far away
from London. I did not come away with any money, but
only a vivid memory and a lot of laughter, after the Night I
Read the News in Regina.

It was on one of a dozen visits to Canada. I was in the
middle of a tour across the country and, spending a few
days with the B.B.C.'s counterpart, the Canadian Broadcasting Corporation, in the prairies, found myself in
Saskatchewan whilst a British Week was being held, trade
fair, English beer, London Bobbies, Scots pipers an' a' an'
a'. After I had broadcast for the C.B.C. some commentaries and interviews, and had myself been variously interviewed, at a big exhibition in the provincial capital, Regina,

I was telephoned by the main private TV station in the city to say that they would like, as their contribution to the Week, to invite me to do something on the air for them too. 'You're an old hand from the Old Country,' said the manager, 'and we'd sure appreciate having you guesting for us tonight. May we send a car round to your hotel?' I consulted the local C.B.C. manager, who seemed to find nothing terrible in the thought of my working for our commercial rival. 'Good for community relations, Godfrey,' was his word. 'Go and show them how to speak.'

That was all very well, but when I got to the station I discovered that what they wanted me to do was read the main television news that evening. This filled me with apprehension. The speed of my broadcasting speech is much slower than the rapid machine-gun rattle of American and Canadian newscasters; and they, moreover, omit prepositions and articles in their sentences, which is something quite foreign to the British way of talking. I told them they would have to rewrite the scripts and leave out a lot of items if I were to read the news. The timing would go haywire too, because I was totally unaccustomed to stopping at a certain second on the clock to let the 'commercials' pop up in the middle of bulletins. 'Not a thing to worry about,' they replied. 'You can *write* the news as well as read it.' So I was there and then plunged into what was to me a frenzied session with a young sub-editor and a typist, wrestling with paragraphs studded with ministerial names like Romanow and Smishek, and places ranging from Assiniboia to Esquimalt and Moose Jaw to Medicine Hat, new sounds which I found very strange to say. The typist even chortled at my pronunciation of cities she called 'Ahrawah' and 'Tarrana'—Ottawa and Toronto to me.

The subsequent performance when we actually put the news out was memorable. I wished that the Regina viewers could have seen, not merely me in shirt sleeves at the announcer's desk reading the bulletin, and the bits of news-film which we had, but the complete studio pantomime. The entire staff of Station CKCK, grinning broadly, seemed to be capering about behind the cameras, waving at me to look this way and hat, flagging me down to stop read-

ing, pointing at me to start again after the advertising spots
had been flashed on, and crawling about the floor, below
camera-lens level, to whip stories off my table and slide
other, late-item sheets in front of me. I finished the bulletin
in an exhausted state, feeling that the whole thing must have
been disastrous. But the station switchboard was deluged by
telephone calls from delighted (and astonished) viewers
saying how much they had enjoyed the new announcer.
It seemed as though half the inhabitants of the surrounding
prairie were emigrants from Britain lusting for nostalgia.
'Just like old times; let's have some more' was the general
message. Even young Canadians declared with surprise
that they 'could understand every word the guy said'.

The result was that the station and I went through all the
trouble again the following night for the sake of the novelty
of my 'cute English accent'; and my second experience of
'guesting' precipitated more studio antics and more telephone calls from customers after the show. The next two
days of my stay in Regina were positively embarrassing.
I was accosted in the streets and almost every shop I entered,
with: 'Say, aren't you the B.B.C. man in town? Saw you on
TV. We'd like to have you come to supper in our home.' It
was Old Home Week with a vengeance. As so often in the
New World, I was beaten down with hospitality. And also
inured to the ways of commercial broadcasting: in fact,
when I left Canada after that trip I was almost signing-off my
B.B.C. dispatches with, not: 'Now I return you to London,'
but: 'Now here's a word from our sponsor.'

Although being a guest announcer was not my usual line,
being a guest commentator on big occasions was a routine
job on most of my overseas visits, for teaming with the
resident commentators of other broadcasting organisations
was a B.B.C. public relations exercise. I usually found it a
refreshing exercise too; and when a local station asked me to
help, I always said yes, provided that the spot of talking for
them did not get in the way of B.B.C. commitments. But on
one occasion my 'guesting' did just that.

I was covering one of the Queen's and Prince Philip's
sweeps through the Caribbean and had arrived, ahead of the
royal party, in Dominica, to my mind the most attractive

West Indian island, wildly mountainous, and boasting
365 tumbling rivers, tree-frogs that are better eating than
chicken, and the world's best lime-juice production (though
that is *not* why the island's capital is called Roseau!).
The Windward Isles Broadcasting Service asked if I would do
a couple of minutes' description as part of their broadcast of
the royal arrival at the harbour quay in Roseau before I
jumped into the radio car in the royal procession across the
island. When the moment came, a dark and smiling gentleman at the waterfront opened the commentary, introduced
me, handed me a large black microphone on a stick the size
of a shillelagh—and promptly skedaddled. Standing in the
broiling sun, I talked for a good six minutes whilst the
formal welcomes were taking place, and, when the cars
were about to move off, looked round to see to which of the
home commentators I should pass the mike. But the microphone and I were quite alone with each other on the
broadcasters' rostrum: my W.I.B.S. colleagues were nowhere
to be seen. The royal 'motorcade' began to draw away, with
a technician and a fellow correspondent beckoning frantically
to me from my inexorably accelerating car in the middle of
the line. It was a moment of desperate decision. Was I to
say to the listening Caribbean: 'I'm sorry, I have to go now,'
ending a 'live' transmission in mid-flow? I felt I could not do
that; and, watching my procession disappear, I went on
talking on my own for the remaining part of the scheduled
O.B. from the port. Only when it was over did my West
Indian friends turn up again, full of apologies, buttoning up
their happy-snap tourist's cameras. They'd been over the
wall and in the crowd, taking pictures for their family
albums, so carried away with the excitement of seeing the
Queen in their remote homeland that they had forgotten
both the time and their promise to relieve me.

The assurances that my broadcast would never be
forgotten, and the gift of two of the finest bottles of clear,
golden rum I have ever tasted, did not compensate for my
'missing the boat', or for the hair-raising drive of two hours
through the mountains in a very ancient taxi to overtake
the official party.

In another island of the Caribbean, Barbados, full of sugar

cane and soft Colonial echoes, I was once asked—again
during a royal visit—if I would go to a Bridgetown club-
restaurant to take over the stage microphone and compère a
'suitable charity show'. I declined the honour this time, but
went to see the show. They certainly made collections for
orphans, not too noticeably. And they certainly made a
salute to the royal tour in their own curious way. The
swarthy proprietor of the establishment erupted on to the
bandstand to make a fulsome John Bull-ish speech in terms
which suggested that he had studied but failed in the school
of Henry Irving. He did, however, achieve the feat, during
his oration of praise for Good Ole Britain, of getting both
Horatio Nelson and Horatio Bottomley almost simul-
taneously into his story. A special turn by his Negro strip-
tease girls was then introduced: they shed Union Jack
brassières to mark the occasion, and joined in what were
described as patriotic island songs in salute to the Queen.
One of these, if I remember correctly, began: 'Long time,
Lizzie Girl, no see you—come, let me hold you close.'
Later, I was invited to meet the strippers, with the recom-
mendation: 'You will find all our ladies very loyal.'

I should have found the compèring of their performances
beyond my powers.

My trips to the West Indies have often been made on the
way to or from Canada (not so strangely: Canadian influence
is strong in the Caribbean), with Ottawa as a starting and
finishing point. In (their) winter, some Canadians almost
commute to the warmth of the Caribbean islands. Myself,
perversely, I liked to be in Ottawa, snow or sun. I always
managed to get the Federal capital included in my Canadian
itineraries, even making detours to do some broadcasting
from there rather than from Toronto or Montreal. Ottawa is
my favourite city, the most dramatically situated Centre of
Government in the world. To many people it may be a
dreary dump of uninspiring ministerial blocks; but to me the
neo-Gothic Parliament buildings, and the great Peace Tower
rising above the lawns and the scarlet Mounties on guard,
have an unashamed nobility. Every time I have been to the
city I have taken the first chance to go and stand on Parliament Hill and look north from that cliff above the river,

staring across into French Quebec and the vast woodlands of
the Gatineau Valley amid the grandeur of the Laurentian
Hills. It is a splendid sight. I look down to the broad water
150 feet below, and always a giant timber raft is floating
there, a boom of thousands of logs from the far interior.
Just a little way upstream, where the falls are, you see the
foaming white of rapids and the forests hemming them in on
either side. Here, though you are in the modern metropolis,
you get the feel that you are on the edge of the wild,
traditional Canada, the romantic country of the R. M.
Ballantyne stories; and I would never have been surprised if
an Indian canoe had come paddling down the river carrying
a grizzled old fur trapper, rifle across his knees, and on
his head a coonskin cap tattered by the arrows of Huron
braves.

But the trader would have got an almighty surprise when
his birch-bark bumped up against today's sawmills, the
Interprovincial Bridge, the bottom lock of the Rideau Canal,
Pierre Trudeau's prime ministerial front garden—and the
river bank overshadowed by the green gables and pepper-
pot turrets of the Château Laurier.

'The Château', the only Ottawa hotel I would ever stay in,
is more than an inn: it is an institution, a community, a way
of life, a grand period piece, vast and picturesque and
expensive, warm and old-fashioned and rambling, floor upon
floor of little windows and long wide corridors. It is full of
plushy comfort and character; and I love it.

The Château is both on the river and in the main square.
More than once I have done a whole running commentary
from my bedroom window overlooking ceremonies round
the square's massive war memorial. Moreover, at the
Château I had the permanent link to London almost in my
bedroom: one of the joys of being in Ottawa was that the
C.B.C. radio station, which I always used for broadcasts to
London and talks with my office, was right there in the
hotel, a whole top floor full of offices and studios immediately
above my bedroom. Sheer bliss it was, especially in the
arctic winters which Ontario gets, to walk only a few steps
without even putting on a jacket—and one night in my
dressing-gown—to find 'Station C.B.O.', the allotted micro-

phone and a cheerful B.B.C. traffic manager at the other end
of the booked circuit. No wonder I liked Ottawa.

The task of catching the fixed-time radio circuits which
London used to arrange in advance so that I could put over
my dispatches from distant places was not always so easy.
When on tour, traffic jams, aircraft delays, missed trains and
sudden switches in routes were constant hazards; all too
often, very late, I have burst into some small-town broadcasting station or remote radio transmitter house, panting
like a fox terrier, to hear a tired local engineer wailing into
the microphone: 'No, I don't know where your Mr. Talbot
is, B.B.C., or why he's not here, or what he's done about
sending your television film, but we can't hold this circuit
much longer: Montreal Control are getting testy, and the
N.B.C. reporter is breathing down my neck; it's his turn
and he's wanting New York. We'll have to give Talbot up if
he's not arrived in two minutes.'

I remember that during one train journey in Canada (I
have liked trains and am sorry the long-distance passenger
ones have declined in North America) I was doing a trip by
Canadian Pacific Railway westward through the Rockies,
and as I sat watching the scenery through the windows of
the parlour-car I realised I would never be in time for the
circuit scheduled for me in Vancouver next day. So, when we
stopped at a small station I hopped off, with the intention of
sending a cable to London telling them to make the booking
at a later time. The telegraph office seemed shut; and on an
impulse I thought I would try the vaunted telephone system
of the country. I went to the station phone. More as a lark
than anything—for overseas calls really have to be pre-
arranged—I asked the switchboard operator if she could get
me LANGHAM 4468.

'Where would that be?' said the girl.

'London.'

'Oh, no problem.'

'But I mean London, England; not London, Ontario.'

There was a short pause, then: 'That's different. Still, let
me see. Hold the line. Whom are you calling? Will they pay
for the call? Who are you?'

'It's the B.B.C. This is Godfrey Talbot. But really it's not

much use trying, is it? Anyway, my train's going in a
minute.'

'Hold it, sir, here's Montreal. They're trying London
now.'

To my astonishment, only a minute later a voice said:
'This is Foreign News Traffic here. Where are you speaking
from, Godfrey? Didn't know you were back in England.'

'I'm not. I'm still in Canada, as you know I should be. In
fact I'm over five thousand miles away, and this is coming to
you over two ordinary telephone wires across the Rocky
Mountains and the entire prairie provinces. I didn't book the
call, but I got through inside two minutes. Marvellous.
Anyway, will you take a message?'

'Well, you're clear as a bell. What's the message? Go
ahead: I am recording. And if you have a news piece for us,
better speak it now: you'd hardly get a better circuit.'

In fact I did have with me a scribbled story, which I was
going to put over from the Vancouver studio next day, so I
fished it from my pocket and began to speak it into the
telephone.

What I did not tell London—they were incredulous enough
anyway—was that I was using an ordinary public coin-box
telephone which was not even in a booth but was stuck up
on a thin wooden partition just outside the door of the
station Gents'. And as I started to speak my piece, several
travellers came panting up, anxious to patronise the
convenience. If they were to do so, the noise would ruin my
call; and I was now desperately keen to use this unexpected
opportunity to get my story through. So I held my arm
across the doorway of the loo and said to the urgent
gentlemen: 'Do you mind waiting a minute or so; I'm just
doing a broadcast.'

They gaped at me. I think it was their certainty that they
were face to face with a lunatic that made them retreat.
With one eye on the train and the other on my notes which I
could scarcely see in the dim lamplight, I talked my report to
London, received a 'Splendid, thank you; pretty good
quality; we shall use your dispatch in voice,' and dashed
back into the train just as it was moving off.

I have never been so impressed with the North American

telephone system. And that was the only time I broadcast
from a public lavatory.

Later, when I was in Montreal, I went and thanked the
operators of the international telephone exchange. I was in
Montreal to commentate on the opening of the billion-dollar
extravaganza on the St. Lawrence River with which
Canada celebrated her hundredth birthday as a nation: the
great exhibition called 'EXPO 67', a thousand acres of
fantastic pavilions displaying everything from a Dead Sea
scroll to Elvis Presley's guitar.

Super-show though EXPO was—they even built a whole
palace specially to accommodate the world's broadcasters—I
found the city of Montreal itself even more wonderful: the
new Montreal, rushed to completion to bedazzle the millions
of EXPO visitors. In particular, the underground city with
its miles of shops and brilliant promenades linking hotels,
office blocks and railway stations. It was delightful to stroll
without an overcoat along warm and seemingly sunny
pedestrian precincts even when there was, as on one
occasion when I was there, about twenty inches of snow on
the freezing streets above. And I liked to ride, just for the
sake of riding, in Montreal's clinical new 'Tube' which has
different French décor at each underground station and
rubber-tyred carriages on the trains which go with great
speed and quietness. I attended the gala opening of that
Underground. Come to think of it, I went to the opening of
many things in North America: newsmen are obsessed with
inaugurations.

When, away back, I was reporting the early days of the
United Nations in New York, when they used to meet at
Lake Success and Flushing Meadow, I had to do a special
programme on the ceremonial laying of the cornerstone of
the new U.N. buildings in the city itself by President Truman.
It was on a springlike October day in 1949. The General
Assembly met in extraordinary plenary session out on the
open site in Manhattan beside the East River. Four thousand
policemen were on duty: there were not only the Assembly's
world statesmen to protect, but hundreds of V.I.P. guests too,
everybody sitting on little chairs set out in rows right across
42nd Street. I tried to get some colour and informality for

my programme by interviewing official visitors. With tape
recorder at the ready, I started to comb the audience before
the ceremony began, and fell with joy upon a picturesque
bunch of incomers sitting, erect and solemn, in the fortieth
row: six Red Indian chiefs in full feathered war bonnets and
suits that were all doeskin fringe and gay wampum. Here, I
thought, was a chance to get the views of redskins from the
far reservations on the paleface pow-wow in the big city.
I introduced myself, held out the microphone, and in my
best pidgin English asked the nearest of the warriors what
he thought of the occasion. The Indian promptly handed me
a Rotarian visiting card and a fat cigar and, in the accents of
Brooklyn, declared that he was happy to know me but was
not, right then, available for comment. He added: 'Come to
my suite at the Waldorf-Astoria after the show and have a
drink. Our Six Nations P.R.O. will be happy to see you get
our Press Hand-Out statement.'

So much for my untutored savages!

The President of the United States arrived at the foundation site in deafening circus splendour. His car, on which
descended welcoming showers of coloured streamers and
torn-up paper from skyscraper office windows, was escorted
by a hundred police motor-cyclists with red lights blinking,
engines growling and sirens screaming. And yet as soon as
Mr. Truman stepped out of the limousine he twinkled around
so casually, shaking hands, patting people on the back and
generally behaving in a homespun manner, that he made the
U.N.'s moment of history seem like the opening of a village
bazaar. President Truman specialised in taking the starch out
of official proceedings when he had a mind to do so, which
was often. Almost exactly two years after that 42nd Street
party, I watched him at a party for the British Queen.
It was when he was host to Her Majesty—she was Princess
Elizabeth then—on her visit to Washington. He led her
round the town like a benign uncle presiding over a family
outing for a favourite niece, taking her by the arm, 'my
dear-ing' her, telling her funny stories, explaining everything
she saw, but doing it in such a natural and homely way
that there was no offence in it. He was nothing but pleasing.

If you want free-and-easy manners and a classless way of

life, America is the place. New York cab drivers will tell
you their troubles, ask who you are and call you by your
Christian name, all in the first few minutes of your ride.
One of the nicest social evenings I ever spent was in the little
house of Joe Podgorski, the taxi-man who used to ferry me
to and from the U.N. committee meetings in the old Sperry
Gyroscope factory buildings at Lake Success, Long Island.
It was a Thanksgiving Day holiday, though not a complete
holiday for the delegates. I spent the morning listening to an
interminable First Committee debate—largely, as usual, an
hour-long tirade by Russia's vitriolic Andrei Vyshinsky—
and was weary when I got to Joe's for the Thanksgiving
dinner to which I had been invited. But I was soon restored.
The meal, which lasted from four in the afternoon until
eleven at night, could not have been more lavish. We kept
adjourning from table to armchairs, and then going back for
another eating session. The turkey was huge, the cranberry
sauce was in an ice-bucket, and the pumpkin pie looked like
a cartwheel. Joe and his wife—she was fat and very jolly
and a taxi-driver too—had also assembled on the sideboard
twenty-seven bottles of liquor of every conceivable sort,
their idea being that their guests should sample *all* the
tipples.

London never knew why they got a message cancelling
the New York circuit that night.

Coping with copious liquid entertainment is routine
duty in a foreign correspondent's life; and fortunately
I have always had a strong head (I have a rogue theory that
it is because my forbears were teetotallers). Stamina is
needed to keep afloat in the seas of transatlantic alcohol.
Once I was nearly drowned—in South America this time.
With the B.B.C.'s then Latin America correspondent, Noel
Clark, I was on a train from Valparaiso to Santiago at the
end of the Queen's tour of Chile late in 1968. We had left the
royal party, who were going off for a private week-end, and,
returning from a hard day's work covering the Sovereign's
activities on the Pacific coast, we were looking forward to a
rest and a quiet meal during the four-hour train ride back to
the Chilean capital. But alas for tranquillity! Our brief-cases
bore royal emblems, a Union Jack, and the words 'B.B.C.'

N

We were patently English on a railway which rarely saw.
Englishmen anyhow; and we had come from the Queen—
that was enough: we must be British royalty. In that belief,
waiters and ticket collectors buzzed fawningly round our
dining-car table, assuring us that the line's best facilities,
the galley's finest viands, would attend our repast. They were
honoured that we were riding with them. Clark, in his best
Spanish, tried to convince them that we were journalists
and wished only a gentle bottle of wine and a simple meal.
But the matter was taken out of our hands. If we weren't
absolutely Royal, we were at any rate something quite out of
the ordinary run of their railway passengers, and certainly
official representatives of Britain.

We were bowed and pushed into the little kitchen to see
our dinner being prepared, to shake hands with the chefs,
sign their autograph books, and marvel at the great steaks
which were to be ours. Presently, relays of hors-d'œuvres
and soups and fish were being placed proudly in front of us
at table, followed by the main dishes and fruits and selec-
tions of cheese. And all accompanied by assortments of
drinks. Whisky and brandy, both, came with red and white
wines. Our protests that we did not need the ramparts of
bottles and glasses filling the table were of no avail. Euphoria
and enthusiasm over the British royal visit to their country,
which had momentarily gripped the Chileans, crystallised in
that train, and the chief steward assured us that on this day
of Anglo-Chilean celebration we two were the guests of the
railway and the State. Healths were drunk; the conductor-
in-chief took off his uniform hat and sat with us; so, for a
time, did the guard and, to my dismay, the driver of the
train, sloshing down glass after glass and urging us also to
'drink like true men'.

Garbled word sped through the train that two excellencies
from the Palace of Buckingham were aboard, and streams of
passengers from other coaches flowed into the diner. Each
visitor insisted on raising a glass of fiery spirit with Clark
and me. Their friendly exuberance was touching; and it
would have been terrible discourtesy for the two helpless
milords to refuse. Gulp away though I did, the glass of *pisco*
beside me was never anything but full, as new friend after

new friend appeared, usually with a fresh bottle in hand.
Two Ganymedes from the train's wine store stood beside
our table on permanent duty. One of the passengers was the
chief catering officer of the line, who took post beside us,
waving imperiously to his minions to bring out better
vintages.

Hospitality knew no bounds. When Clark and I got up for
a breath of air in the corridor, a man who seemed to be an
inspector sidled up and asked if, when we came to the next
station, we would like to have some 'warm chicken'. To
which I replied that I personally had eaten more than
sufficient. Everybody laughed then. Innocence and schoolboy Spanish had let me down: it was explained to me that
the suggestion was that some willing female company might
be brought on board at the next halt. Clark politely declined
for both of us and we returned to the bottles.

As the train lurched through the coastal mountains and the
night, the dining car became full of people jostling about us.
Time and again we had to stagger to our feet to drink the
health of the Queen, her Filipe, the President, the glorious
B.B.C., and the friendship of Britain and Chile. Cooks and
stewards gathered round and drank too. As the wine took
effect, we were embraced and slapped on the back. Jolting
train and jolting men caused glasses and bottles to spill. I
found a plant-pot into which I contrived surreptitiously to
keep pouring my *piscos*; but it was not that which flooded
the car. By the time we reached Santiago, the floor, and my
tape recorder on it, was awash. The fog of cigar smoke and
the smell of the pools of brandy were indescribable. The
stewards and the catering man, drunk and asleep, were
sprawled across the tables; the ticket collectors, their duty
and their defences done, had slid to the ground in the
doorway, happily snoring. I can remember leaving the
train, bearing two gift bottles, three flags and a pocketful of
Chileans' visiting cards. I recall getting into a taxi and saying:
'Hotel Hilton Carrera, pronto!' Then a blackness denser
than the Andean night descended on me. But I think the
British had kept their end up.

South America served up an *actual* black-out, upsetting at
the time but engaging in retrospect, when an electrical power

failure hit us in the Brazilian city of Recife at a royal visit reception in an old colonial palace, causing every light to go out. The Brazilians didn't know that one of the things happening was the overloading of circuits by the TV cameramen's lights—but the Queen guessed it. She knew that Richard Cawston and his team were filming; she remembered that when they had been filming her at Covent Garden Opera House in London, some time before, her party had been plunged into darkness by a similar over-burdening of power plugs; so when the lights fizzed out in Recife the first voice I heard calling out loud and clear was the Queen's: 'Where's Cawston?'

That party in Recife was one of the most elegant and romantic of the Latin American occasions—largely because, thanks to the power failure, it took place by genuine candle-light. Recife was the start of a journey through Brazil, which seemed to me the most exciting country in the world. Some of the reasons why I enjoyed it so much were that it is a world of its own, vast in variety, and that I found the names easy and musical to say (I had been suffering from Mexico; and in Mexico City, breathless anyhow because of the altitude, had been wrestling with tongue-twisting horrors like Quetzalcoatl, Xiuhtecutli and Teotihuacán, which places were probably unrecognisable in my broadcasts). Recife has a touch of old Amsterdam and of Venice about it; Salvador de Bahia, once the Portuguese capital, is a fascinat-ing, though crumbling, city of history; and Brasilia, the brand-new capital carved out of a plateau six hundred miles from anywhere, is an architectural wonderland in the sun, a planner's dream come true.

Another thing about Brazil: the coffee, wherever you drink it, really *is* better than any coffee on earth.

But it is Rio de Janeiro which remains the most enchanting place. The very name is almost a song (though a nonsense too: a figment of the early Portuguese sailors' imagination, for there never was a 'River of January'). For all the rhythmic parkways of Brasilia, for all the skyscraper sophistication of the biggest city, São Paulo, Rio stays the capital in the hearts of most Brazilians, certainly the hearts of its volatile citizens, the Cariocas. I did not like the

cigarette-butt squalor of the famous golden beach of
Copacabana, strewn as it was with peanut shells, ice-cream
papers, Beach League goalposts and noisy volleyball teams;
but the city itself, with its hills and bays and grand boule-
vards, is a perpetual spectacle of South American life and
beauty.

It was in Rio that I saw a theatrical sight, a compound of
music and movement more stirring than anything I have
ever seen on a stage or in a stadium, a sight which I should
think will never be repeated. As a Latin carnival, it had an
improbable setting in the garden of the British Residence;
and its impresario was an Old Etonian diplomat (son of the
police chief Russell Pasha I had known years before in
Cairo): Sir John Wriothesley Russell, then our Ambassador
to Brazil, the tall and aristocratic Englishman who had
organised the evening. The spectacle which this diplomat's
brio caused to be produced that velvet night—the excuse for
it was the need to have an 'entertainment spot' during a party
for the Queen—was too big for the cameras, too big indeed
and too purple for my words. But I tried:

'At midnight there came swaying and throbbing up the
drive, through the palm trees hung with fairy lights and
golden floodlamps which made the heat even more tropical,
an amazing stream of five hundred samba dancers moving as
one. As they approached towards the point where Sir John's
two great greyhounds crouched like fireside ornaments on
either side of the entrance to the house, beneath the balconies
and terraces where the Queen, the elegant Ambassador
and a thousand guests watched, the rhythm of that brilliant
snake of dancers quickened and the black and coffee-
coloured figures whirled and jerked with native suppleness
to the beat of drum and cymbal and tambourine. They sang
and they played as they advanced, men and women and
children in fantastic costumes: some of the girls half-naked
in wisps of silk bikini, golden slave-chains on hands and
feet; others in crinolines, pompadour wigs and parasols;
men dressed as eighteenth-century Portuguese grandees.
The lights flashed back from jewels and gowns and dazzling
teeth in dark, dark faces. Music and song reached a crescendo;
and the twisting bodies, sensuously writhing as they had

been, now, at their climax, seemed in their repeated caressing contortions to be making love to both the earth and the stars. And all the time, above the whole pagan pageant, spotlighted two thousand feet up in the sky, stood the enormous statue of Christ the Redeemer on its Corcovado mountain peak, arms flung wide as though embracing all Rio: a Saviour unnoticed as Samba reigned. It was a night of African intoxication which could not have happened in Africa. . . .'

Of that sight, and so much else in America, North, Central and South, I can only say: Thanks for the memory.

Those American journeys, those experiences, could not happen again now. I am afraid to return across the Atlantic. Today could not live up to yesterday.

16

Return to Egypt

Never go back, they say. Never return to a place where you were happy, where you savoured something rare. It won't be the same. But it is precisely *because* of change that a journalist does return, by order. For change makes news.

The particular country to which I had no desire to travel again after the war, I thought, was Egypt. Going to wartime Egypt had been the making of me as a broadcasting reporter. It had special memories; and I believed it would be better to leave them roseate rather than revisit the place and risk disillusion. My masters, however, decreed otherwise; and in fact Egypt was a country with which I became particularly familiar, and of which I became fond all over again, through a series of assignments there in the years when Nasser reigned. They were the years of shaky emergence from British tutelage.

The first mission that took me back was in the tense autumn of 1954. I went as commentator on the unveiling of the Alamein Memorial. British troops were still stationed in Egypt then, but only just. They were penned in the Suez Canal Zone. The situation had been deteriorating for two years, since the military coup, led by Colonel Gamal Abdel Nasser with General Neguib as a front, the rising tide of republicanism and nationalism, and the forced abdication of the obese and dissolute King Farouk. The strain on Anglo-Egyptian relations had been increasing steadily; and on the very day I flew into Cairo the British representatives and Nasser—now Prime Minister and soon to be President—signed an agreement for the evacuation of the Zone and the withdrawal of British soldiers from the country. I expected hostility at the airport, but the customs and immigration officials gave me a smiling and patronising welcome: their land was going to see the back of the khaki British and they were that night feeling magnanimous in victory.

There were difficulties all the same. The British troops attending the Alamein Memorial ceremony, as guards of honour and comrades of the men who had died in the war, were forbidden to emerge from the Canal Zone into Egypt itself—that was the law the Egyptians had laid down. The authorities in Cairo grudgingly admitted that it would be reasonable for Britain to wish some of her soldiers to be present at the memorial on the day of its inauguration; but Alamein was far away from the Zone, and the authorities insisted on the letter of the law being observed. So every soldier had to be provided with civilian clothing before being allowed to travel, albeit in a troop train, from Ismailia and across the Nile Delta to Alexandria and El Alamein. They came in civvies then, all uniforms hidden away in packs and suitcases. On arrival at the memorial—the land around which had been given by Egypt to be international territory in the care of the Commonwealth War Graves Commission—officers and men went into a tented camp, unpacked their military belongings, changed, and became properly dressed soldiers again.

For Field Marshal Viscount Montgomery, however, there was no restriction—it was Monty, of course, who was the unveiler of the memorial, and the day chosen for the ceremony was just twelve years after the beginning of his great battle. Monty, lean and ascetic still, flew out from England in state, and travelled up the old desert road from Alexandria to Alamein in full tropical khaki-drill uniform ablaze with decorations, and with the famous two-badge black beret on his head. But not in a military car. He rode, incongruously, in a vintage, sit-up-and-beg, hearse-like black limousine—the old Rolls from the stables of our Embassy in Cairo. It was an oddity of the occasion, but not the only one. Four old International Wagon-Lit coaches from the Egyptian State Railways had been shunted into a siding in the sand behind the little Alamein station-halt to provide sleeping accommodation for officials concerned with

the ceremony; and to those who had known this desert only
as a cockpit of privation and hard soldiering it was strange
to see this blue civilian train stuck in the middle of the
scenery. I slept in one of the train berths for four nights
whilst we were preparing for the broadcast of the ceremony,
but my nights were far from sweet or sybaritic. I wished I'd
had a bivouac in the open, for the wagons-lit were decrepit
and their fleas were not.

On the day, we broadcast, 'live' into Britain's Home
Service and the B.B.C. overseas network, the entire inauguration and dedication ceremonies, an O.B. an hour and a half
long. It was a great strain for me as commentator, but
probably a greater strain to many of the listeners. I wondered
how many endured to the end, for our transmission included
not only Monty's long oration, endless band playing and the
lament of the pipes, a church service in the Anglican manner
and a full Roman Catholic mass, but also the voice of an
aged imam reciting protracted Mohammedan prayers.

In order to make the broadcasting of this miscellany
clearer and less burdensome, I arranged to have with me
beside the microphone two helpers who would whisper
information into my ear and who could be called upon to
explain to listeners what was happening during the specialised
parts of the religious services. The two were a Moslem from
Radio Cairo and a Catholic padre; and I began the broadcast
with the pair of them safely in position on seats just behind
me. But the event, or rather the weather, proved too much for
my assistants. Our commentary point was on the roof of the
memorial, with no shelter from the scorching sun. This was
hard to bear, and I remember that during the three hours I
had to sit there my clothes became black with sweat.
Before his part of the proceedings came, my Mohammedan
asked to go below for a drink of water—and never returned.
My Roman Catholic did not retreat, but when, with the
Low Mass of Requiem in progress, I turned to him for his
few words, it was to see him slumped on the floor in a
dead faint.

But in spite of everything, that October afternoon of
remembrance had its own impressiveness and lasting beauty.
The Alamein Memorial was, and is to this day, an oasis in the

wilderness of the Western Desert: a long, low, honey-coloured cloister of local rock and marble and Portland stone. On its tablets are inscribed the names of twelve thousand officers and men of the Commonwealth forces who died in the Middle East fighting of the Second World War and have no known grave. The memorial forms the seaward side of a walled cemetery in which are buried over seven thousand. Miraculously, as it seems—though it fact it is thanks to the old wartime water supply piped from Alexandria, and the labours now of seven Bedouin workmen permanently stationed at Alamein—this lonely graveyard is also a beautifully kept garden where lawns of fresh grass, bright shrubs, bougainvillaea, polyanthus and English tea roses spring from the alien sand and soften the geometric outlines of row upon row of white headstones.

Two more memorials have been built a few kilometres further along the coast road through the field of Alamein, two more military shrines where the dead of the desert war are buried. Each has something of the character of the nation which erected it. Whilst the British have made a garden, the German memorial is a stark and massive building, an octagonal fortress bulking almost brutally from its hillock a mile from the dazzling white shore of the Mediterranean. The Italians have put up their war memorial too. This one is like a tall white temple, architecturally clean and handsome, with a huge picture window through which you see the blue and lonely sea beyond the cross on the altar. Here, in caskets let into the smooth marble walls, have been gathered the ashes of thousands of the Giuseppes and Luigis and Marios who were killed whilst serving with Mussolini's desert divisions.

Dotted along that little-used road, a ribbon of tarmacadam which runs westward to the Libyan frontier, are other reminders: small concrete cairns, historically inscribed. One, for instance, recalls the Eighth Army's fine Springbok division, saying: 'South Africans outspanned and fought here during their trek from Italian Somaliland to Germany, 1939–1945.'

There is still no town, not even a village, at Alamein. There is little more than the memorial and the forlorn

railway halt. But nearby, where buses stop on their way
from Alexandria to Mersa Matruh, a little restaurant and
motel have been planted. They possess a small electricity
generator, so patrons have permanent light and a refrigerator
—and a blaring juke-box and two-channel television. Nearly
on the same spot, the Egyptians have built a war museum of
their own and have filled it full of relics, mostly consisting of
old weapons, maps, models and photographs. Rommel and
Montgomery are given equal space, their armies' deeds
impartial treatment. The surprise here, however, is that the
Egyptian army seems to have got into the Alamein act:
there are showcases and pictures to the glory of the United
Arab Republic's fighting forces. Israel is not mentioned.

The strangest, also the pleasantest, transformation I saw
on recent visits along that coast was at Mersa Matruh, which
was just a jumble of ruins in the 1940s, but nowadays is a
new town and gay little seaside resort full of cafés and beach
umbrellas. The old German underground command post on
the headland across the harbour has been turned into a
tourist cave, selling ice-cream and bearing a signboard
saying: 'Rommel's Grotto.'

They were very kind in Matruh. I went back there reporting for a programme about the changed scenery and the
holiday possibilities of the northern coast, and was impressed
by the new mosque built on the edge of the town. One hot
evening, hearing a resounding call to prayer coming from
the top of the high minaret, my producer and I set about
recording the evocative sound of it. But our tape-machine
jammed, and we called at the mosque to see if we could find
out when the next announcement would be. A young
bearded priest, the local imam, came up and in English
asked if he could help. When we explained ourselves he told
us that it was he who was the muezzin and, to our surprise,
asked if we could get our recorder going again and, if so,
he would climb the tower once more, there and then, and
repeat the cry for us. This he duly did (I wonder if the
astonished faithful of Matruh prayed twice-over that night)
and we made the recording. Afterwards the priest invited us
to step into his bare little room at the back of the mosque
and asked if we would take a little liquid refreshment.

We said yes thank you, and were steeling ourselves for mint tea or Turkish coffee when he added: 'Will a Coke be all right?' and produced a few piastres from beneath his robes, gave them to an attendant small boy, and watched the lad shin through a window out into the street and its little shops. In a moment the boy was back, his grimy hands over the open mouths of three dusty bottles. From these we politely drank, praying to Allah that the germs would be dormant.

The Victor of Alamein himself went back to the North African battlefields once more, in 1967. He was eighty years old and it was his last return. He was still sprightly and self-confident when I saw him jeeping up and down the sands with an Egyptian army patrol in attendance. The occasion this time was the twenty-fifth anniversary of the battle (and only a few days before Egypt's disastrous Six Day War with Israel) and Monty had gone out this time as the guest of the Egyptian Government—though he had virtually invited himself. He told me that he had wished to see the desert just once more and so, with no reference to the British Foreign Office or anybody else, had 'looked up the address of President Nasser and written him an airmail letter'. Nasser wrote back a 'very civil' reply to Monty's house near Alton in Hampshire, and bade him come. This time Monty stayed not in Alexandria but in the desert —in surprising comfort and cleanliness, however: they lodged him and his party in a new, large, and otherwise empty new hotel which had been hopefully built near Sidi Abd-el-Rahman, on a beautiful beach miles from anywhere.

I was making my eighth visit to Egypt then. I wandered a little more deeply into the desert than Monty did—wandered rather nervously after I had heard a bang and seen a puff of sand on the other side of a wadi, and found an unwary Bedouin maimed by stepping on one of the mines laid a quarter of a century before. Straying camels and donkeys, men too, are still killed from time to time in old minefields whose charts were lost and therefore were never cleared. Most of the danger areas were swept safe very soon after the war; and scavengers and scap-metal dealers long ago removed almost all traces of the great conflict. The dealers had a good haul: a lot of broken ironmongery had been left. But now it is hard to find even a bit of rusty barbed wire, fragment of tank-track or punctured jerrican. The desert is empty again, miles and miles of stony, khaki plain; the only Desert Rats are the native ones, tiny jerboas scuttering about under the scrub of saltbush and camelthorn.

My own Egyptian friends were not very keen on my visits to the 1942 battle zones. For them, those were days when they were an occupied country—days *not* to be recalled. But my hosts were zealous to show me the changes and improvements in Alexandria and Cairo: no beggars and no dirty postcards; but plenty of new schools and new roads. But I did not find everything improved. The smells, the flies and the poverty were still there. So indeed were the baksheesh brigades. It is true that the pashas have gone, but a new 'boss class' of party officials and senior army officers are satraps in their stead. Alexandria looked very shabby indeed, and the Cecil Hotel an empty ghost of its old self. Farouk's Montazah Palace still looked grand, largely because they have kept it as a museum (as they have the Abdin Palace in Cairo) just like it was when the king lived there. His boots and suits and uniforms are laid out ready, as though at any moment he would waddle in and put them on; his erotica is to be seen in bookshelves and bathrooms. His bed is made and turned down, and looks clean. The tear-off calendars on the walls still show the date when he left for his exile, for good.

I had walked into the former palace imagining that in setting up the place as a museum they would have given at least some rein to derision and vilification of a hated ex-ruler. But not a bit of it. The preservation of Faroukiana seemed almost loving; and the museum curator was very sharp with me when I remarked that the king had been a monster. He also made it clear that he preferred the days when the royal children were playing in the grounds to the present scene with day-trippers screaming up and down the gardens and holiday crowds littering the once-private beach. 'No, sir,' he whispered. 'Not everything in old times was bad. Alex was properous and smart, and the shops full of fine goods. But not now—though, please, I am not speaking for your record.'

In Cairo I did find improvements, though the city is becoming seedy again. The surface, at least, was brightened in Nasser's years. A fine Corniche road now sweeps along the Nile river-bank from the Delta to the heart of the modern city and the better residential areas, running southwards to join the highway to Helwan. Tall blocks of buildings fringe the river road: the new Shepheard's, the radio and television headquarters skyscraper, and the Nile Hilton, built on the spot where the verminous old Kasr-el-Nil barracks used to be. Across the river on Gezira Island the trees are now dominated by the Cairo Tower, a slender, latticed concrete and steel landmark six hundred feet high, with a revolving restaurant at the top. As you eat your kebab up there, you get the most superb eagle's-eye views of city, river and desert in turn. The restaurant floor makes one complete revolution every twenty-nine minutes—a sedate and almost imperceptible rate, though one evening when I was up in the tower there was a sudden juddering and the revolving stopped. A party of V.I.P. but very rustic Yemeni visitors found the business of eating a meal on the move up there in the sky altogether too sophisticated and upsetting; and they asked for the world to stop to let them get off, leaving their dinner uneaten.

Each time I visited Cairo I discovered not only a lot of new construction going on but new entertainments too: *Son et Lumière* at the Citadel and the Pyramids, a tented night-spot called 'Sahara City' in the desert beyond the Sphinx, and more cabaret shows in new hotels and old houseboats. There was no decline in the popularity of the belly-dancers, but a year or two ago a prudish Government order was issued making the girls put thin white muslin over their acrobatic tummies. At the same time an attempt was made to ban bikinis on Egypt's beaches. I think the edict stemmed from some old and very orthodox Moslems behind Nasser, but I did wonder at the time whether the move had anything to do with the Muscovite killjoys I used to see, in greater and greater numbers, in the Egyptian capital—the clutches of sober-suited, square-faced Russian 'advisers' of various kinds who always seemed to be ensconced in strength in those strongholds of the wicked capitalists, the large Cairo hotels. At any rate, the men from the Soviet Union were noticeably unpopular with the Egyptian people.

As to changes, the Gezira Sporting Club in Cairo experienced one of the most striking. I found the once famous playground of the sahibs extraordinarily altered. I could not see one British person there. Egyptian youths and girls were playing football and throwing javelins on that beautiful old green oasis of a cricket ground which in the old days used to be so lavishly watered and lovingly barbered. The turf was now patchy, rough and browned. But the cricket scoreboard was still standing, and moreover it still showed figures: 47 for 3 wickets, last man out for a duck. The boys and girls said they didn't know what the score figures meant, but nobody was going to change them, they thought. The board was like those carefully preserved rooms that used to be Farouk's—a love-hate souvenir of something that had been kicked out. But there were few to whom the Gezira Club mementos meant anything.

Egypt has gone on wanting the tourists to come back, to be undeterred by wars. Beside the saddle camels outside Mena House, and in Old Cairo's dark little curio shops of the Khan-al-Khalili bazaar, the dragomans and the shop-keepers wait and hope. But when can the small stream of tourists to which the holiday trade was reduced swell again to a rich river? I have watched the decline of the country economically and internationally as militarisation and Sovietisation has spread. It has been sad to see: America's withdrawal (and so our own) from the Aswan Dam project in 1955; Nasser's retaliation by taking the Canal for Egypt's own (and, incidentally, before it was blocked, running it very efficiently, contrary to foreigners' expectation); the attacks of the very able Jewish army; Anthony Eden's Suez War; defeat at the hands of Israel, twice; the sinking of ships in the Canal; the Russian take-over on the Canal's West Bank and down at the Aswan Dam—all these events discouraging, to put it euphemistically, to holiday visitors and the needed money they could bring.

Individuals and organisations have been welcoming to me personally, and few countries in the world have more fascinating things to see than Egypt can show; but it has not been a comfortable country to be in, teetering on the edge of new war. Mine were business visits through the years, and I found, naturally, fewer and fewer visitors who were there just for pleasure: tourists are not going to patronise in large numbers a land which may blow up at any moment. The sad thing is that Canal dues and travellers' dollars were the great sources of revenue from abroad—and Egypt almost killed both. The surprising thing is that, in spite of all the tension, Cairo hotel business picked up well as the 1970s began.

The atmosphere became more and more jumpy as the years, and my assignments, went on; but the country always strongly attracted me, and the stories I was sent on were unique. Four times I went south to Aswan to report the building of the Sadd-el-Aali, the Aswan High Dam, one of the major engineering achievements of the twentieth century, which cost 500 million pounds and has brought the promise of new industrial power and, through controlling the floods of the river, the possibility of increasing greatly the areas of agricultural fertility on the borders of Africa's biggest river. The High Dam is a working reality now. It was financed and eventually master-minded by the Soviet Union; it is now guarded by Russian guns and is virtually unapproachable except to those who run it and defend it.

But I was there as it grew, saw it from the first coffer dam which blocked the Nile above the First Cataract and the old, inadequate British dam to the turning of the whole river into a new course blasted deep through the native granite, and then watched the work move gradually forward to the completion of the immense rock-fill dam, 350 feet high and two miles wide, and the harnessing of the throttled torrent by the tunnels, gates and turbines of a hydro-electric power station. The unforgettable sights were the picture that thirty thousand Arab workmen made as they sweated night and day in gigantic canyons gouged by monster machines in an inferno of dust and noise—a task and a work force greater than those of the building of the Pyramids—and the

The view I *should* have had from my official chair at the Caernarvon Investiture (page 147)

Crowded royal occasions in Castle and Palace

A garden party in London where the Queen walks the 'lanes' between ranks of guests on her own lawns. 'It is quite a scrum' (page 137)

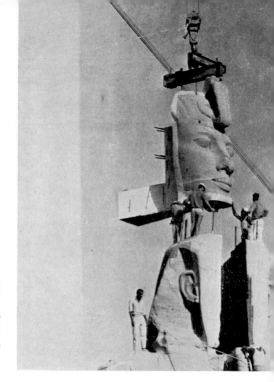

The face of the Pharaoh, thirty tons of it, lowered into place at Abu Simbel, where the temples of Ramses II were rescued from the rising waters of the Nile

The Great Temple in its original position, now drowned. Today the temple stands reassembled on the clifftop

sweltering, deafening tunnels deep in the rock where a thousand red-shirted Russian foremen, blond and unsmiling, directed more hordes of Egyptian labourers in turbans and grimy long gowns, whilst improbable lemonade sellers crouched impassively behind their orange boxes, and grinning little black urchins darted in and out of the gangs to peddle sticky sweets and chewing gum as though it was the most natural thing in the world.

Aswan itself—once quiet and backward, far away in Upper Egypt, peaceful and remote, with the domed mausoleum of the great Aga Khan the Third lonely on its hill across the water—Aswan swelled into almost the capital of the country, such was the concentration of men and materials during the years of the High Dam's building. I saw the little town, to which failed civil servants used to be posted as a punishment so that they should be out of the world and forgotten, become the magnet for Egypt's best engineers and administrators (it was Egyptians, not Russians, who sat round the High Dam board-room table). I saw Aswan burst into a boom city of huge blocks of flats, acres of stone and concrete villas, cinemas, meeting halls, factories and railway marshalling yards—and separate housing estates, clubs, shops and schools for the families from Russia.

I saw Nikita Khrushchev, grinning and clowning at the side of President Nasser on the deck of the ship which was once Farouk's royal yacht, casting the final stones into the river on the ceremonial day of closing the last gap in the Nile's old course and beginning the Dam itself.

And I remember how the Soviet Premier threw me out of my hotel, for when he arrived he took over the entire New Cataract Hotel and had it surrounded by troops and armed police. I transferred to a small hotel on an island opposite the Cataract, but that night, after the ceremonies, I was unable to get into even that resting place. I had had a long and full day's commentating and tape-editing, and was sailing thankfully towards the hotel in a hired felucca when Ahmed the boatman, frightened by a glint of steel and a shout of command in the Cataract Hotel's garden, suddenly put his helm about and fled back to his town mooring. I commanded him to stop the nonsense and take

o

me home at once, crinkling money under his nose, but it
was no use. 'If I go past the soldiers in the dark they will
shoot at the boat,' he wailed. 'No, respected sir, not for a
thousand piastres will I be dead meat for Russians. They do
not care for us—and I wish to be alive to sail my boat
tomorrow.'

Above the High Dam, the whole geography of the area
has now changed; and boatmen have many miles more of
water on which to sail. Banking up behind the barrier which
has been put across the river, the Nile in Nubia is becoming a
large lake—so large in fact that it will eventually stretch far
down south into the Sudan, so large that the whole of Britain
could be submerged in it.

The rising waters of the penned-up Nile were the cause of
still more reporting missions for me. I went again to Egypt
when a great Noah's Ark operation was evacuating river-
side villages, carrying bargeloads of people and animals to
new communities downstream. And, especially, to report
the years of work on the much more extraordinary operation,
the saving from drowning of the famous Abu Simbel
temples 150 miles south of Aswan. The temples, hewn out of
the cliffs at the water's edge over three thousand years ago,
most dramatic of all the monuments of ancient Egypt, would
soon have been submerged beneath the new Nile lake had
there not been mounted, under the aegis of UNESCO, an
international rescue operation which took five years and cost
fourteen million pounds. The temples were saved in the
nick of time. The site was still being cleared when the water
began to come over the top of the steel piling of the temporary coffer dam which had protected the removal work. But,
with last-minute all-round-the-clock labours in ninety-
degrees temperatures, the last stones were brought out
successfully. The rescue was done by sawing the temples
into bits and hauling them piecemeal to be reassembled on
higher ground.

Today the old site and the old village of Abu Simbel are
deeply submerged and, two hundred feet higher than they
were, the temples stand again, minutely preserved, in full
majesty. Flanking them is a man-made cliff which looks
exactly like the natural cliff which was the old setting. Steel

arches and girders which support cliffs and temple roofs are hidden deep in the new mountainside. The picture is as before. The Pharaoh Rameses II once more sits sculptured in colossal quadruplicate on the towering sandstone façade, gazing impassively towards the rising sun across river and desert as he has done for thirty centuries. The sculptures are marvellous to behold; you cannot tell that they have ever been moved.

Yet moved they had been, in an unprecedented engineering job carried out by a consortium of German, Swedish, French and Italian firms (Britain was one of fifty countries which contributed money, but the only British national I found among thousands of workers was a young Scots landscape architect working for the Swedish company). Every inch of the Great Temple of Rameses and the adjoining Lesser Temple of Nefertari his Queen was brought out of all danger.

It was, of course, the removing which made news. As the archaeologists winced and worried and finally sighed with satisfaction, three hundred thousand tons of stone— including carved figures and beautifully decorated roofs and walls inside the cliff where the light of day had never shone—were taken to safety. Heads and bodies of the colossi, broken into thousands of pieces by the handsaws and chainsaws of expert Italian workmen brought over from the marble quarries of Carrara, were lifted high in the air by giant cranes. The pieces were huge: each of the Pharaoh's faces weighed over thirty tons. Up a specially built ramp they went, to a hill-top storage area, later to be put together again on the new site. It was a fascinating business to see. My visits to the workings produced, in recordings and pictures, a story that was undoubtedly less urgent than most of my assignments, but less ephemeral and more satisfying.

The pity is that Abu Simbel, of the great wonders of Egypt and the whole ancient world, is so far away in the depths of the Nubian Desert, and not easy to reach with speed and comfort. There is no road or railway, and steamers are infrequent so far up the Nile. Even a trip by hydrofoil from Aswan took me over five hours and was a

cramped and noisy experience. Recently, a landing strip for
aircraft has been made not far from the temples and the
Egyptian airline has included flights to it on their schedules;
but Abu Simbel remains out of the range of most people.
A marvellous sight, restored and as yet uncrowded, it
waits for better times. The nearby stone houses and the
little hotel and the swimming pool, all built to form a
village for the men who worked on the moving of the
temples, are now a potential tourist resort; but it may be a
long time before they are turning business away. For,
remote though these astonishing monuments are, far removed
geographically from Suez and Sinai and their tensions, they
are still part of troubled Egypt.

I once felt the long arm of trouble reach out to the temples.
On a visit to Abu Simbel, enjoying the warm hospitality of
country and government as I worked with microphone and
camera on the Abu Simbel story, I became aware one
morning of a sudden coldness, and uncharacteristic curtness
and lack of smiles from my Egyptian hosts. They even told
me that I must take no photographs of 'important national
objects'. Questioning the officials as they crouched in the
shade of a site-foreman's hut to listen to a news bulletin
coming out of a portable radio set, I found that crisis had
come in the north, and the air was charged with the hate
and fear of ominous Arab-Israeli threats.

It was borne upon me that it was high time to get back
from tombs to twentieth century; and I made for civilisation.
With my notebooks and tapes and films, I managed to hitch
a lift that very day in the chief engineer's tiny monoplane,
which dropped me in Aswan. There I caught one of the
regular Russian aircraft flying to Cairo—to find a highly
charged situation and the Six Day War beginning.

I had no wish to be a war correspondent in that conflict,
certainly not on the Egyptian side where there was an
annihilating news censorship and virtually no information
to be got at all. But I stood by and filed what messages I
could until there came out from London a stream of vigorous
young B.B.C. reporters eager for blood and glory (soon to
wish, from a professional point of view, that they were on
the other, the Israeli side, the winning side, where news

stories were flowing full and free and army P.R.O.s were only too eager to get correspondents to the front). I flew out of Cairo to Rome and then on to London before the Egyptians closed their airport to civilian traffic. I was thankful, that time, to be away from a city, where, even before the war erupted, I had become a foreigner to be glowered at and shied away from, shadowed by policemen, who took such laborious and ostentatious note of every cab I took from Shepheard's or the Semiramis or Hilton that for a while the taximen were reluctant to have anything to do with my custom.

Egypt was a dirty and a dangerous place, I told myself when I had got out of the place. But that feeling didn't last long. After a few days I knew the country was enticing still, in spite of everything. Back in England and resuming my Palace rounds and the duties of reporting on our own monarchy, I soon felt the old desert nostalgia pulling again, making me look forward to the next visit to the Nile and its relics of other kings and queens whose world was wonderfully contrived and civilised in the days when Britain was still nothing but woods and woad.

17

Retirement is just a Word

My journeys as a staff correspondent, and as what my Welsh friends called 'Talbot the Palace', stretched over thirty years of my life. When I left the staff at the end of 1969 it didn't feel that long—though a woman in Amersham wrote: 'The first time we heard you broadcast our small daughter thought you said, not "Godfrey Talbot" but "God Victoria". In our family you have always been known as God Victoria. You have been talking to us for so long that you seem eternal. We're sure you must have been with the Old Queen.' It was a backhanded compliment.

My retirement from the B.B.C. ration strength was made widely known because an official announcement about it was issued from Portland Place; and this precipitated a new flood of letters. Of the hundreds, only one really stabbed: it simply said: 'Thank God!' and was unsigned. Another note, nearly as short but nicer, was: 'Thank Godfrey.' A message from a man in a Lincolnshire village cut both ways: 'You have been sometimes a cross between a flunkey and a funeral director—but fun.' Many letters were plain—and varnished—compliments.

The announcement also brought a procession of interviewers to my door: newspaper reporters and magazine and gossip-column editors as well as colleagues wanting reminiscences for assorted radio and television programmes. It ought, I suppose, to have been refreshing to be the interviewee instead of the interrogator; yet, even though I was being asked simply to tell something of my own story, I didn't feel happy with myself when answering the reporters' questions—I felt I would have been better doing the questioning. A matter of being in the unaccustomed seat. I noticed that few of the Press visitors were able to 'take a note' (they told me: 'If you write shorthand you get put on dull jobs'), but several bore a tool of *my* trade, and at the beginning of our talk placed a microphone and small tape recorder on my table. When I raised an eyebrow, one young man answered: 'Perhaps it's lazy to do it this way rather than with a notebook and pencil, but at any rate we can get the quotes right, and our victim can't deny afterwards that he said it!'

But, taped or not, the modern interview can still have the reporter's and sub-editor's gloss on it when the conversation gets into print. Inevitably, there ensued headlines like 'Royal Flush' and 'Good-bye Gracious Godfrey'. The whole business seemed absurd and unrealistic: I wasn't ancient and I wasn't retiring from work or broadcasting; but, having reached the statutory age, it was a case of off the staff-list and on to free-lancing—an arrangement, indeed, which suited me. Gone today and here tomorrow.

The personal publicity did at least give me an opportuniy to set one or two things straight. For instance, one journalist wrote: 'Talbot belongs to the old style of broadcaster, with his correct, well-groomed voice investing any ceremonial occasion with a sense of hushed importance', but he had the goodness to print my riposte: 'You suggest that I'm in the habit of making oral genuflections. Not a bit of it. There's usually a reason for what may sound like whispered reverence. There come moments when you are chattering away happily into the microphone against a considerable background, and then suddenly the organ or the band stops and there you are shouting your head off and everyone's looking round and saying hush. Of course you lower your voice. And another reason for "whispering" sometimes is that, as you are talking about them, Royalty is passing a foot or two away from you—and you don't want to be describing them into their own ears.'

Some of the interviews took place in the North of England, for I was sent on a sort of farewell tour of Yorkshire and Lancashire to revisit some of the scenes of my early days, partly because it was thought I would like this (and I

did) and partly because the never-known-to-miss-a-trick
B.B.C. editors wanted to get out of me some stories about
the Changed North.

Much *was* different, of course. Rebuilt city centres made
some of my old haunts unrecognisable. The new towns,
the pedestrian precincts and the bold fly-over highways had
transformed the scene. But the phenomenon that most
astonished me was in the shape of the enormous modern
theatre-clubs, some of them accommodating a thousand
diners, built in the middle of grimy places like my old Batley
and Wakefield. They were old music-halls, really; but now
the settings were new and bright, and the cloth-cap patrons
were sitting at tables demolishing scampi and Spanish
plonk.

A lot of the North, to my pleasure, had not changed:
Ilkley and its moors, lovely Upper Wharfedale and the folds
of the hills at the heads of those West Riding valleys,
Fountains Abbey and Studley Royal, the Trough of Bow-
land, Leeds Market, Morley Town Hall, the rhubarb fields
near Wakefield, the old road to Lancashire over the tops by
Nont Sara's, the broad views round Haigh Hall in Wigan,
Blackpool promenade and all its grand professional vulgarity
and my favourite backwater in all Victorian England—
Grange-over-Sands, which has stood sedate and half asleep
beside Morecambe Bay, not altered since the place was born
when they built the Furness railway to Barrow.

There were old friends in the North who greeted me still
with: 'Na lad' or ' 'Ow ista?' and who said 'Hey up!' when
they meant 'Look out!' They stopped me, when they thought
I was talking London rubbish, with the dry, salutary: 'Nay,
give ovver.' Someone even called me 'You daft ha'p'orth'.

It was all heart-warming. It was the sort of affectionate
abuse that I had been brought up with. And flat vowels
didn't mean flat lives. Some of those folk I met were hard up,
but grumbled very cheerfully indeed. Most people were
enjoying themselves in one way or another. I found more
natural politeness and more zest for life than in London;
and more independent thinking. Also, there still seemed to be
a better chance of *moving* as individuals and not as herds:
not even Manchester or Liverpool at rush-hour has anything

quite so depressing as the treadmill stream of human ants scurrying back and forth across London Bridge in the night and morning surges between office and suburbia.

Universal television and Southern ways have *not*, it seems to me, ironed out the North as an entity, or a series of entities; and the Northern accents have not been destroyed. I even found Yorkshiremen who went to Southern public schools and used to talk standard B.B.C. English, but who are now deliberately and aggressively adopting a broad Northern speech because they reckon that in business it helps to stamp them as successes, reliable go-ahead types. The short 'a' is almost a status symbol; and Pennine vowels have cash value.

I had a good nostalgic wallow in reminiscences with old journalistic colleagues, too, as I shuttled about ' 'twixt Trent and Tweed', but it was in London that most of my retirement celebrations happened. Newspaper friends in Fleet Street threw a party for me. Men and women journalists with whom I had shared the joys and sorrows of many an overseas Queen-watching journey presented me with a handsome silver wine jug. They did not put their names on the vessel (they wrote those on the champagne corks during the party), but on it was engraved 'Now the Royal Tour is Over . . .'. The words were a reminder of the song which the Press Party, exhausted but thankful and letting its hair down, used to sing on the last night of each tour. They were always the first line of the song, and the second line was also always the same ('O How Happy we Shall Be'—sung to a well-known and for decades profanely used hymn tune); but the rest of lines were new each time, written for the particular royal visit we had just endured. They consisted of ribald recollection of misadventures experienced and irreverent comment on the foibles of ambassadors, aides and information attachés with whom we campaigned. I had been the author of most of the verses, plentifully helped by the couplets of fellow travellers.

When I received the jug in London it was the second time the memento had been given to me. The first time was in Norway at the end of what was officially my final royal trail—reporting the tour which the Queen and her family made through the fjords and coastal towns. The last engagement was a big dinner at the Britannia Hotel in Trondheim, a full-dress civic occasion attended by all the royal and official personages. It was followed, later that night and in the same hotel, by another dinner, delightful though less decorous, given specially for me by the press corps who, in an enthusiastic and generous shopping spree that afternoon had combed the city and bought me an armful of books—and the jug, which was formally handed to me at this Dinner Number Two. That press 'do' was a long and splendid carousal. Everybody made speeches and told stories, and the champagne flowed copiously in and out of my jug until we all tottered off to bed in the clear Scandinavian dawn. The jug was firmly removed from me, then, so that it could be inscribed and handed to me once more at that second party in London.

The whole Trondheim evening had turned out to be almost one long Presentation Party. At the end of the earlier, the official dinner, the Queen, without any warning, stopped at my table as she was leading her party out of the banqueting room, to present me to her host King Olav and to tell him about my years of commentating. Crown Prince Harald and his wife, pretty young Crown Princess Sonja, and the Queen's own family gathered round and listened to recollections of all sorts of tour experiences. In fact the halt developed into a general chat and trading of reminiscences apropos my work and my retirement— whilst the rest of the guests were left standing at their places and wondering what was going on. Her Majesty at length moved on with a 'See you in London'.

There was indeed further talk in London when I was received by the Queen at the Palace, was kindly bidden to family lunch, was approved by the corgis and received at the royal hand what the old reports used to describe as 'tangible tokens of appreciation'. It was a particular happiness to be received also by Queen Elizabeth at Clarence House, where the conversation was full of ease and full of fun. The Queen Mother is a charmer still.

The royal households took it upon themselves to lunch me too, extra busy though they were, especially at Buckingham Palace with the long task of providing detailed material for Parliament's vast review of the monarchy's costs (and indeed the monarchy's functions) through the Select Committee on the Civil List, whose recommendations of increased expense allowances to meet, at last, the increased cost of living caused predictable but misleading newspaper headlines about 'Pay Rises for Royalty' and 'The Million Pound Queen'.

It was also a time of change for the principal servants of the Queen as well as for me: the retirement of Her Majesty's sage Private Secretary, Sir Michael (now Lord) Adeane, came; and it was to lead to promotions including the elevation of the able young Australian, Bill Heseltine, to the post of Assistant Private Secretary only four years after he had succeeded Richard Colville—who became Sir Richard—as the Palace Press Secretary.

Meanwhile I was having some eventful weeks in Broadcasting House. I cleared out the accumulations of years in my office cupboards. I grappled with Salaries officers and Welfare ladies. I saw my insurance card for the first time, for it was now handed me to stamp for myself because I was now becoming self-employed. I acquired personal experience of the agreeable customs with which the B.B.C. says *au revoir* to senior members of its staff: lunches, dinners, and a tea-party in the Council Chamber beneath the portrait of John Reith, with speeches and the presenting of gifts and a handsome album full of the signatures and scribbled salutes of colleagues. The large number of pages in that fat album was a measure of my three decades and many friendships. Fellow workers all over the Corporation had signed. To read their written messages was to take a sentimental journey through the years. The Director-General occupied the first page, but I think I was most touched by the last page. On it was written: 'Love from the Third Floor Tea Lady' and there were three kisses underneath.

Everybody professed to be amused when, on being asked what leaving presents I would like to have, I had asked that a stop-watch might be one of them. Such a watch had long been an instrument of my profession, for the timing of spoken dispatches and the editing of tapes, and they had assumed that I should no longer want to be burdened with such a device. But the point was that I now required a stop-watch of my own instead of a B.B.C. one. I was still working.

I required an office too, outside Broadcasting House. My house provided that. My study at home soon became more a place of business than ever it was, well used though it had been. I continued to go into B.H., and also into our World Service studios at Bush House, after I had left the regular ranks there; but now did the bulk of my writing work in my own Surrey home. My desk there became a clutter of files and letters and scripts, the typewriter a permanent piece of domestic furniture. The telephone rang at all hours, and my wife knew the full rigours of secretarial message-taking, and the coping with requests from people who thought I had nothing to do: 'Well no, he's still terribly busy. I don't know why they say retirement —except that I have him at home for more meals just now . . . No, he's not one for joining clubs . . . No, he'll be setting off early tomorrow morning . . . No, I don't think he can be on any more committees.'

There was not much leisure; and, to be honest, I didn't want it. I have never been good at holidays; my job has always been my hobby, and I regard gardening and golf as in the same category as washing-up, chores to be avoided if possible. We did take a couple of weeks of swimming and dodging the sun in Malta before I settled down squarely to organising my professional life without the B.B.C. dictating its entire shape for me. Once back, I was busier than ever. New enterprises were taking up a great deal of time, particularly when I started recording commentaries to guide visitors round historic places such as Hampton Court Palace and the State Apartments of Windsor Castle. This was work which I found both demanding and satisfying. It consisted of researching, then writing and speaking on to tape, a half-hour spoken guide to each place. The recordings were copied on to hundreds of tiny reels and then, one to each machine, they were put into small individual tape-players, equipped with minute earphones and shoulder slings, so that, having hired these devices at the entrance, tourists could wander through the famous buildings with me talking to them with informality and accuracy—not audible generally but clearly heard by each customer—describing the pictures and the history and pointing out items of special interest in the rooms. This sort of conducted tour needs something of the broadcasting technique and is more personal than the recitations of the all-too-visible bear-leaders who tow flocks of sightseers round London and harangue them at fixed halts. The guide-on-tape needs to be an easy companion to the tourist, nothing of the dry schoolmaster, pouring out information but doing it in a simple and friendly and almost casual way, with an occasional nudge and a touch on the arm. And, as in radio, talking to one person, not a hundred. Material and manner must be just right, entertaining and painless to absorb. When they are so, the tapes are very popular indeed.

I was heavily engaged in these and other new labours, and a lot of my old ones, when there came, on top of it all, another big change—this time a domestic change. We moved house. Other people, thank heavens, did much of the work and worrying which this involved, but I could not escape the necessary though traumatic process of weeding out my own accumulated belongings in face of the smaller premises to which we were going.

Though a strain, the move was sensible. The family house had become too big, its garden too much a burden, for its remaining two people. Our sons had flown the nest and were now married men with lives of their own. The elder was a schoolmaster-turned-college-lecturer-turned-education administrator; Number Two, in spite of my warnings that he couldn't expect the good breaks I had experienced in my career, had progressed through weekly and daily journalism into B.B.C. news. So my wife and I found an attractive small bungalow, excellently built but *newly* built (we went into occupation with the walls scarcely dry: in any future move I shall wish not to be 'first in', so that someone else shall have the teething troubles of a house's first year). 'Holmwell' we called our new abode, a Lake District echo. The place is a joy, though, since I am no handyman, it took a little time for rapture to break through.

Holmwell became both my home and my professional headquarters, the springboard of a life of writing and talking. Theoretically, I now had more time for writing: practically, the talking part increased, and became talking on platforms and postprandially in dining rooms as well as into accustomed microphones. There were times when I had to say no to B.B.C. producers who telephoned and asked me to come to the studios to do pieces for their programmes, because I found that lecture bookings stood in the way.

I had become an extra kind of public speaker: a lecturer— not just a sound and an image but a performer in the flesh, alive, aloud, in person and in captivity.

18

Platform Performance

I had been doing lectures for years whilst still on the staff of the Corporation; but most of the dates had to be on my days off or sandwiched between B.B.C. jobs, which, of course, had to come first. Now that I could accept speaking engagements more freely, and in my diary dovetail them in whatever pattern I wished around the writing and broadcasting commitments I undertook, lecturing became something of a habit and a way of life.

But in my case 'lecturing', though the word has to be used, is strictly a misnomer. Except on a few occasions, my kind of public speaking is describing in my own vein some of the things I have seen, some of the people I have met and some of the things that have happened to me. Audiences like being told stories, and I enjoy telling them. It is really as simple as that. I drifted into 'giving talks' quite casually, hesitatingly accepting a few of the invitations which came to me as a B.B.C. reporter. When, as time went on, the invitations snowballed—I have never *sought* a speaking engagement in my life—I had perforce to pick and choose. And I still do. Even today, in demand and my own master, I do not by any means spend the major part of my time at the business—though once not long ago I found myself contracted to make seven hour-long speeches in seven widely separated towns in one week. That was exceptional. What I try to do is space the bookings, or take a few on a run and then get on with other things for a while until the next bout. So I keep a good but limited number of speaking dates each year. I enjoy them, and have got to know the ropes of public appearance. It is a world of its own, this lecture-tour trade, which in America booms and is inelegantly called 'the gab racket' and which in the United Kingdom, where its pace is gentler, has experienced a great revival. It is this that I know.

Thousands of clubs and societies are avid for good speakers. The women's luncheon clubs and tea clubs— which lie thickest in the North and Midlands of England and meet from October to May—are numerous beyond counting. From them come the biggest demands for paid talkers. The secretaries arrange their programmes a year ahead.

There are the Inner Wheels and Ladies' Circles, whose special occasions I know. Then the Business and Professional Women's Clubs, the conferences of Soroptimists, the Conservative Women, the Literary Societies, the dining clubs, the county gatherings of the Women's Institutes and the Townswomen's Guilds. But it is not an all-female world. Municipalities run series of celebrity lectures on winter evenings; Round Tables and Old Boys' Associations, professional bodies such as doctors' and dentists' associations hold annual dinners, big firms put on public relations lunches for clients; Rotarians stage thumping great district conventions in seaside pavilions; and schools make a considerable to-do over prize-givings, speech days and parents' society evenings. All these gladsome goings-on are capably organised by officials who know perfectly well that their special assemblies need, besides their own company and their own business discussions, some particular interest and entertainment from without. All the occasions, in fact, require guest speakers. Carefully and hopefully, the organisers invite to their tables and platforms the more articulate of the nation's explorers, politicians, novelists, cooks, couturiers, hoteliers, photographers, musicians, broadcasters, buyers of antiques and breeders of silkworms.

Many of the club secretaries who have booked such people have done so by shopping at one of the Speakers' Lunches which a lecture agency holds each year at a large London hotel. These Talkers Parades are attended by both secretaries from all over the country and some speakers who are available for bookings. They are unique events. By being

present at them, the women secretaries—almost all the
secretaries *are* women, from the provinces, and incidentally
they always seem to me to be infinitely more smartly dressed
than the average London female at a West End lunch—
are able to meet and expertly size-up the assembled candi-
dates for their meetings. They know their stuff, these
secretaries do. They are delightful and at the same time
direct. A lecturer may well be accosted with questions
like: 'Our people would be thrilled to have you, but can
we afford you? Do give me an idea what you would cost?'
Or it may be: 'Would you be anywhere near Heckmondwike
next March?' Or: 'Do we have to pay your first-class fare,
and can you face an early train so that an overnight hotel
doesn't come into it?'

Speakers' Lunches are pleasant and popular as well as
profitable. Those buyers in the smart hats are really absolute
darlings; and, quite apart from the money, lecturers genuinely look forward to the possibility of meeting them
again on their home ground.

This some of them do when the season comes. It is then,
in the autumn, that the major speakers pack their throat
lozenges and take to the road. Through the peak six months
from October to March these wights errant ride bravely
out and venture the highways and byways in the cause of
oratory. They are intrepid travellers, and physically tough.
They have to be. Day and night they go, by slippery roads,
draughty railway stations and dilatory trains taken at
godless hours. Their travel expenses increasingly erode
their fees as they journey to parish rooms and provincial
hotels, school halls and Masonic parlours, fighting frost
and fog and missed connexions and incipient influenza
to keep their trysts and say their pieces.

And their quality? Perhaps twenty of the regular talkers
are good. Word of their appeal to audiences gets around,
and the clubs clamour for them, save up for them. It is
they, of course, who can command the best payment.
There are also something like a hundred lecturers who are
bearable for a short time; and these speakers are used to fill
up the societies' schedules. The rest of the talkers are eminently forgettable, and they talk seldom. Just a few of them

see the light, work hard on their material and its delivery, study the market, and so they improve and mildly prosper. But most, regrettably, are the dolorous 'would be's' who plague the agencies' telephones and send in letters with such chilling openings as: 'I have been collecting butter-flies for many years, and my friends tell me that I have a modicum of that precious gift of rhetoric which, I feel sure . . .'

Perhaps they think it is all terribly easy but that they just need a start. But the hard truth is that speaking accept-ably and entertainingly to non-academic audiences is a tricky task which is often underestimated. You have to work at it, and yet make it seem like anything but work. Moreover, you do not become famous *by* lecturing. You have to be known first—in politics, literature, television or sport.

I am myself one of the itinerant company I describe (and deep down inside me I am still a bit awed by the whole thing). That I turn an objective reporter's eye on the lecture world does not mean that I love it not, or that I am not beholden to it. I find it vastly interesting and agree-able. And I have been lucky. I was a name before I dared the lecture circuits. In my job I had had to be raconteur as well as reporter. I do very much like (whilst liking doses of solitude and silence too) to move about amongst people in widely differing communities, and I am simple enough to be rarely bored. Though I am sometimes scared for a moment when I stand up and face five hundred expectant human beings, I don't show it because I can dissemble nervousness. I have things to tell. I possess a grin and a reasonably clear voice. I have never had an elocution lesson and therefore do not, for I cannot, 'elocute'—thank heavens, for it is death to informal speaking. I am neither quick enough nor erudite enough to 'fright the ladies'—who indeed often say let him roar again.

Most of the invitations which come to me beg for a talk on the Royal Family or behind-the-scenes stories from historic occasions of the first twenty years of the Queen's reign. The club secretaries and their members also seem to like, next best, to hear about interviewing V.I.P.s: 'Face to Face with the Famous.' Sometimes the letters say: 'Please come and talk—on anything you like', but more often it is: 'Please suggest a subject, because we like to have a title for our printed programmes for the year.' But, if I agree to go, I send them a list of subjects and let *them* choose. 'Pitfalls of the Spoken Word' gets a number of takers: the errors of the years have an enduring fascination.

If they prefer illustrations, I travel with a hundred colour slides—I have taken pictures with a simple little camera of my own in recent years—and give 'Royal Occasions Then and Now' or 'Abu Simbel Saved—New Egypt Rescues Old'. And so on.

Pictures are popular. But personally I enjoy giving a straight talk rather more than talking with illustrations: doing my own pictures in words. I find that showing slides is not for me a *rest*: I talk just as much when the room is dark and the screen is the focus of attention, and oddly the pictures seem sometimes to get in my way. I have been known to pop a slide in upside-down purposely to break the mechanical tyranny of my own picture sequences—a perverse practice but a reminder of human fallibility, and it gives the audience the relief of a laugh. (I did not, however, think it so funny when a nervous helper, working the projector, cascaded a whole tray of my slides all over the floor halfway through my performance.) Slides and films, however, undoubtedly have a great appeal; and there are lecturers on the circuits who have really magnificent pictures to show and who can dilate technically on how they obtained them. Some lecturers cannot perform without pictures. Others—and I expect I am in this category—would be better if they did not chatter so much *with* them.

Even luncheon clubs like slides sometimes, though I myself think that a picture show in the middle of the day is unnatural, and often it is difficult to black-out the room properly. Not long ago I arrived, complete with my colour transparencies, at a club rendezvous to be met by a doleful secretary with the lament: 'We've discovered that the hotel has sent its window curtains away for cleaning, and they've no way of shutting the daylight out.' I did not share the lady's chagrin that I had to talk without illustra-

tions; and I must say that her members did not seem to
mind listening to my reminiscences over their coffee cups at
the luncheon tables instead of shuffling into rows in front
of a screen and peering round each other's heads at the
pictures.

I have given talks on every day of the week, Sundays
included. But Thursdays are easily the most popular days
for meetings of all kinds. I have held forth in every county
in England and Wales and many in Scotland. I have gone
from addressing prisoners in Wandsworth Gaol (a keen and
intelligent audience) to arguing with Sixth Form boys at
Gordonstoun School on the Moray Firth, and from dodging
unmentionable missiles at riotous Round Table charter
celebrations as I shouted through the young men's late-
night frolics to debating questions of belief and the ethics
of journalism at sedate morning seminars.

But by far the greatest number of my encounters with
live audiences have been with the women's—they are often
still called ladies'—luncheon clubs. These have grown
phenomenally in numbers and in membership since the
war. There are eight, I am told, in one city alone—the
prosperous city of Leicester. Women who tire of being
on a club's waiting list for membership start a club of their
own; and when that one in its turn becomes full, yet another
sprouts. The clubs have become popular because, in an age
of social mobility, they provide a chance for women to
meet new neighbours, widen their contacts, exchange their
views, eat a meal cooked by somebody else and hear a
talk about somebody else's job.

I am usually met at the railway station by one of the
committee members in a well-washed car and driven
straight to the hall or hotel. If I go by road I find that they
have thoughtfully fixed a parking space for me, and at
the place of the luncheon I know the chairman will be
waiting in the lobby to greet me and introduce the president
and secretary and treasurer. The treasurer is sometimes to
be seen sitting at a little table at the entrance, her assistant
beside her, taking the tickets and the money as the members
come streaming in. Occasionally, before I have even had
time to look round, the treasurer beckons me and surrep-

titiously slips me an envelope with my cheque in it, and whispers: 'Do forgive me if I hand you this now. It gets it out of the way and done with—and I know you can't escape!'

The room and the bar at the end of it are already busy and buzzing. Many of the members have arrived early, have put their gloves down on the chairs they wish to occupy at lunch, and have been happily sitting around sipping their good sherries and chatting to their good friends for the best part of an hour. I am led round to have a word with as many members as possible, once I have met the committee; and there is a general flurry of questions well before the meal starts.

Contrary to a widespread idea that all women's luncheon clubs are millinery parades, and that the prime aim of members is to show off their more frivolous hats, many of the luncheons I have visited have been noticeably hatless ones. True, I have admired some frilly confections on dainty heads—and there are clubs which sport plenty of these—but the growing tendency nowadays is *not* to wear hats.

When we go in for the meal I sit in the middle at the top table, where the committee are. I can relax for a while—just a little. The talk abates momentarily as we tackle our minestrone. Then the conversation wells up again and comments and questions dart about: these well-informed women are not committee members for nothing. I have to keep my ears open—and my eyes on the look-out. One day I was placed next to a cartwheel hat which just about obscured its wearer but which nearly put my eye out every time she turned her head. We progress to the chicken or occasionally lamb or steak pie. These are not always gastronomic treats: meal prices have to be kept down. After the coffee, the chairman bangs the table, introduces me, and I stand up and make my speech, which usually lasts for about forty-five minutes.

Sometimes there are questions at the end—after a pause during which you think none is coming. But nobody likes to be first. Someone usually says: 'Who was the most attractive woman you ever met?' and I can answer that safely with the Queen of Tonga. Another question often is: 'Can you tell us what was your most embarrassing moment?' Of course there have been plenty of such moments, but one answer I give is quite truthfully to say: 'The moment when I was introduced at a luncheon club by a chairman who declared: "We are all eager to hear Mr. Talbot who, as we know, has for years been intimate with the ladies of the Royal Family".'

No after-speech question has ever been so uncompromisingly to the point as that put to me by one of 400 schoolboys who, when the headmaster at the end of my talk about jobs in broadcasting said I would answer their queries, shot his hand up and demanded loud and clear: ' 'Ow much do *you* get?'

Generally, luncheon club presenters, questioners and givers of votes of thanks are polished performers and serious seekers after information and the broadening of their minds. When they speak they are accurate and succinct; and they have done their homework. But that cannot be said of all the *men* who preside at the civic dinners, town hall lectures and public forums—which, incidentally, though hit have been by no means downed by television. By one of these chairmen I was once introduced to the audience as: 'Sir Geoffrey Turbot, the well-known co-respondent.' Another ended his preliminaries with a not wholly jocular: 'Now we'll see whether he's worth what he's costing.'

Whether the occasion is a lunch or an evening with the magic-lantern, to me the business of talking to a visible audience is something I find stimulating, a little frightening, always demanding. Every audience is different, every date has in it something of a 'first time'. It will be years, I think, before the experience of being able to watch the people I am addressing ceases to become a change and a challenge after half a lifetime spent in talking only to a microphone or camera lens. In lecturing, as distinct from broadcasting, you can see how the customers are reacting; you can change gear to suit the nature of the audience. Some are sophisticated and serious. A few, at lunches, have come to be seen and to see what Godfrey Talbot is really like. Some of them smile encouragingly. Some sit straight-backed and forbidding, faces immobile. Some organisations place their aged and deaf founder-members in the front row, where they are prone to doze off disconcertingly under the nose of the speaker. They rarely actually do sleep ('they hear better with their eyes closed', I have been told by more than one secretary), and in any case I have sympathy for those who do 'drop off'. I myself find the steady drone of a human voice immediately after a meal immensely conducive to torpor.

When you get to your feet at the start of a lecture you know what sort of an audience you've got within five minutes. The response—or lack of response—to a light-hearted anecdote at the beginning will almost always give you the clue.

Once you are launched, the occasion becomes not so much a solo performance as a *situation* in which you and your hearers are taking equal part: you tell, they take it in, and the attention they clearly give to you completes the relationship and the bond. If you have got the meeting on your side you can coast along and enjoy the whole thing. The audience becomes, not a sea of faces but an assembly of separate people; and you dare to look at them one by one, selecting a person here and there and for a second or two talking directly to her. But this, and the 'coasting along', needs some practice. Beware lest you lose control and concentration. I once directed myself so particularly to a lady in the second row who had been alternately scanning her fingernails and staring at the ceiling that I became obsessed with her fidgets and her fallen handbag, and was suddenly panic-stricken at the realisation that I had let go the grip on my narrative and floundered before I remembered what came next.

It is also dangerous to address too long some pretty face looking directly towards you with rapt attention. Her expression, you suddenly find, doesn't change even when everybody else in the house squirms and laughs: behind the glazed eyes she is probably thinking, not of you, but of last night's party or the dentist she is going to after lunch.

However, it is exceptional, in my experience, to find the company anything but kind and co-operative. Most clubs are pleasantly free and easy. They want to learn from you, but also to enjoy themselves; and they want you to be happy too. Just now and then, though, there comes a tiny flick of the whip, even if from a gentle hand. Before I visited one old-established society, I received from the secretary a duplicated typescript headed: 'Notes for Speakers'. It valuably outlined the organisation's history and sketched the nature and probable size of the audience, stressing the experience and cerebral potential of the membership because, as the paper put it, 'it has sometimes happened in the past that a visiting speaker has mistaken his audience . . . You may find members with considerable interests, and sometimes high personal attainments, in your own field.' The nine pithy paragraphs of advice ended with this verb. sap.: 'There have been some unfortunate, though happily rare, occasions when a speaker has quoted extensively, or sought to *read* the whole or part of his address.'

All of which was unexceptionable; but that dedicated secretary, having put her hand to that particular plough, might have typed even more hints whilst she was about it. Indeed she might usefully have written very many. My own Guide to Talkers, distilled from my mistakes over the years, would be something like this:

Don't talk over the listeners' heads, figuratively or literally. Aim your voice at the back rows, but look at every part of the house in turn. Use a microphone only if the hall's acoustics demand it and if you are accustomed to the device.

Use plenty of voice and speak fairly slowly. Watch lest your volume drops at the end of a sentence or gets progressively weaker as your talk goes on.

Don't be dispassionate in your manner, even though your material may be clinically objective. Project your personality: don't be afraid of being an enthusiastic and provocative human being, prejudices and all. Be a little larger than life: 'act' yourself. Seem as though you are enjoying talking, for then your hearers are the more likely to enjoy themselves too.

Smile, but not all the time. Never be patronisingly comic. Slide your funny stories in, boot-faced, between the serious slabs of information. Don't let them see you ponderously change gear and laboriously begin: 'That reminds me of the tale of . . .'

Don't keep gulping from the glass of water on the table. If you must take a sip, do it during the laughs.

Be flexible. Feel for your audience's taste at the outset, and insert or omit anecdotes to suit it.

Never be over-technical, even in specialised company. And beware the error of thinking that audiences of women want 'women's topics'. Jam-making and knitting are out. Short of a full mannequin parade, they like the inside stories of the haute couture trade rather than a chat about fashions.

Travel and international affairs are steadily popular.

But, if you are showing slides or films, the holiday-snaps prattle won't do. 'My Trip Through the Sun-Drenched Paradise of Corfu' will empty the hall. You must have hard, newsy information and some good stories—and up-to-date pictures—on places which are interesting in themselves and not just because you've got some pictures of them.

Never say: 'Next slide, please', keep the mechanics of the operation so unobtrusive that the audience is hardly aware of them. So, in your commentary, anticipate what picture comes next and signal it up (by click or press-button) whilst your words flow on and fit.

See that the smuts and whiskers are cleaned off your slides. They may not be very noticeable on your little home-viewer, but will appear like boulders and tree-trunks when the slides are projected in a hall (the screen at Dundee is twenty feet square).

What you say, with or without pictures, must be your own stuff and not other people's—as more than one television 'personality' has discovered when, asked to talk at a meeting, he has floundered abysmally without script and producer.

Never 'spin it out' garrulously or overrun your allotted time. Leave them wanting more, not shaking their watches.

Be polite, if not flattering, to the people whose invitation you have accepted. (More than once, I have been told by Madam Chairman: 'So-and-so was brusque and bad-mannered when he came to us, and complained throughout the meal. So we didn't enjoy him, and he can't have been very happy either. Shan't have *him* again!')

Finally, be chary of accepting too much extra-luncheon hospitality from club officers; it may mean more hard work than the actual lecture—even though the invitations come with the nicest of intentions. When I have stayed overnight or had a meal at someone's home, invariably the house and the bed have been most comfortable, my hosts kind and delightful. And some have been discerning enough to give me an hour or two of quiet and rest. But occasionally my hosts have unwittingly put me on quite strenuous parade by throwing coffee parties for me and inviting large numbers of their friends to meet me. This requires bright conversation for hours—sometimes into the small hours of the morning. So, if in doubt, have a hotel bed-and-breakfast and relax. You will lecture the better for it.

Such are the suggestions I would make to those longing to lecture. Critics might say that they should be put under the heading of Gratuitous Advice or Giving the Game Away. But I think not. It is certainly to me both harmless and helpful to put a few guide-lines down; for I still need to be reminded of a great deal of the advice myself. Knowing the ropes does not mean that you want no ropes. Familiarity with luncheon-club land breeds contempt indeed—but not for the clubs and the ladies. Rather, contempt for those who underrate the clubs as a lot of silly women. The committees are professionals who know their stuff: the speaker who approaches them thinking otherwise does so at his peril. I much respect these organisations which have crept into my career. I take the clubs

seriously. I have not the slightest doubt that these committees, and the great majority of the rank-and-file members,
are naturally clear-headed people and possess more individual common sense than you can find in any comparable
male gathering round the luncheon tables. Their minds
are healthy and their reactions sound, their judgments
palpably mature. If I had known such women earlier in
my professional course I should have been a lot wiser.

I would like to see more of them as arbiters of taste
and public affairs. I wish some could infiltrate one or two
of the programme boards of the B.B.C.

Which brings this story of mine almost to where we came
in. But by a different entrance and to a different scene.

19

Whatever Happened to the B.B.C.?

I should be aberrant if I finished my book without running my old eyes over the state of broadcasting in the Seventies, the present condition of the craft I have followed and loved for so long.

The heading of this chapter is the burden of many letters I receive. But I get cross with the people who write them. They say: 'You must be glad to be out of what has become a rather undignified profession in which the Players have taken over from the Gentlemen.' What rubbish! As if there was something bad about a business being conducted by experts!

The fact is, of course, that the programmes and policies of television and radio daily arouse the easy joys of righteous indignation. The B.B.C., at fifty years old, is the whipping-boy of the world. As every journalist, if not every schoolboy, knows, an essay on the current sins of broadcasting can be churned out on even the dullest morning with no trouble at all. And it is all too simple for one who has stepped out of the regular ranks to sit back at leisure and indulge in senseless scolding of his successors, snorting that his old service has 'gone downhill since my time'. I am certainly not going to pretend that the Old Guard were all spotless paragons of probity who knew more about producing broadcast programmes than any of today's new lot. For Broadcasting House and Television Centre are the present homes of practitioners whose brilliance makes my eyes goggle and whose processes fill me with admiration and envy. I feel like an idiot child when I am in the midst of the talented men and the technical miracles to be found in the studios nowadays.

Something *has* happened to the B.B.C., however. It was bound to. The world has changed; and the B.B.C. is a microcosm of the world. Almost everything on the air, for instance, has expanded—and brassily accelerated. Fast talk is the accepted norm. We have become so used to young broadcasters firing at us like smart insurance sales-men that when we happen to hear a recording of Richard Dimbleby's voice it seems strangely measured and dated.

The overpowering thing that has changed the total B.B.C. has been and is of course the rise of TV. Not only the physi-cal rise of that modern complex of offices, workshops and studios which is the Television Centre, the Corporation's vast entertainment factory at White City in West London, but the rise, the dominating rise, of the great god Vision. TV gobbles the B.B.C.'s audiences and money, forcing Sound to play the poor relation. It is not surprising, for the Telly is the wonder of the age and every household's window on the world. It is really not surprising, either, that some trendy young programme men at the Centre refer condescendingly to 'steam radio', or 'blind broad-casting', if indeed they mention the older medium at all. Perhaps they are too busy with themselves and their ex-pensive productions to notice that radio still exists, let alone to be aware that it is still the paramount giver of information to the world, swifter than television and far from moribund. Most of the British public stare at 'the Box' every night of their lives—that is the thing the new telly-boys know, that is what they naturally care about, as they weave their theatrical ways through the labyrin-thine corridors and club bars of Shepherd's Bush and see the universe in terms of TV spectaculars. It is a spectacle itself, the TV Centre—its inhabitants as much as its archi-tecture make it so.

For all the television takeover, however, Broadcasting House remains the hub and administrative centre of the Corporation. 'B.H.', the Old Lady of Portland Place, now in her forties and one of something like forty buildings

which the B.B.C possesses in the London area, has changed
too. The exterior looks just as it did in 1932 when the place
came into full use and Reith was the giant in charge: a
concrete battleship, bows-on to Oxford Circus, bearing
down from Regent's Park. But, inside, much is different. The
offices with their maddening little windows, the panelled
committee rooms and the sound studios in which the
acoustics boys played eternal games of wall-changing in
the early days—they are all still there and, up Portland
Place, the B.H. Extension has been tacked on. But these
haunts are peopled by a new race of administrators, technicians, talkers and producers, men and women of impressive skills and iconoclastic principles. True, there
are still a number of workers in B.H. who dress con-
servatively and value the old traditions of steady public
guidance and the old standards of good taste; there is
indeed something left of that backbone of the Corporation-
that-was, the band of devoted secretary ladies in neat
tweeds and twin-sets; and in the back rooms there works an
engineering staff which is still of unexampled efficiency.
The great difference to be discerned is among the radio
producers and programme performers—a change of aim
and attitude. The watchword now is, so often, novelty
and change for change's sake. I get the impression that with
some of the new boys, the very clever new boys, it is a
point of honour to question all outside authority and
suspect any established precedent. They are very keen.
They are keen to win the approval of their departmental
bosses, keener perhaps than they are to find out what
the licence-payers, their customers, think and want. (But,
happily, at the same time one of the new ideas of radio
in the Seventies has with great success brought listeners'
views right into the programmes—the telephone-the-
experts shows such as 'It's Your Line'.)

The appearance of the new race of workers swarming
in and out of the Broadcasting House hive is striking to
those who knew B.H. as the sober-suited Reithian temple
of the arts. Boys in beards and blouses, typists in rainbow
slacks or hot-pants, computer operators in casual coats,
cute little clerks in minimal smocks and maximum eye-

lashes, brisk reporters in flowered shirting, they swing
jauntily through corridors where gaunt Sir John walked
and studios where Stuart Hibberd was once mellifluous
king. In a wonderland of recording rooms and tape-editing
suites sit a special breed of shirt-sleeved technical operators,
men and girls, marvellously swift and sure, who cut down
the world to size—the size and length of the tape each
sound programme needs.

There is a brand-new radio News Room now in Broadcasting House, lighted like a stage and carpeted like a boudoir,
where even the dictation typists sit in armchairs to work
and the sub-editors have specially built desks to which the
'copy' flows from batteries of high-speed mini-teleprinters
which endlessly spew computerised news agency messages.
The subs are surrounded by microphones, headphones,
instant duplicators, television screens and a telephone
system with a hundred intercom push-button links. They
still write stories, but not so many as we used to do: a lot
of their work consists of listening to recorded tapes on
which correspondents and reporters have told their tales,
cutting the tapes, and giving the news-announcers little
links to say between the tape snippets.

A lot of snippety stuff goes out nowadays. For a radio
news bulletin all clearly written by first-class subs and
broadcast 'straight' by a trained announcer would appear
to be regarded by the News Division as old-fashioned—
although a few such bulletins do remain in the schedules.
Mostly, the ten or fifteen minutes of news now has to be
broken into a series of voices, no matter if the voices are of
varying quality and clarity, and indeed no matter sometimes
whether the news items merit the distinction of a change of
voice.

The News itself is still concise, well balanced, objective
and accurate. It is the best news service in the world. But
news bulletins are only part, a relatively small part, of a
vast output of topical information, including parliamentary
reports, briefings on the political scene, serious debates
and foreign correspondents' analyses of current events—
all of which are clear and responsible. What are less palatable
to some of the B.B.C.'s listeners are the long, dressed-up

news programmes of 'feature' type put out at fairly frequent
intervals from before breakfast until after bedtime. These
programmes seize each major news item of the day and,
again and again as the day goes on, they probe it, stretch it,
explain it, speculate on it, interview on it, shake it, gut it
and nearly flog it to death. If the listener switches on more
than very occasionally, he is in danger of being battered
insensible by the reiteration and the extreme assiduousness
of the radio journalism. He is also battered by noise. Some
of the programmes, and the news summaries, are distress-
ingly introduced and punctuated by the loud sounds of
'musical' signatures which might have escaped from bedlam
and strike the ear like a confusion of demoniac fire engines
and escaping bath water. Radiophonic jingles are, to me,
aural hell.

The news magazine programmes are put on the air by
cultivated editors at the backroom desks and capable
producers at the studio panels, and some are well announced
too. But not all. There are programmes which are put in
the hands, or at any rate the voices, of whipping-up,
wisecracking compères. Sometimes the compère will be
a reporter, sometimes one of those manifestations of showbiz thinking, a 'personality', unclassifiable and not noticeably qualified in the art of communicating by the spoken
word. Not content to give us the facts and the views of
persons involved in the facts, and letting us judge it all,
they impose their comments and strive to make each
contribution unnaturally red-hot and provocative as they
quip their way through their hours and half-hours. I
find it hard to accept the gratuitous personalising which
goes with the modern style, the trivialising of news items
which are not unassailably grave and important, the compères' childish domestic jokes and their bogus enthusiasms.

Let us by all means have cheerful announcers who are
known human beings, but they must beware of taking
over and influencing their material. The patent exalting of
broadcasting's new blue-eyed creature, the 'presenter'
—which is the fashionable label for the compère—is
dangerous because he can so quickly become an interference,
making the listener's task of absorbing information more

difficult instead of more easy. The public may become as punch-drunk with news *chatter* as with the relentless caterwaulings of Radio One which keep the Pop boiling. The poorer presenters are soul-mates of those facetious disc-jockeys who deal in cackle rather than clarity. They broadcast for adolescents.

Another change which grieves old hands at the B.B.C., and which is a particular sadness to me, is the way pronunciation has taken a beating. Most of the regular announcers are admirable; they speak correctly with pleasantly modulated voices, and so are immediately understandable. But there are so *many* people presenting programmes, reading and reporting, that their ranks, perhaps inevitably, include a number of misusers of the Queen's English; and it is this minority's slipshod performances, the grotesque saying of words, which have disproportionate effect and remain jarringly in the mind. Unfortunately, this kind are also pickers of the fancy words and pedlars of the wrong ones. To them the poor are the 'underprivileged', cripples are 'the handicapped' and drunkards are 'alcoholics'. The good, robust word 'begin' becomes 'commence', and instead of 'expect' we get 'anticipate'. Split infinitives, tautology and solecisms such as 'different than' are three a penny. And, alas, the coming of Local Radio has added to the tally.

There ought to be a moratorium on the improperly employed 'definitely', and all the talkers who say 'This is so' should be made to write out a hundred times the words they mean: '*That* is so.'

Mispronunciations, however, are the main misdeeds of the irksome few. English is a heavily stressed language, so when the twisters of our ancient tongue bungle the inflexions and put the accent on the wrong syllable the mistakes are palpable. They speak of '*figh*-nance' and '*dis*-pute' and 'ha-*rassment*'. When they try to tell us that a bomb was de-fused they so mis-say the word as to suggest that the very opposite happened: the bomb was '*diffused*', they declare.

Often, when the tackling of bombs has been reported, the scene has been Northern Ireland. But sometimes

Q

what has fallen upon our ears has been a province called 'Northern *Eye-land*', whose problems have been spoken of by someone called the 'Pry-Minister', who has called for '*lor* and order' whilst he was 'droring' conclusions about 'rasial' strife and trying to 'ensewer' justice. We have from time to time been presented with dispatches from a being called 'Our Rhone Correspondent'. The second month is called 'Febuary', and sometimes its weather is 'partickerly' cold. We hear of countries committing 'ax' of aggression; and zealots have distributed religious 'tracks' through letter-boxes. Detectives are trying to 'soulve' crimes and many suspects are 'involved'. We are sadly accustomed to 'lenth' and 'strenth', without the 'g'. Fifth becomes 'fith'.

It is not terminological inexactitude, but sheer sloppy speech—and nothing to do with welcome colloquialisms or pardonable national habits (the Welsh give us 77 as 'semty-semm' but their meaning is unmistakable). To hold the mispronunciations up and object to them is not fussy pedantry. The point is that oral reporting must be such that it is immediately comprehended. If the words are not said properly, clearly and in the accepted and civilised way, the message may well not be received and understood. What is said must be at once easy to take in. For you cannot say 'What was that you said?' to the man on the radio or the television. He cannot turn back the page and repeat it for you: he is already hurrying on with the next item. When the listener does not 'get it first time', it is usually bad broadcasting which has caused the breakdown of communication.

Nor is a plea of 'lack of time to prepare' a sufficient excuse for these sins—or for another sin: getting names wrong, names of people and names of places. In these days not enough effort seems to be made to get them right. Pronunciation has lost priority. In the old days tremendous effort was made to get the names and sounds of every word correct, to set an example and to be authoritative. Our watchword used to be: 'Have someone check it.' Nowadays one gets the impression that the motto is: 'Have a bash at it.'

Incidentally, I except the overseas programmes from rebuke: the B.B.C. World Service seems to me to remain admirable. In the programmes in English heard throughout the world, the News is given in a steady succession of presentations seventeen times in each twenty-four hours; and these are straight, full, lucid radio bulletins well spoken each time by one professional voice, innocent of cleverdick mannerisms. The World Service, in fact, in its basic news output steadfastly declines to tie brash ribbons round the unvarnished branches of factual reporting, and admirably maintains the B.B.C.'s old reputation as exemplar of English speech to the whole world.

And indeed the hard news, the facts, as given by the B.B.C. in all its outlets both home and overseas is unexceptionable. The basic commodity has nothing wrong with it: the national and international news given from London is as un-rivalled as always in its swiftness and reliability. I am not unhappy about the essential core of news. What shakes me is the jazzy and jackanapes versions of it which occasionally pollute the domestic air. It is the home listener who may get his ear twanged by gimmicks.

But I must not let my complaints get out of proportion. I would not have my last chapter sound like The Last Judgment. If I am captious about one or two of the things I hear nowadays it is simply because I am out-of-date enough to *care* about quality and manner in broadcasting. Actually, I admire much more than I abhore in the stuff of the new radio, in which bad performances are few—but they do irritate out of all proportion to their number. And, to be fair, even the new and slangy words which make me bristle, they have a case—and I would be a grouch not to admit it. The English Tongue must be free to move and grow, and it is the B.B.C.'s legitimate business to keep it fluid and alive, current as well as correct. Like the broadcasting medium itself, the language is constantly absorbing changes. It has to be sensitive to the contem-porary tastes of society. New but generally used terms must be brought into accepted employment. A language dies if it does not develop. So, innovations there have to be; and the B.B.C. rightly dares them.

And, heaven knows, I am not advocating any sort of flat, academic 'oral print' on the air, as though the speaker reads from a book, for that is the negation of good broadcasting. The finest and most delightful talkers who have ever been in regular communication with listeners—I am thinking especially of the late Sir Walford Davies, the late Professor John Hilton, the so lately dead Franklin Engelmann, and the far-from-late but immaculately enduring Alistair Cooke as examples—have always respected the radio medium enormously and prepared with care for their broadcasts, but not with the grammar and full-stops of the printed page. Such men always punctuate with pauses and hesitations and tones of voice. They speak, person to person, in the way people talk to each other in a room—not as though pounding a platform or penning a treatise. Alistair Cooke remains a model of the right way because he speaks correctly yet with calculated informality. I wish more performers would study him, though I admit that the style does not come easily to many.

It is a style with a deceptively simple, conversational approach which makes the hearer feel individually addressed, as though the talker was visiting his home. Even on television, where you can nod and smile and be seen, few have the real knack which breaks the barriers between speaker and listener. The knack is pure joy (and pure gold to those who have it). There is a moral in the story of the lady who every night in her parlour tidied her hair and put on fresh lipstick before sitting down to join her favourite news commentator.

Of course no broadcasting is easy—no broadcasting *ought* to be. If you come across a performer who tells you he finds it as simple as falling off a log, you can usually be sure he is a second-rater.

And it must be acknowledged that nothing is so fraught with trouble as the business of getting and giving the news. Newscasting not only has its own peculiar domestic problems and difficulties but has to take uniquely hard criticism simply because News and Current Affairs programmes are with us constantly and have the greatest audiences and the deepest impact. Their irritant potential

exceeds even that of the poor salacious plays which parade
long-haired violence and lust, even that of the features
which denigrate heroes of history or those occasional
interview programmes in which interviewers of aggressive
scepticism are permitted ill-mannered grilling of their
betters. The vices of the News tend to hit us in excessive
measure, much more than the taken-for-granted virtues.
Since news mirrors realities which affect us all, we have a
porcelain sensibility towards the treatment given to them.
The determined critics also overlook too easily the other
pressures which bear upon the producers of news at the
present time, pressures from vested interests and all kinds
of governmental, political and public bodies—pressures
far greater than the Reith era knew. Accusations of bias
come from all sides; they often cancel each other; and they
are certainly a measure of the importance of the medium as
well as of public anxiety over the turbulence of our times.

B.B.C. news is not biassed—except against such things
as incitement to murder and the destruction of society
by violence. In holding up a looking-glass to our times, it
reports, truly and with maximum effect, what is happening
in the world. Ours is a bad world, and so there is a pre-
ponderance of bad news. The bulletins have no editorial
opinion in them. They are produced by honest and dedicated
professionals who are no more and no less infallible that
other human beings. The B.B.C.'s reporters, cameramen
and sound-recordists nowadays face problems and hazards
surpassing those which I and my colleagues experienced
even during the war and the frustrating and unsettled years
which followed. In Ulster, for example, war and peace have
been bloodily fused into a state of boundless danger
which broadcasting reporters must court as they struggle
to meet their unending series of news deadlines. It is hard
to write of the fortitude of my successors without indecent
enthusiasm. The young reporters I know today are both
skilled and dauntless.

And the broadcasters' audiences—how have *they* changed?
They have, I think, become both more pernickety and more
pliant. More picture-minded. Just as today's reporters, the
ones who work in television, are increasingly the servants

of the camera, so the public are for the most part slaves of the television sets in their homes. Impact of programmes which hit the eye is greater, and is easier, than the impact of those which strike the ear only—that is why we remember that the news-reader's tie was askew even though we have forgotten what he said. That is why there is such concentration on Vision, on pictures as storytellers and newsgivers. Indeed, that is why the spoken word, and the use of it, has suffered since TV bagged the mass audience.

We are in some danger of becoming a nation of supine watchers, sour spectators, pleased and informed up to a point, but less and less intelligent *participators*. Television, which can be the supreme stimulant, is often a soporific instead—because of our too many hours spent in front of its magic lantern and because of the indiscriminate nature of the watching. In many homes, slumping in a chair and staring at everything on the little screen night after night is almost the sole after-work 'activity'—time-killer might be a better description. Television becomes a substitute for real life. Sated with its particular form of education, some of our young people do not take easily to the education of their schools. The risk is that the faculty of reason (because everything is 'served up') and the moral sense (because of sordid behaviour seen uncondemned in plays) may both become gradually paralysed. And the marvellous technological advances in communications seem to be in inverse ratio to people's ability to communicate. In short, it seems to me that television, the most powerful instrument of enlightenment and persuasion ever invented, becomes more of a master and less of a servant every day.

Of course, provided that you pick and choose your viewing, switch off frequently and do not have the TV set everlastingly dripping like an unattended tap, then television is marvellous and a 'must'. It provides some superb programmes; and, to housebound people especially, gives pleasure beyond reckoning. I am not tut-tutting because I do not like it or because millions enjoy *Coronation Street*. I am not suggesting that highbrows should be arbiters of taste. I am simply afraid of the television set becoming a Frankenstein.

In the years ahead, as the world becomes ever more disordered, it will be necessary for television and radio to review their own power and to think more responsibly, not only about the nature of their programmes but about the effects of them on society. Certainly, demands for control and for censorship will increase; and the B.B.C. will be fighting hard to keep its independence and to resist what is seen as outside interference with programme decisions. I believe, nevertheless, that more and more outsiders will graduate through advisory panels to programme boards, and that they will in fact bring some salutary air with them. Whatever happens, the B.B.C. as a monolithic monopoly is gone for ever. Though still a public service, it is today in full competition for audiences with commercial broadcasting—in radio now as well as in the field of television. There are now other Voices of the Nation. What the Corporation will be, I hope, is the best of the voices.

The old firm's hours of output, local radio stations and all, will inevitably increase still more. Its commercial rivals also will rend the air almost without stopping. (To my mind, the increases are lamentable. We are in a gadarene gallop to all-round-the-clock noise. If I were God I would bestow on mankind the inestimable boon of a few hours of compulsory silence each day.) Standards of popular programmes will slide as ratings soar; but, with more splitting of output, several parts of the B.B.C., and of the commercial broadcasting services too, will probably specialise more and more in catering for the minorities of viewers and listeners who are still contriving to think for themselves. I am sure that sound radio will wax rather than wane, the small stations as well as the pervasive networks. The new local commercial radio, with its jangling advertisements, will become *national* commercial radio. Soap powders will wash the country's ears as well as its eyes.

These, however, are the guesses and generalisations of my crystal ball. I do not by any means wish to end my tale despondently, with the piping prophesies of Old Godfrey's Almanac, for I am neither seer nor doomwatcher. I am, in fact, only eager to be there to see what *will* happen to my trade. The golden days of broadcasting, my early days, when to say 'B.B.C.' meant magic and brought instant respect, will not come back. That is understandable, and I have no illusions about the change. The days we live in are days not of gold but of plastic, days of smartness but— for all the B.B.C.'s euphoric jubilee—of little sentiment; days of clinical efficiency, words without end, and music without melody. But at any rate it is impossible, or so it seems to me, to be bored or idle, to be dull or disinterested, in the present days—not if you are in the news line, anyhow.

And so long as mankind's cliff-hanging story goes on at all, broadcasting will be there telling it, vitally and inextricably, instant historian to the end.

I am glad to be out of the centre of the frenzy. All the same, I have the feeling that if I were starting a career again, I would wish to go into it fortified by the same disciplined upbringing as I had before. I would not change my occupation, nor choose the moves differently. I would find myself edging once more, unrepentant, towards some junior reporters' table at a parish council meeting, and then taking that course which would lead deep into journalism and on to the microphone. I would, in a word, do it all again. I would at all costs get into the inquiring profession, the news business, the talking trade. Because if you are in broadcasting you are in everything. As I have been.

Index